I0649791

PHYSICAL MEASUREMENT AND ANALYSIS OF THIN FILMS

PROGRESS IN
ANALYTICAL CHEMISTRY
Based upon the Eastern Analytical Symposia

Series Editors:

Ivor L. Simmons
M&T Chemicals, Inc., Rahway, N. J.

and Paul Lublin
General Telephone and Electronics Laboratories, New York, N.Y.

Volume 1
H. van Olphen and W. Parrish
X-RAY AND ELECTRON METHODS OF ANALYSIS
Selected papers from the 1966 Eastern Analytical Symposium

Volume 2
E. M. Murt and W. G. Guldner
PHYSICAL MEASUREMENT AND ANALYSIS OF THIN FILMS
Selected papers from the 1967 Eastern Analytical Symposium

In preparation:
Volume 3
K. M. Earle and A. J. Tousimis
X-RAY AND ELECTRON PROBE ANALYSIS
                    IN BIOMEDICAL RESEARCH
Selected papers from the 1967 Eastern Analytical Symposium

PROGRESS IN ANALYTICAL CHEMISTRY
VOLUME 2

PHYSICAL MEASUREMENT AND ANALYSIS OF THIN FILMS

Edited by **E. M. Murt**
Philco-Ford Corporation
Blue Bell, Pennsylvania

and **W. G. Guldner**
Bell Telephone Laboratories
Murray Hill, New Jersey

Ⴔ PLENUM PRESS • NEW YORK • 1969

Library of Congress Catalog Card Number 68-31239

© 1969 Plenum Press
A Division of Plenum Publishing Corporation
227 West 17 Street, New York, N.Y. 10011
All rights reserved

PREFACE

This volume contains eight papers on the measurement and analysis of thin films presented at the Eastern Analytical Symposium held at the Statler-Hilton Hotel in New York City on November 8–10, 1967.

In view of the widespread interest in thin film technology and its applications to electronics and space technology, the Eastern Analytical Symposium agreed that the proceedings of two sessions devoted to this subject should be made available to all workers in the field *via* publication in this series.

Included in this volume are discussions of the electron microprobe, nondestructive optical techniques for measuring film thickness, the use of radioisotopes in specific applications, characterization by electron microscopy and diffraction, analysis by source mass spectrometry, the chemical and structural evaluation of thin glass fims, and a comprehensive review of X-ray methods.

On behalf of the Eastern Analytical Symposium we wish to express our appreciation to the authors for their efforts in making this material available for publication. We would also like to thank The Electrochemical Society, Inc. for permission to publish the paper by Richard Brown, "Density Determination of Sputtered Tantalum Films by a Beta-Backscatter Technique."

Edward M. Murt
William G. Guldner

CONTENTS

Chapter IV
Density Determination of Sputtered Tantalum Films by a Beta-Backscatter Technique 93
  by Richard Brown

Chapter V
The Characterization of Solid Thin Films and Surfaces by Electron Microscopy and Diffraction 105
  by R. B. Marcus

Chapter VI
The Emission-Spectrographic and Atomic-Absorption Analyses of Metallic Thin Films 138
by J. D. Nohe

Chapter VII
RF Spark Source Mass Spectrometry for the Analysis of Surface Films 148
by D. L. Malm

Chapter VIII
Chemical and Structural Evaluation of Thin Glass Films.... 168
by W. A. Pliskin

I. NONDESTRUCTIVE OPTICAL TECHNIQUES FOR THIN-FILM THICKNESS MEASUREMENTS

W. A. Pliskin

IBM Components Division
Hopewell Junction, New York

Nondestructive film-thickness measurements of transparent films can be made by optical or spectroscopic reflection techniques. One of the oldest and simplest techniques for thin-film thickness measurements is based on the interference colors produced by the film. However the accuracy of this method and the thicknesses which can be measured by it are limited. Another very simple but accurate technique is the use of VAMFO, a special interferometric microscope equipped with a rotating stage and a monochromatic filter. The film thickness d is given by $d = N\lambda/(2n_2 \cos \theta_2)$, where N is the fringe order at which a maximum or minimum occurs, λ the wavelength of the filtered light, n_2 the refractive index, and θ_2 the angle of refraction of the incident light in the transparent film. By the use of this technique, film thicknesses from several hundred angstroms to several microns can be determined. With this technique it is also possible to determine the refractive index of the transparent film.

Film thicknesses can also be determined spectroscopically by measuring the reflection from a wafer at a fixed angle. In this case, instead of varying the angle of observation as in VAMFO, the wavelength of radiation is varied spectroscopically. From the wavelengths at which the recorded maxima and minima occur the film thickness can be determined.

Use of ellipsometry provides another nondestructive method for measuring both the thickness and the refractive index. This method is most useful for extremely thin films; however, for most transparent films the previous two methods are more practical.

1. COLOR COMPARISONS

Since in silicon technology there is a wide use of silicon dioxide in glass films for passivation, it is necessary to have accurate nondestructive techniques for film-thickness measurements of silicon dioxide and glass films. This paper will cover the use of nondestructive optical and spectroscopic techniques for making accurate measurements of the thicknesses and refractive indexes of transparent films.

The thicknesses of transparent films on reflective substrates can be measured optically by various nondestructive techniques. The simplest technique consists of color comparison between the unknown film and a step gauge consisting of films of varying thickness but having a refractive index close to that of the unknown film. The variation of color with film thickness has long been known. Newton was the first to relate the color of thin films with thickness. His color chart was reproduced by Rollet ([1]) many years ago, but it can also be found in more recent publications ([2]). A description of the colors formed by interference upon oxidation of various metals and references to early work in the field are covered by Evans ([3]).

The reason for the colors is shown in Fig. 1. Here part of the incident ray (B_0) is reflected at the top surface, i.e., the interface between media 1 and 2, giving rise to ray B_{12}, and part of it is reflected at the interface between media 2 and 3, giving rise to reflected ray B_{23}. If the refractive indexes of the three media are related by $n_3 > n_2 > n_1$, and k_3 is small, then the 180° phase changes on reflection at the two interfaces cancel each other, and, as is shown in any elementary optics text, it follows that

$$N\lambda = 2n_2 d \cos\theta_2 = 2d(n_2{}^2 - \sin^2\theta_1)^{1/2} \tag{1}$$

where N is integral for constructive interference or maxima and half-integral for destructive interference or minima for radiation having a wavelength λ.

Thus at normal incidence for a 2000-Å silicon dioxide film ($n_2 = 1.462$) on a silicon substrate, we would have in the visible region of the spectrum only one maximum corresponding to $N = 1$ and $\lambda = 5840$ Å. Therefore the film would have a yellow color. With a 3100-Å silicon dioxide film, the only maximum in the visible region would correspond to $N = 2$ and $\lambda = 4540$ Å and the film would have a blue color. With thicker films the number of maxima and minima in the visible region will increase and the color will depend on their relative distribution; in addition, because of the mixture, the color will become less pure or less saturated, and at a sufficiently large thickness the color will disappear. The brilliance of the color also depends on the completeness of the interference occurring between rays B_{12} and B_{23}, which in turn depends on the reflectivity at the two interfaces [see Eqs. (4) and (5)]. Thus with silicon dioxide ($n_2 \simeq 1.46$) on silicon ($n_3 \simeq 4.05$) the reflectivity at the 1–2 interface is significantly less than that at the 2–3 interface, and the colors are not as vivid as with films of silicon nitride ($n_2 \simeq 2.03$) on silicon. If k_3 is negligible, then the reflectivities at the two interfaces are equal when $n_2 = \sqrt{n_1 n_3}$.

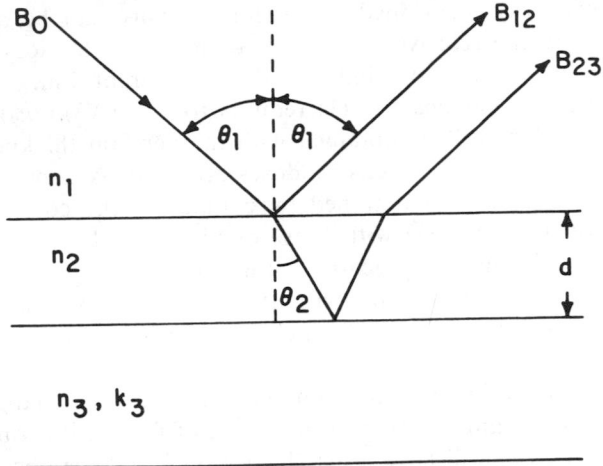

Figure 1. Schematic diagram of the reflections from a transparent dielectric film on a reflecting substrate.

One of the first precise color-thickness gauges was made by Blodgett [4,5], who prepared a very colorful and useful thickness gauge consisting of layers of barium stearate deposited on a lead glass plate. However, this gauge must be protected by enclosure in a transparent package since the barium stearate film can be damaged easily. A much better thickness gauge can be made with silicon dioxide on silicon. In this case, a silicon wafer is oxidized to a predetermined thickness and then various areas are etched away under controlled conditions so as to give films of various thicknesses. This type of gauge is much better than the barium stearate step gauge because thicker films can be grown and the silicon dioxide is more stable to heat and most common solvents and chemicals. It is also better because the oxide can be formed on a relatively thin wafer so that intimate direct comparisons can be made with an unknown sample.

In making color comparisons one must be careful not to confuse film thicknesses of different orders which give rise to similar colors. Errors can be avoided by comparing the colors of the films when observed at various angles. For films with refractive indexes close to that of silicon dioxide, color comparisons are limited to thicknesses between 500 Å and 15,000 Å with an accuracy of $\pm$ 100 Å over most of the region. A detailed color chart for silicon dioxide on silicon as well as unusual color differences to look for in order to establish the proper order have been described by Pliskin and Conrad [6].

The refractive index of the film can influence the color in three ways:

1. As previously mentioned, the color intensity can be affected by modifying the relative reflectivity at the two interfaces through a change in the refractive index of the transparent film.

2. At normal incidence Eq. (1) reduces to $d = (N\lambda)/(2n_2)$, and thus similar colors will be obtained with thinner film thicknesses when films having high refractive indexes are used. A good example of this phenomenon is obtained by comparing the colors of Ta_2O_5 films on tantalum ([7]) with those of SiO_2 on silicon ([6]). However there is a further complication here in that there is a larger phase-shift thickness correction with the films on tantalum than with films on silicon. Phase-shift thickness corrections will be discussed later.

3. The refractive index of the film also influences the change in color with incident angle. From examination of Eq. (1) it is obvious that a change in θ_1 will have less influence on λ and the observed color for materials having a high refractive index than for those with low refractive indexes. Thus low refractive index films will be seen to undergo more color changes as one changes his viewing angle from normal incidence to higher angles of incidence.

2. REFLECTIVITY THEORY OF TRANSPARENT FILMS ON ABSORBING REFLECTIVE SUBSTRATES

The rate of publication of papers on nondestructive techniques for measuring the thickness of transparent films on reflective substrates making use of the interference phenomenon between the radiation reflected from the dielectric–air interface with that from the dielectric–substrate interface, has increased tremendously in recent years ([6-34]).

These interferometric techniques can be divided into two general categories. In the most commonly used technique the radiation is reflected from the sample film in a spectrophotometer with fringes being formed as a function of wavelength. This technique has been named CARIS (constant angle reflection interference spectroscopy) by Reizmann and Van Gelder ([32]). In the other technique which is called VAMFO (variable angle monochromatic fringe observation), interference fringes are formed by varying the angle of observation ([6,18,20,22]). In both techniques the film thickness d can be given approximately by Eq. (1). However more accurate thicknesses are obtained from fringe minima according to the relation ([30])

$$d = \frac{N\lambda}{2n_2 \cos\theta_2} + \Delta t_\varphi + \Delta t_r \qquad (2)$$

where N is the order given by $N = 1/2, 3/2, 5/2, \ldots$; n_2 is the insulating film refractive index at wavelength λ; θ_2 is the angle of refraction in the insulating film; Δt_φ is the phase-shift thickness correction; and Δt_r is the reflectivity correction.

The phase-shift thickness correction for SiO_2 on silicon has been adequately covered for the visible region ([6,18,20,22,23,30,31,33]) and for the ultraviolet region ([30,38]) of the spectrum. Phase-shift thickness corrections for various insulating films on commonly used substrates have been determined and universal type charts which simplify the calculation of phase-shift thickness corrections have been constructed ([35]).

Reflectivity corrections have been determined for the spectrophotometric technique ([33]) and for VAMFO ([34]). Experimentally, with CARIS approximate compensation for reflectivity corrections are obtained by reflection off a silicon wafer in the reference beam of the double-beam spectrophotometer ([24]), but more complete compensation can be obtained by using a silicon wafer with a thick nonuniform SiO_2 film in the reference beam ([33]). With both VAMFO and CARIS the reflectivity corrections are approximately inversely proportional to the order N and thus become insignificant with thicker films ([33,34]).

The phase-change corrections are the same for both VAMFO and for CARIS; however, the reflectivity correction for VAMFO differs from that for the spectrophotometric technique. In the former, one must consider the reflectivity variations for a fixed wavelength and varying incident angle; whereas with the latter, the angle of incidence is fixed, but the wavelength is varied. Using VAMFO, reflectivity corrections can be eliminated experimentally by making a 100 Å step in or on the film ([6,18,20]).

The reason for the reflectivity and phase-change corrections can be seen from examination of the more complete equations describing the reflectivity of a nonabsorbing (transparent) film on a reflective substrate. For simplification we will consider only that component of radiation which is perpendicular to the plane of incidence. At normal incidence the relations are the same. The reflectivity for the perpendicular component is given by ([30,36,37]) [see Fig. 1 and also Eq. (37) of section 5]

$$R = \frac{r_{12}{}^2 + \rho_{23}{}^2 + 2r_{12}\rho_{23}\cos(2\beta - \varphi_{23})}{1 + r_{12}{}^2\rho_{23}{}^2 + 2r_{12}\rho_{23}\cos(2\beta - \varphi_{23})} \tag{3}$$

where

$$r_{12} = \frac{n_1 \cos\theta_1 - n_2 \cos\theta_2}{n_1 \cos\theta_1 + n_2 \cos\theta_2} \tag{4}$$

is the reflectivity at the air–SiO$_2$ interface,

$$\rho_{23}{}^2 = \frac{(n_2 \cos \theta_2 - u_3)^2 + v_3{}^2}{(n_2 \cos \theta_2 + u_3)^2 + v_3{}^2} \tag{5}$$

is the reflectivity at the film–substrate interface,

$$\tan \varphi_{23} = \frac{-2n_2 v_3 \cos \theta_2}{u_3{}^2 + v_3{}^2 - n_2{}^2 \cos^2 \theta_2} \tag{6}$$

is the phase change at the film–substrate interface,

$$2u_3{}^2 = w + (w^2 + 4n_3{}^2 k_3{}^2)^{1/2} \tag{7a}$$

$$2v_3{}^2 = -w + (w^2 + 4n_3{}^2 k_3{}^2)^{1/2} \tag{7b}$$

$$w = n_3{}^2 - k_3{}^2 - n_1{}^2 \sin^2 \theta_1 \tag{8}$$

and

$$\beta = 2\pi d n_2 (\cos \theta_2)/\lambda = N\pi \tag{9}$$

Reflectivity minima as given by Eq. (3) do not coincide with those determined using Eq. (1) because, first, the factors r_{12} and ρ_{23} vary with angle of incidence giving rise to reflectivity corrections [33,34] and, second, the presence of φ_{23} in the cos $(2\beta - \varphi_{23})$ term leads to the phase-shift thickness correction. The phase-shift correction can be expressed in terms of thickness as [22,23,30,33,35]

$$\Delta t_\varphi = -\left(0.5 - \frac{\varphi_{23}}{2\pi}\right) \frac{\lambda}{2n_2 \cos \theta_2} \tag{10}$$

This will be discussed in more detail later.

3. VAMFO

3.1. Thickness Measurements

This nondestructive technique involves the use of a microscope equipped with a monochromatic filter and a stage capable of rotating on an axis normal to the optical axis of the microscope so as to observe the reflected light at various angles [6,18,20,22]. Only reflected monochromatic light is observed either if the microscope objective is covered with a monochromatic filter or if the film is illuminated with monochromatic light. For improved accuracy, a polarizing filter is used in conjunction with the monochromatic filter so that only the perpendicular component is observed. The light source need not be collimated, and optically flat substrates are not necessary. A schematic diagram of the apparatus is shown in Fig. 2.

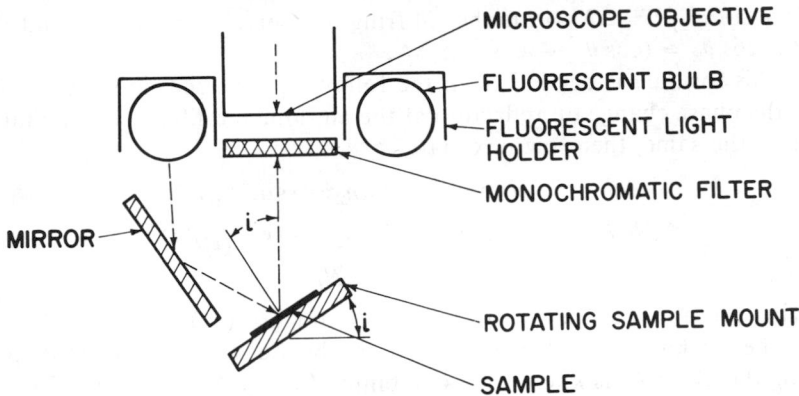

Figure 2. Schematic sketch of the essential portions of VAMFO [Pliskin and Conrad ([6])].

It should be noted that the fluorescent bulb can be replaced with a mercury bulb ([20]) and thus the accuracy of the system is not limited by the lack of monochromaticity of the light source. Even with the fluorescent bulb and filter combination the effective wavelengths can be determined to an accuracy of 1 to 2 parts in 5000 which is more than sufficient for most cases ([20]). As an example of the precision possible with VAMFO using a mercury bulb, the thickness of a thick film of SiO_2 grown thermally on a silicon wafer was measured using in one case the 5460.7 Å green line and in the other, the 4358.4 Å violet line. The measured thicknesses were 42,782 Å using the green line and 42,778 Å using the violet line.

As the stage and sample are rotated, one observes maxima (bright) and minima (dark) fringes on the sample film. During stage rotation the mirror is hand rotated and positioned to maintain the proper reflected light on the sample. With a vertically illuminated microscope, a fixed mirror mounted nearly perpendicular to the rotating stage can be used if it is close to the point on the substrate under examination. Since the positions of minima can be determined more accurately than maxima, the angles at which minima occur are noted. The angles of incidence (θ_1) are read from a calibrated dial attached to the shaft of the rotating stage or from a Decitrak unit which is connected to the shaft. The film thickness (d) is given by ([6,18])

$$d = \frac{\Delta N\lambda}{2n_2(\cos\theta_{2i} - \cos\theta_{2j})} = \frac{\lambda}{2n_2(\Delta\cos\theta_2)} \tag{11}$$

where θ_{2j} is the angle of refraction at that fringe for which the angle of incidence is θ_{1j} and $\sin\theta_{2j} = (\sin\theta_{1j})/n_2$ by Snell's law, thus $n_2\cos\theta_{2j} =$

$(n_2{}^2 - \sin^2 \theta_{1j})^{1/2}$; ΔN = number of fringes observed between θ_{1i} and θ_{1j}; and $\Delta \cos \theta_2 = (\cos \theta_{2i} - \cos \theta_{2j})/\Delta N$.

This formula is derived from the following considerations. Assuming that the phase change on reflection at the air–film and film–substrate interfaces is the same, then for maxima

$$N_i\lambda = 2n_2d \cos \theta_{2i} = 2d(n_2{}^2 - \sin^2 \theta_{1i})^{1/2} \tag{12}$$

$$N_j\lambda = 2n_2d \cos \theta_{2j} = 2d(n_2{}^2 - \sin^2 \theta_{1j})^{1/2} \tag{13}$$

$$\Delta N = N_j - N_i \tag{14}$$

Solving the above equations for d, we obtain Eq. (11).

The thickness can also be determined by Eq. (12) [or Eq. (13)] providing the order N_i is known. By combining Eqs. (11) and (12) we find the order N_i given by ([6,18])

$$N_i = \frac{\cos \theta_{2i}}{\Delta \cos \theta_2} = \frac{\Delta N(n_2{}^2 - \sin^2 \theta_{1i})^{1/2}}{(n_2{}^2 - \sin \theta_{1i})^{1/2} - (n_2{}^2 - \sin^2 \theta_{1j})^{1/2}} \tag{15}$$

Nomograms are sometimes useful for thickness determinations as shown in Fig. 3, where we have plotted the thickness as a function of the angle of incidence for both minima and maxima ([6,18]). The minima are indicated by the curves without circles; the maxima are indicated by the curves with circles. Each curve was determined from Eq. (12) for a particular value of N and λ. The nomograms can in practice include curves for other wavelengths in addition to those shown ([6]). Using this nomogram the thickness of a silicon dioxide film 2000 to 12,000 Å can be determined. The minimum thickness on this particular nomogram is only 2000 Å. In general, the minimum thickness that can be measured by this technique is slightly greater than $\lambda/4n_2$ as can be seen from Eq. (12) and the technique is applicable to about 800 Å. At $\theta_1 = \theta_2 = 0°$, a minimum fringe should occur at $\lambda/4n_2$ but in order to be certain that one passes through a minimum, it is necessary to have $\theta_1 > 0°$, resulting in an approximate limit of about 800 Å using short-wavelength visible radiation ([18]). However, when the VAMFO is limited to visible radiation, there is a dead-spot region from about 1350 Å to about 1500 Å where there are neither maxima nor minima. Furthermore, the maxima are generally not as accurate as minima ([6,18]) and if visible radiation is used, only maxima are possible in the 1500 to 2250 Å regions. Minima are more accurate than maxima because they are sharper. This can be determined from plots made of R vs. θ_1 from Eq. (3).

3.2. Refractive-Index Measurements

By dividing Eq. (12) by Eq. (13) we obtain ([20])

$$F = (N_i/N_j)^2 = (n_2{}^2 - \sin^2 \theta_{1i})/(n_2{}^2 - \sin^2 \theta_{1j}) \tag{16a}$$

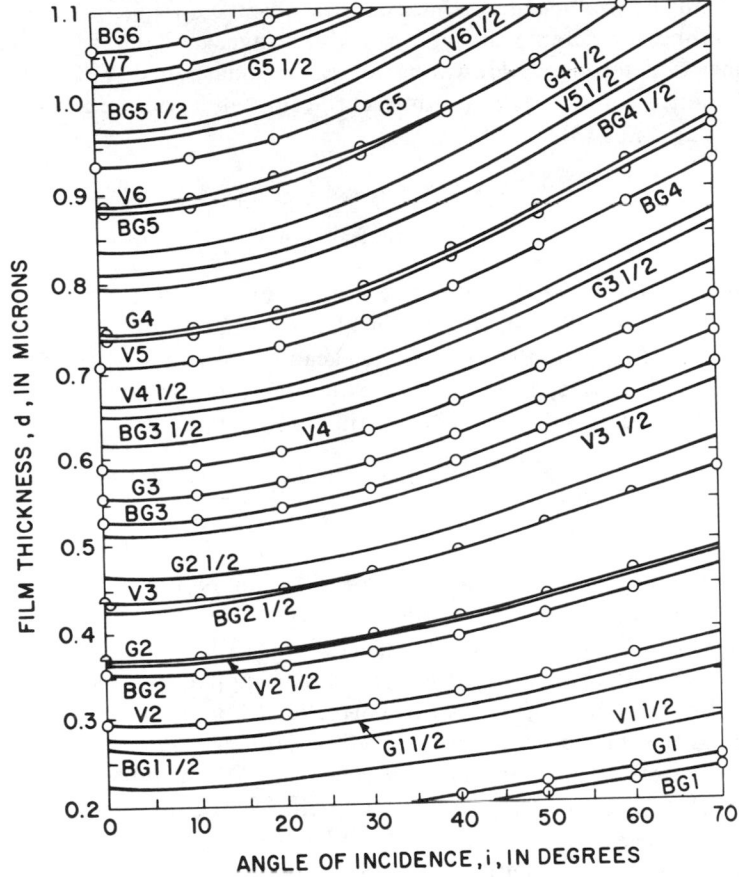

Figure 3. Positions of interference maxima (⊖) and minima (—) for a silicon dioxide film on silicon with filters 4340 Å (V), 5190 Å (BG), and 5450 Å (G) [Pliskin and Conrad [6]].

or

$$n_2 = \left[\frac{F \sin^2 \theta_{1j} - \sin^2 \theta_{1i}}{F - 1} \right]^{1/2} \tag{16b}$$

Thus n_2 can be determined if the fringe orders N_i and N_j are known. The fringe orders can be determined by counting the fringes at a step, by the nondestructive techniques described by Pliskin and Conrad [6], or by the CARIS technique, which will be described later.

With the thinner films, one does not observe a fringe-order difference on rotating the sample through a usable range, and the refractive index cannot be determined. However, it can be determined if fringe minima are obtained for two or more different accurately calibrated filters. Equations (12) and (13) become

$$N_i \lambda_i = 2d(n_{2i}^2 - \sin^2 \theta_{1i})^{1/2} \qquad (12')$$

$$N_j \lambda_j = 2d(n_{2j}^2 - \sin^2 \theta_{1j})^{1/2} \qquad (13')$$

where n_{2i} and n_{2j} are the refractive indexes of the film for wavelengths λ_i and λ_j. From the known dispersion of a substance similar to that of the transparent film being measured, one can write $n_{2j} = n_{2i} + \delta$, where δ is small, and assume, as a first approximation, that the same relation holds for the film being measured. Neglecting the δ^2 term, we obtain ([20])

$$n_{2i} = \left[\frac{F \sin^2 \theta_{1j} - \sin^2 \theta_{1i}}{F - 1} \right]^{1/2} - \frac{F\delta}{F - 1} \qquad (17)$$

where $F = (N_i \lambda_i / N_j \lambda_j)^2$. On many of the thinner films $N_i = N_j$ and F reduces to $(\lambda_i / \lambda_j)^2$. After obtaining the refractive index by Eq. (17), the thickness can be determined by Eqs. (12') or (13').

Phase-shift thickness corrections can be applied to the thickness by use of Eq. (10). In most cases this correction is practically independent of angle. Phase-shift corrections can be used in determining the refractive indices from Eqs. (16) and (17) by decreasing the N values by δN where $\delta N = 0.5 - (\varphi_{23}/2\pi)$. The effect of such phase-change corrections on refractive index can become significant at smaller values of N (0.5, 1.5) and at shorter wavelengths ([20]). The phase change expressed as δN or $\varphi_{23}/2\pi$ does have a slight angle dependency as shown in Section 3.4.

As was mentioned in Section 2, due to reflectivity changes with angle of incidence, highest accuracy is obtained on films of uniform thickness by forming a thin (~ 100 Å) step by controlled etching ([6,18,20]). The average thickness across the step is determined from the angle at which the two portions of the wafer are equally dark (for minima). With this technique, it is possible to increase the accuracy of determination of the incident angle to better than 0.1°. If an etched step is undesirable, a step can be formed by the deposition of a few monolayers of a metal stearate by the Blodgett technique ([4,5]). A slight correction for the refractive index and thickness of the deposited material may be necessary, but the deposited step has the advantage of easy removal with solvents without harm to the film. In addition, a small correction is necessary with stereomicroscopes to obtain accurate angle readings ([6]).

3.3. Simplified VAMFO Interpolation for Thickness and Refractive Index Measurements

The calculations involved in the previous equations for determining refractive indexes and thicknesses have been eliminated by tabulating the thickness in sets of tables ([20]). The thickness is given by

$$d = N\lambda_j/2n_2 \cos \theta_2 \tag{18}$$

Each table gives the thickness (d) as a function of θ_1 for a particular wavelength (λ), refractive index (n_2), and value of N. The tables also include stereo-angle corrections and phase-shift thickness corrections for films on silicon. Each set or book of tables is identified by the refractive index at 5456 Å (the actual effective wavelength of our "standard" filter in two of our VAMFO models). The corresponding refractive indexes used in tabulating the thicknesses associated with the other filters within the same book are based, in one volume of books, on the dispersion of fused quartz; in another volume, on the dispersion of lead silicate glasses; and, in still another, on an assumed mixed silicon dioxide and silicon nitride system. The dispersion details will be discussed later.

In compiling the tables, corrections were made for the stereo angle of the microscope ([6]) and for phase-change differences at the silicon–film interface. The refractive index and thickness can then be determined by interpolation between books to obtain consistent thicknesses for different readings. This simplified method has been applied to thin films where different filters are necessary to obtain at least two readings, and to thicker films where two or more minima can be obtained with the same filter. By these techniques, we have measured films with refractive indexes from 1.30 to 2.10. When the refractive index of the film is known and the order known it is only necessary to obtain one reading for a thickness determination from the tables based on Eq. (18).

An example showing both the interpolation accuracy and the method of using the tabulated thicknesses for various orders for a particular wavelength is shown in Table I. In preparing this table we assumed a refractive index of 1.475 for the film and a thickness of 18,257 Å. Such a film would have minima at observed angles of incidence of 23° and 48.36°. The tabulated values include corrections for stereo-angle and also for phase-change corrections which will be covered in more detail later in this paper. The apparent increase of thickness with angle of incidence in the 1.45 refractive-index column indicates that a refractive index of 1.45 is too low and the apparent decrease with incident angle of the thickness taken from the 1.50 book indicates that a refractive index of 1.50 is too high. Interpolation between the two shows that the same thickness would be obtained at a refractive index of 1.476_4, which is only 0.001_4 different from the actual refractive index. The interpolated thickness is only 12 Å different from the actual thickness. Since in this refractive index range we have books of tables for intermediate refractive indexes, it is concluded that the maximum error in the refractive index due to interpolation is less than 0.001 and the maximum error in thickness is significantly less than 0.1%. For best accuracy two successive minima should not be taken unless they are separated by a large difference in angle of incidence.

Table I. Interpolation Accuracy

N	λ, Å	i	Assumed actual $n = 1.475$	$n = 1.450$	$n = 1.500$	Interpolated $n = 1.4764$
9.5	5456	23.00	18,257	18,597.7	17,929.0	18,245
8.5	5456	48.36	18,257	18,685.7	17,850.2	18,245
				−88.0	+78.8	

When several minima are observed in the range from about 20° to 65° angle of incidence, the refractive index and thickness are determined by the best least squares fit. The results of such a procedure are shown in Table II for a thick thermally grown SiO_2 film, whose thickness was determined to be 44,802 ± 5 Å [22]. The determined refractive index of 1.4613 is slightly greater than that for fused quartz, but we believe the difference is real. It is attributed to the presence of a region near the interface which is oxygen deficient resulting in a higher refractive index for that portion of the film near the silicon. It is not seen as a distinct layer, however, it results in an overall refractive index for the entire film which is slightly greater than that for fused quartz whose refractive index is 1.4601 at 5459 Å [45].

The situation becomes more complicated if the film is too thin to obtain at least two minima for the same wavelength. The difficulty is overcome by using calibrated filters to obtain the minima with well separated incident angle positions. In this case the effects of dispersion must be considered, as was previously mentioned. The simple relationship which we have used to relate the refractive index at any wavelength to the refractive

Table II. Refractive Index and Thickness Determination of Thermally Grown Silicon Dioxide [22]

N	λ, Å	θ_1 front reflection	θ_1 back reflection	$\Delta\theta_1$	θ_1	d, Å $n_2 = 1.4619$	d, Å $n_2 = 1.4500$	d, Å $n_2 = 1.4613$	Avg. d, Å $n_2 = 1.4613$
22.5	5459.0	29.77°	30.14°	+0.19°	29.96°	44,784	45,203	44,805	
21.5	5459.0	39.85°	40.20°	+0.17°	40.02°	44,772	45,231	44,795	
									44,802 ± 5
20.5	5459.0	48.89°	49.34°	+0.23°	449.12°	44,779	45,285	44,805	
19.5	5459.0	57.93°	58.36°	+0.21°	58.14°	44,773	45,333	44,802	

N = Fringe order number
λ = Wavelength of observed light
θ_1 = Angle of incidence and reflection (observed)
n_2 = Refractive index
d = Silicon dioxide film thickness

index at 5456 Å is given by

$$n_{G,\lambda} = n_{G,5456} + \delta_\lambda \frac{D_G}{D_O} \qquad (19)$$

$$D_G = n_{G,4358} - n_{G,6235} \qquad (20a)$$

$$D_O = n_{O,4358} - n_{O,6235} \qquad (20b)$$

$$\delta_\lambda = n_{O,\lambda} - n_{O,5456} \qquad (21)$$

where the subscript G refers to the glass film and the subscript O to fused quartz. The second subscript for the refractive index n refers to the wavelength in angstroms.

To show that this is a reasonably accurate fit for lead silicate glasses, we have tabulated in Table III the refractive index as determined by that simple relationship and the actual refractive index for a sample of dense flint glass. As shown in Table III the approximation is valid for dense flint glass. Similar calculations for other lead silicate glasses, borosilicate grown glass, sapphire, and crystalline quartz showed agreement within 0.001 in the calculated and actual refractive indexes for the wavelengths given in Table III. With silicon nitride the agreement was within 0.002.

Table III. Example of Accuracy of Simple Dispersion Relationship. Data for Dense Flint Glass

λ, Å	Calculated n	Actual n	Difference
5456	1.6602		
4361	1.6797	1.6802	+0.0005
4916	1.6682	1.6680	−0.0002
5150	1.6645	1.6643	−0.0002
5775	1.6565	1.6567	+0.0002
6145	1.6527	1.6532	+0.0005
6230	1.6520	1.6525	+0.0005

Since the greatest emphasis has been on silica and silicate type glasses, the dispersions of various materials were compared with that of silica. In Fig. 4 the dispersion ratio as given by D_G/D_O is plotted against the refractive index at 5456 Å for various materials. The data indicate that we can group the materials of interest into three series of dispersions. The highest dispersion series are used for lead silicate glasses, the lowest for most other silicates or aluminosilicates, and the medium dispersion series for a mixed

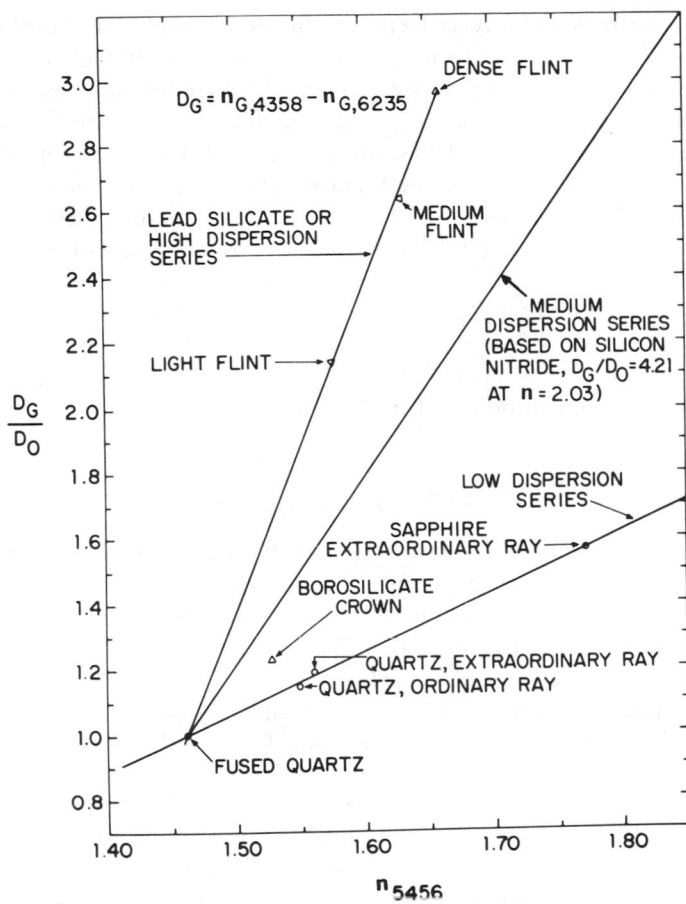

Figure 4. Dispersion ratio D_G/D_O for various materials as a function of the refractive index of the material at 5456 Å (or equally well at 5461 Å).

silicon dioxide–silicon nitride system. For each dispersion series we have a volume of books as had been mentioned near the beginning of this section. The refractive index for each filter within a book in a volume is calculated from Eq. (19) and Fig. 4.

3.4. Phase-Change Corrections

The phase-shift thickness corrections are the same for VAMFO and for CARIS. The phase-shift thickness correction arises because the phase shift of the ray reflected from the dielectric–substrate interface is generally not

180° (π), whereas the ray reflected from the air–dielectric interface does undergo a 180° phase shift on reflection. In the case of SiO_2 on silicon it had been found that the phase-shift thickness correction is essentially independent of the angle of incidence for the perpendicular component [6,18,20,22,23,30,33]. Thus, in the case of VAMFO, where only the perpendicular component of monochromatic visible radiation is utilized, the small phase-shift thickness corrections were originally given irrespective of the angle of incidence [6,18,20]. In the ultraviolet region of the spectrum where the phase-shift thickness corrections become appreciable, it was found that the change with angle was insignificant for the perpendicular component but did vary to some extent for the parallel component [30,33].

With silicon in the visible region, k_3 is quite small, and, therefore, for the perpendicular component Eq. (6) reduces to [22,23]

$$\tan \varphi_{23} = \frac{2n_2 n_3 k_3 \cos \theta_2}{(n_3^2 - n_2^2 \sin^2 \theta_2)^{1/2} (n_2^2 - n_3^2)} \tag{6'}$$

where $k_3 \ll 1$. Thus the phase-shift correction in terms of δN, where $\delta N = 0.5 - \varphi_{23}/2\pi$, is slightly angle dependent as shown in Fig. 5. The phase-shift thickness correction is virtually independent of angle because the $\cos \theta_2$ term in the numerator of Eq. (6') is counteracted by the $\cos \theta_2$ term in the denominator of Eq. (10).

The general invariance of the phase-shift thickness correction with angle for the perpendicular component was found to hold with many other combinations of insulators and substrates [35]. On the other hand, it was found that the phase-shift thickness correction for the parallel component increases with an increase in θ_1 as $1/\cos^2 \theta_2$ in most practical cases [35].

The phase-shift thickness corrections will vary with wavelength due to the variation of the refractive index (n_2) of the dielectric film and due to variation of the refractive index (n_3) and extinction coefficient (k_3) of the substrate with wavelength. The optical properties n_3 and k_3 of the reflecting substrate have more influence on the variation of the correction with wavelength than does the refractive index of the transparent film. Some examples of the variation of the correction with wavelength are given in Fig. 6 for sputtered SiO_2 films on silicon, on germanium, on copper, and on aluminum [35]. Determinations of the phase-shift thickness corrections have been simplified by the use of special phase-shift thickness correction charts [35].

3.5. Multiple Films

VAMFO can also be used to measure the thickness and the refractive index of a second transparent film applied over an initial transparent film.

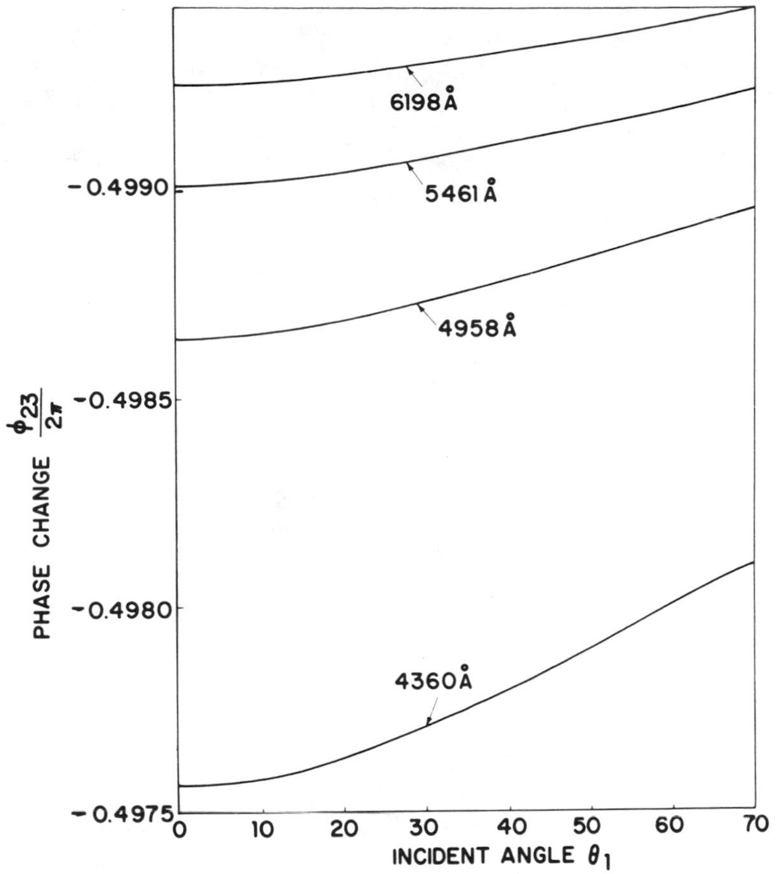

Figure 5. Phase change at the silicon dioxide–silicon interface of the perpendicular component as a function of incident angle θ_1 [Pliskin and Lehman ([22])].

As with a single transparent film, there are several equations which can be used for measuring the thickness of the second film. If the fringe orders N_i are not known, but the refractive indexes of the two layers as well as the thickness of the bottom layer are known, then it is easily shown ([6]) that

$$d_G = \frac{\lambda}{2n_{2G}\Delta \cos \theta_{2G}} - \frac{n_{2O}\Delta \cos \theta_{2O}}{n_{2G}\Delta \cos \theta_{2G}} d_O \tag{22}$$

where the subscripts O or $2O$ refer to the first transparent film and the subscripts G or $2G$ to the second transparent film which is on top of the first. The reasons for using subscripts G or O in our nomenclature is that in

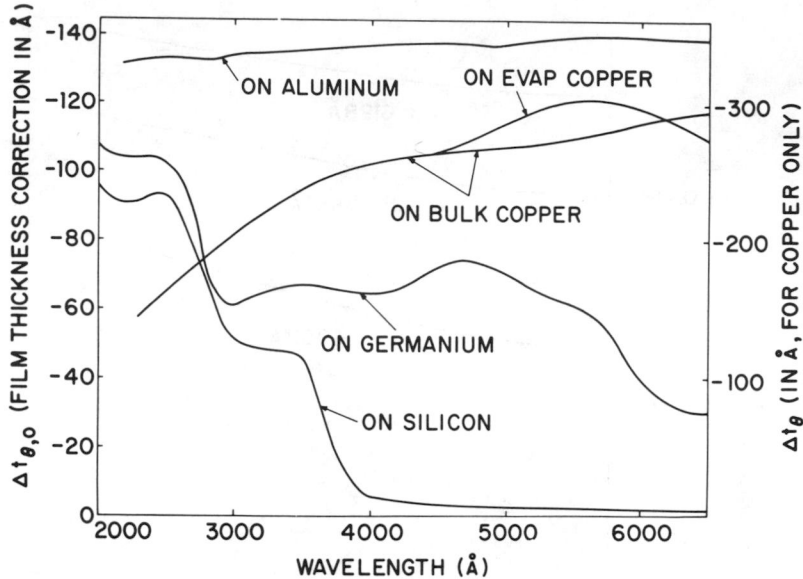

Figure 6. Phase-shift thickness correction for sputtered SiO_2 on various substrates [Pliskin [35]].

studying multiple-film systems we have made most of the measurements on the thicknesses and refractive indexes of fused sedimented-glass films [38] formed on silicon-dioxide-covered silicon wafers [29,39] and on similarly constructed semiconductor devices [40]. Although we shall for simplicity speak in terms of glass films on oxides, the same formulas are applicable to other two-component transparent-film systems on reflective substrates. The Δ cos factors are defined the same as with Eq. (11). Equation (22) was derived from the basic formula

$$N_i\lambda = 2n_{2G}d_G \cos\theta_{2Gi} + 2n_{2O}d_O \cos\theta_{2Oi}$$

$$= 2d_G(n_{2G}^2 - \sin^2\theta_{1i})^{1/2} + 2d_O(n_{2O}^2 - \sin^2\theta_{1i})^{1/2} \tag{23}$$

If the order is known, then it is seen from Eq. (23) that we can determine the thickness of the second film using

$$d_G = \frac{N_i\lambda}{2n_{2G}\cos\theta_{2Gi}} - \frac{n_{2O}\cos\theta_{2Oi}}{n_{2G}\cos\theta_{2Gi}}d_O$$

$$= \frac{N_i\lambda}{2(n_{2G}^2 - \sin^2\theta_{1i})^{1/2}} - \frac{(n_{2O}^2 - \sin^2\theta_{1i})^{1/2}}{(n_{2G}^2 - \sin^2\theta_{1i})^{1/2}}d_O \tag{24}$$

An expression for the refractive index is obtained from Eq. (24) in the exact manner as Eq. (16) was obtained from Eqs. (12) and (13)

$$n_{2G} = \left[\frac{F' \sin^2 \theta_{1i} - \sin^2 \theta_{1i}}{F' - 1}\right]^{1/2} \tag{16'}$$

where

$$F' = \left[\frac{N_i - [2d_O(n_{2O}^2 - \sin^2 \theta_{1i})^{1/2}]/\lambda}{N_j - [2d_O(n_{2O}^2 - \sin^2 \theta_{1j})^{1/2}]/\lambda}\right]^2 \tag{25}$$

In some cases the thicknesses can be determined most conveniently by ([29])

$$d_T = \frac{N\lambda_j}{2n_{2j}\cos\theta_{2j}} = \frac{N\lambda_j}{2(n_{2j}^2 - \sin^2\theta_{1j})^{1/2}} \tag{26}$$

where n_{2j} is the average refractive index at λ_j for the composite film of glass and oxide. If the thickness is sufficient for the observation of more than one minimum, then both the average refractive index and d_T can be determined by finding the refractive index for which d_T is the same from sets of tabulated values, as previously discussed with Eq. (18). If the glass refractive index is not known beforehand, it can be determined by use of the relation

$$n_{2G} = \frac{n_{2j}d_T - n_{2O}d_O}{d_G} \tag{27}$$

where

$$d_G = d_T - d_O$$

With thinner films, different filters are used and the sets of tables used in making the interpolation are based on a dispersion system corresponding to the type of dispersion expected for the mixed glass–oxide system. If the total film consists of two fairly distinct components of significantly different refractive indexes and comparable film thicknesses (and d_O is known) then Eq. (22) or (24) is more accurate than Eq. (26). For example, if the two components had refractive indexes of 1.5 and 1.7 and were of comparable thicknesses, then it can be shown that the thickness determined by Eq. (26) is 0.27% greater than that determined by the more accurate Eq. (24). If the two components are significantly different in thickness or if their refractive indexes are not significantly different then the thicknesses determined by the two equations are not significantly different. Similarly the refractive index of the glass or second film can be accurately determined by the relatively simple Eq. (27) if the second film is significantly thicker than the first film even though their refractive indexes are significantly different. If their refractive indexes are not significantly different then it is merely necessary for the second film to be of comparable thickness to obtain reasonably accurate refractive-index measurements from Eq. (27).

Equations (22)–(27) have been used by Pliskin and co-workers for measuring the thicknesses and refractive indexes of fused, sedimented-glass films ([38]) formed on silicon-dioxide-covered silicon wafers ([29,39]) and on semiconductor devices ([40]). Schwartz ([41]) investigated in detail the refractive indexes and film thicknesses of photoresist films deposited on silicon-dioxide-covered silicon wafers using some of the same VAMFO techniques and equations which we had previously used for the investigation of glass films formed on oxidized silicon wafers.

4. CARIS

4.1. Thickness Measurements

Utilization of transmission- and reflection-spectroscopic techniques for determining film thickness can be found in the literature ([7-17,19,21,22,24-28,30-33,42-44]). In this technique wavelength is varied rather than the angle of observation. In the case of reflection, the technique has been named CARIS by Reizmann and Van Gelder ([32]). The use of the reflection-spectroscopy technique was given impetus after Corl and Wimpfheimer ([19]) showed its applicability to the thickness measurement of SiO_2 films on silicon. The spectrum they obtained of a thermally grown silicon dioxide film on silicon is shown in Fig. 7. For homogeneous films, the thickness is often determined by

$$d = \frac{\Delta N \lambda_i \lambda_j}{2n_2(\lambda_j - \lambda_i)\cos\theta_2} = \frac{\Delta N \lambda_i \lambda_j}{2(\lambda_j - \lambda_i)(n_2{}^2 - \sin^2\theta_1)^{1/2}} \tag{28a}$$

or

$$d = \frac{\Delta N}{2n_2(\nu_i - \nu_j)\cos\theta_2} = \frac{\Delta N}{2(\nu_i - \nu_j)(n_2{}^2 - \sin^2\theta_1)^{1/2}} \tag{28b}$$

where ΔN is the number of fringes between wavelengths λ_i and λ_j or frequencies ν_i and ν_j. Equation (28b) is included as it is advantageous to obtain spectra on charts that are linear with frequency (cm^{-1}) since the fringe system is then more sinusoidal and the extrema can be measured more accurately. Due to the variation of the refractive index with wavelength Eqs. (28a) and (28b) are not strictly correct and for greatest accuracy

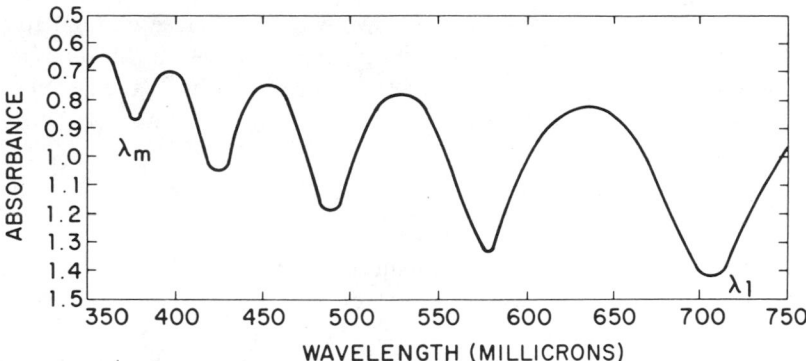

Figure 7. Interference spectrum by reflection from a thermally oxidized silicon wafer [Corl and Wimpfheimer ([19])].

the thickness is given by ([22])

$$d = \frac{\Delta N \lambda_i \lambda_j}{2(\lambda_j n_{2i} \cos \theta_{2i} - \lambda_i n_{2j} \cos \theta_{2j})}$$ (29)

where subscripts i and j refer to wavelengths λ_i and λ_j.

Taking into consideration phase-change corrections and dispersion, the author prefers using the relation [see Eq. (2) and Section 2]

$$d = \frac{N \lambda}{2 n_2 \cos \theta_2} + \Delta t_\varphi = \frac{N \lambda}{2(n_2{}^2 - \sin^2 \theta_1)^{1/2}} + \Delta t_\varphi$$ (30)

where for minima the order N is half-integral with reflection spectra and integral with transmission spectra. The degenerate nature of the silicon substrates used in device fabrication necessitates that reflection rather than transmission techniques be used for these measurements.

A simple method for determining the order which is most applicable at longer wavelengths is given by the approximate relation ([42])

$$N'_i = \frac{\nu_i}{\Delta \nu}$$ (31)

where N'_i is approximately the order for the extremum occurring at frequency $\nu_i = 1/\lambda_i$. This relation is only approximately accurate due to variations in the optical properties with wavelength (or frequency) ([30,42]). The order N'_i is generally slightly greater than the actual order N_i and if the film thickness is not too great or if the calculation were made at sufficiently long wavelengths, then the N'_i would be close enough to the actual N_i as to leave no doubt as to its proper value. With thicker films it is sometimes necessary to make corrections to N'_i to obtain the correct N_i. Equation (31) can be written as

$$N'_i = \frac{\nu_i}{|\nu_j - \nu_i|} = \frac{\lambda_j}{|\lambda_i - \lambda_j|} \tag{32}$$

where the subscripts i and j refer to successive minima. The average N'_i is determined from Eq. (32) using the extrema positions to either side of i. This value is then decreased by the percent given in Fig. 8 to obtain the current order N_i. It should be noted that the corrections above 5000 Å are practically independent of film thickness, and, therefore, there should be no doubt in the determined order N, since it could only be integral or half-integral depending on whether it is a maximum or a minimum. In the case of insulating films with greater dispersion, the corrections are larger, as shown for dense flint glass and for silicon nitride.

After establishing the order for one of the longer-wavelength extrema, each successive extremum toward the shorter wavelengths is increased by one. The film thickness can then be readily calculated for each of the

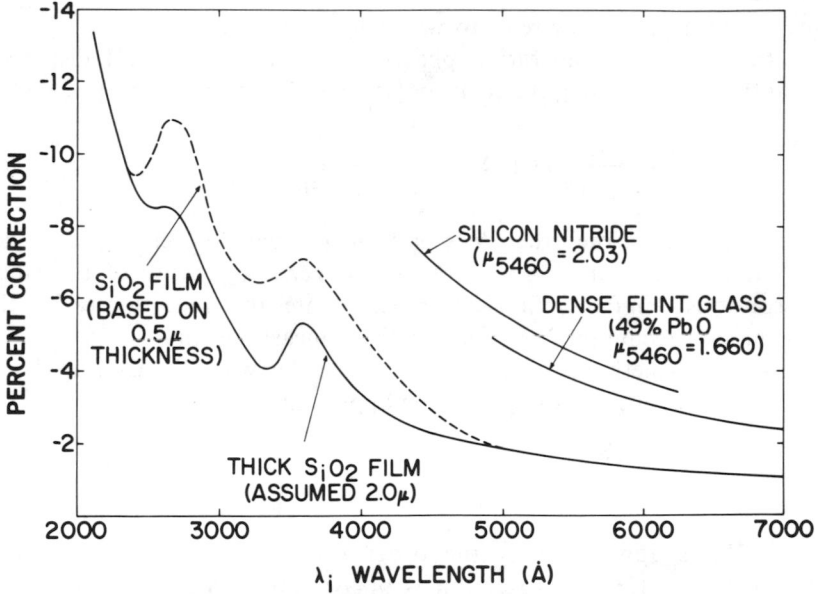

Figure 8. Corrections to be applied to the formula $N'_i = \nu_i/\Delta\nu = \lambda_{i\pm1}/|\lambda_i - \lambda_{i\pm1}|$ to obtain the correct order N_i for thickness determinations of various films on silicon.

extrema by application of Eq. (30). The phase-change correction Δt can be determined from Eq. (10) or taken from a plot as shown in Fig. 6. To simplify matters, the factor $2n_2 \cos \theta_2 = 2(n_2^2 - \sin^2 \theta_1)^{1/2}$ can also be plotted as a function of wavelength.

Excellent agreement in the thicknesses determined from each of the minima in the visible and in the ultraviolet can be obtained. Excellent agreement has been obtained between the thicknesses determined with VAMFO and those determined by CARIS in the ultraviolet region of the spectrum ([30]). This agreement would not have been possible without accurate phase-change thickness corrections.

The film thicknesses can also be determined by use of a nomogram based on Eq. (30) ([30]). This type nomogram differs from those sometimes used with VAMFO in that the film thicknesses for each order are plotted as a function of wavelength for a fixed angle of incidence, whereas with VAMFO the film thickness for each order and fixed wavelength are plotted as a function of angle of incidence.

4.2. Refractive-Index Measurements

The refractive index can be determined as a function of wavelength by these spectroscopic techniques providing the exact film thickness at the region of investigation is already known or can be determined by some independent technique such as VAMFO, multiple-beam interferometry, or ellipsometry. Solving for n_2 from Eq. (30), we obtain

$$n_2 = \left[\frac{N^2\lambda^2}{4(d - \Delta t_\varphi)^2} + \sin^2 \theta_1 \right]^{1/2} \tag{33}$$

Note that in this formula, the absolute value of the film-thickness correction is added to d since Δt_φ itself is negative by Eq. (10). It should be emphasized that for obtaining accurate film thicknesses and refractive indexes by CARIS, the spectrophotometer should be accurately calibrated and the angle of incidence θ_1 accurately determined. If the refractive index and thickness are determined by an external means, as with VAMFO, then $\sin^2 \theta_1$ or the angle of incidence can be determined.

4.3. Multiple Films

Spectroscopic techniques can also be used for the measurement of a second transparent film applied over an initial transparent film. Corl and Kosanke ([27]) obtained the thickness of fused sedimented-glass films ([38])

on oxidized wafers by use of the following equation in the visible and near-infrared spectral regions:

$$d_G = \frac{\Delta N \lambda_i \lambda_j}{(\lambda_j - \lambda_i)(2n_{2G} \cos \theta_{2G})} - \frac{n_{2O} \cos \theta_{2O}}{n_{2G} \cos \theta_{2G}} d_O \tag{34}$$

where the subscripts O or $2O$ refer to the first transparent film and the subscripts G or $2G$ refer to the second transparent film which is deposited on top of the first film. Equation (34) shows that the refractive index and thickness of the first layer must be known as well as the refractive index of the second layer, in this case the glass layer. For most practical purposes, Eq. (34) is sufficiently accurate, but since the refractive index varies with wavelength, the more accurate film thickness is given by

$$d_G = \frac{\Delta N \lambda_i \lambda_j}{2(\lambda_j n_{2Gi} \cos \theta_{2Gi} - \lambda_i n_{2Gj} \cos \theta_{2Gj})}$$
$$- \left[\frac{\lambda_j n_{2Oi} \cos \theta_{2Oi} - \lambda_i n_{2Oj} \cos \theta_{2Oj}}{\lambda_j n_{2Gi} \cos \theta_{2Gi} - \lambda_i n_{2Gj} \cos \theta_{2Gj}} \right] d_O \tag{35}$$

Rather than using the involved Eq. (35) for exact determinations, the author prefers using a modified form of Eq. (24) which had been used for multiple films in VAMFO.

$$d_G = \frac{N_i \lambda_i}{2n_{2Gi} \cos \theta_{2Gi}} - \frac{n_{2Oi} \cos \theta_{2Oi}}{n_{2Gi} \cos \theta_{2Gi}} d_O$$
$$= \frac{N_i \lambda_i}{2(n_{2Gi}^2 - \sin^2 \theta_1)^{1/2}} - \frac{(n_{2Oi}^2 - \sin^2 \theta_1)^{1/2}}{(n_{2Gi}^2 - \sin^2 \theta_1)^{1/2}} d_O \tag{36}$$

where the subscript i corresponds to the various terms for orders N_i and indicates that these quantities vary with wavelength. Basically the same formula as Eq. (36) was used by Murray et al. ([28]) in measuring photoresist thicknesses on oxidized silicon wafers.

Because the multiple component films are usually sufficiently thick, reflectivity corrections are not necessary ([33]), especially if in the reference beam there is reflection off a silicon wafer ([24,33]). In the visible region of the spectrum phase-shift thickness corrections are relatively minor for reasonably thick films on silicon and therefore can be neglected in such cases. However, with other substrates or even with silicon in the ultraviolet region the phase-shift thickness correction is not insignificant. For a two-component transparent film on a reflective substrate where the subscript $2O$ represents the component in contact with the reflecting substrate and the subscript $2G$ represents the component making up the top layer, the phase-shift thickness correction is

$$\Delta t_\varphi = -\left(0.5 - \frac{\varphi_{23}}{2\pi}\right)\frac{\lambda}{2n_{2G}\cos\theta_{2G}} \tag{10'}$$

where

$$\tan\varphi_{23} = \frac{-2n_{2O}v_3\cos\theta_{2O}}{u_3{}^2 + v_3{}^2 - n_{2O}{}^2\cos^2\theta_{2O}} \tag{6''}$$

In many cases use of a nomogram facilitates the glass-film thickness determinations. This has been done for various glass films using the 2.5 to 4.5 μ infrared spectral region [22]. Nomograms for CARIS are constructed by use of Eq. (36), and for VAMFO by use of Eq. (24). In case of VAMFO the film thickness for each order N is plotted against the VAMFO incident angle θ_1. In the spectroscopic nomogram the film thickness for each order N is plotted against the wavelength λ (or frequency v). A different nomogram would be required for each oxide-film thickness d_O, but in the use of many devices d_O is held fairly constant and thus only one nomogram would be required for monitoring glass-film thickness in a manufacturing process.

Before constructing the nomograms, the refractive indexes of the glasses and thermally grown silicon dioxide were determined out to 4.5 μ by use of Eq. (33) on single-layer-thick films for which the thicknesses were first determined accurately with VAMFO prior to reflection or transmission spectroscopic examination. Nomograms were then constructed for glass films on silicon dioxide. The dispersion curve for thermally grown silicon dioxide was found to be practically parallel to that of fused quartz [45] from the visible region [20] out to 3.5 μ [46].

5. ELLIPSOMETRY

5.1. Introduction

The use of ellipsometry provides a fourth nondestructive method for measuring both thickness and refractive index. This technique has also been called polarimetry and polarization spectroscopy. The name of ellipsometry can be attributed to Rothen [47]. This method is much more useful for extremely thin films than any of the previous methods and it can also be used for very accurate measurements of thicker films; however, it is more involved than the relatively simple methods previously described. The body of literature on ellipsometry has become so vast that the references given here are not necessarily complete, but a sufficient number are given to adequately cover the subject. Ellipsometry is mainly based on the work of

Drude [48] and Tronstad [49,50]. Further significant developments were made by Winterbottom [51-54], Vašíček [37,55,56], and Rothen [47,57,58]. In more recent years Archer [59,60] and McCrackin and Colson [61] have made the study more exact by the application of electronic computers. The widespread use of ellipsometry was shown by the symposium sponsored in 1963 by the National Bureau of Standards [62]. For a discussion of elliptically polarized light in itself, the reader can refer to almost any optics text or more preferably to books on the optics of thin films, especially Vašíček [37], Heavens [63], or Mayer [2].

Ellipsometry is based on evaluating the change in the state of polarization of light reflected from a substrate. The state of polarization is determined by the relative amplitude of the parallel (ρ_p) and perpendicular (ρ_s) components of radiation and by the phase difference between the two components, $\Delta_p - \Delta_s$. On reflection from a bare or film-covered surface the ratio of the two amplitudes (ρ_p/ρ_s) and the phase difference between the two components ($\Delta_p - \Delta_s$) undergo changes which are dependent upon the optical constants of the substrate, n_3 and k_3, the angle of incidence, θ_1, the optical constants of the film, n_2 and k_2, and the film thickness, d. If the optical constants of the substrate are known, and if the film is nonabsorbing (i.e., $k_2 = 0$), then the only unknowns in the theoretical equations describing the state of polarization are the refractive index, n_2, and the thickness, d, of the transparent film. In principle, with a complete knowledge of the state of polarization of the incident and reflected light the refractive index, n_2, and thickness, d, can be determined.

5.2. Theory

The basic theory of ellipsometry was developed by Drude [48]. Although not shown in Fig. 1, if one sums the amplitudes of all the reflected beams from the two interfaces for the perpendicular and for the parallel component, one obtains as the amplitudes of the total reflection [36,37,63].

$$R_s = \rho_s e^{i\Delta s} = \frac{r_{12s} + r_{23s}e^{-2i\beta}}{1 + r_{12s}r_{23s}e^{-2i\beta}} \tag{37}$$

$$R_p = \rho_p e^{i\Delta p} = \frac{r_{12p} - r_{23p}e^{-2i\beta}}{1 + r_{12p}r_{23p}e^{-2i\beta}} \tag{38}$$

where the Fresnel reflection coefficients, r, are given by

$$r_{12s} = \frac{n_1 \cos\theta_1 - n_2 \cos\theta_2}{n_1\cos\theta_1 + n_2 \cos\theta_2} \tag{4'}$$

$$r_{12p} = \frac{n_1 \cos \theta_2 - n_2 \cos \theta_1}{n_1 \cos \theta_2 + n_2 \cos \theta_1} \tag{39}$$

$$r_{23s} = \rho_{23s} e^{i\varphi_{23}} = \frac{n_2 \cos \theta_2 - (u_3 - iv_3)}{n_2 \cos \theta_2 + (u_3 - iv_3)} \tag{40}$$

$$r_{23p} = \frac{(n_3 - ik_3)^2 \cos \theta_2 - n_2(u_3 - iv_3)}{(n_3 - ik_3)^2 \cos \theta_2 + n_2(u_3 - iv_3)} \tag{41}$$

where ρ_{23}, φ_{23}, u_3, v_3, and β are defined in Eqs. (5)–(9). Incidently, Eq. (3) describing the reflectivity of the perpendicular component was obtained from Eq. (37) by considering that $R = R_s R_s^*$. The state of polarization is given by the amplitude ratio $\tan \psi = \rho_p / \rho_s$, and the phase difference between the two components $\Delta = \Delta_p - \Delta_s$. The basic equation of ellipsometry is thus given by

$$(\tan \psi)e^{i\Delta} = \frac{\rho_p}{\rho_s} e^{i(\Delta_p - \Delta s)} = \frac{R_p}{R_s}$$

$$= \left(\frac{r_{12p} + r_{23p}e^{-2i\beta}}{1 + r_{12p}r_{23p}e^{-2i\beta}} \right)\left(\frac{1 + r_{12s}r_{23s}e^{-2i\beta}}{r_{12s} + r_{23s}e^{-2i\beta}} \right) \tag{42}$$

Unfortunately for Drude, he had no electronic computers to help him with the calculations. However he expanded the equations in terms of d/λ, where $d \ll \lambda$, and thus obtained the so-called Drude approximations, which are valid for very thin transparent films ($d < 100$ Å) on reflective substrates in air or vacuum. If $\bar{\psi}$ and $\bar{\Delta}$ are the values obtained for the bare surface and ψ and Δ from the film-covered surface, then ([63])

$$\psi - \bar{\psi} = \frac{2\pi d}{\lambda} \frac{\sin 2\bar{\psi} \cos \theta_1 \sin^2 \theta_1\, a_1}{(\cos^2 \theta_1 - a)^2 + a_1^2}(1 - n_2^2 \cos^2 \theta_1)\left(1 - \frac{1}{n_2^2}\right)$$

$$= C_\psi(1 - n_2^2 \cos^2 \theta_1)\left(1 - \frac{1}{n_2^2}\right)\frac{d}{\lambda} \tag{43}$$

$$\Delta - \bar{\Delta} = \frac{4\pi d}{\lambda} \frac{\cos \theta_1 \sin^2 \theta_1\, (\cos^2 \theta_1 - a)}{(\cos^2 \theta_1 - a)^2 + a_1^2}\left(1 - \frac{1}{n_2^2}\right)$$

$$= C_\Delta\left(1 - \frac{1}{n_2^2}\right)\frac{d}{\lambda} \tag{44}$$

where

$$a = \frac{n_3^2 - k_3^2}{(n_3^2 + k_3^{22})} \quad \text{and} \quad a_1 = \frac{2n_3 k_3}{(n_3^2 + k_3^2)^2} \tag{45}$$

Using the Drude equations for films of barium stearate on stainless steel, Rothen and Hanson ([57]) showed agreement for film thicknesses as large as 250 Å. Tronstad extended the Drude formulas for the general case where the film and substrate are immersed in a medium other than air (or vacuum). Archer ([64-66]) used an approximate expression containing even more terms than Eqs. (44) and (45) to give a more exact expression for very thin films on absorbing substrates in air. Burge and Bennett ([67]) have compared the Drude approximation and Archer's more exact approximation with the values determined from the exact ellipsometry equation for Al_2O_3 on aluminum and SiO_2 on silicon. They conclude that Archer's Δ equation is more exact than his ψ equation and it can be used with reasonable accuracy for studying the growth of films as thick as 200 Å. Saxena ([68]) has further extended the approximations, obtaining relations which appear to be more accurate (at least for SiO_2 on silicon) in the thin-film region (< 100 Å) than those of Archer and which are also valid in very limited ranges corresponding to thicknesses in the vicinity of multiple orders of thickness (orders of 2440 Å for SiO_2 on silicon).

Vašíček ([56]) used a graphical method with which he could obtain the refractive indexes and thicknesses of transparent films as thick as 1.5 μ on glass substrates.

5.3. Experimental Applications

With the advent of electronic computers, the application of the exact equation [Eq. (42)] has been simplified tremendously. Computer programs making use of the exact equation have been written by Archer ([59]) and by McCrackin and Colson ([61]). On a particular substrate of known optical values of n_3 and k_3 at wavelength λ and for selected film refractive indexes n_2, Δ and ψ values are determined as functions of the film thickness d, which is related to β in Eq. (42) by Eq. (46) below. Archer's δ is the same as our β, and with δ given in degrees, the film thickness d is given by

$$d = \frac{(180N + \delta)\lambda}{360(n_2^2 - \sin^2 \theta_1)^{1/2}} \qquad (46)$$

where the order N takes on integral values depending upon the thickness of the film. Using this technique, Archer made a graphical plot as shown in Fig. 9 for transparent films of various refractive indexes on silicon. This plot is applicable for $\lambda = 5461$ Å, $n_3 = 4.05$, $k_3 = 0.028$, and $\theta_1 = 70.00°$. Each curve represents a particular refractive index for the transparent film, with δ values for every 20° indicated on the curves. Arrows indicate the direction of increasing δ or thickness. Once Δ and ψ have been determined from ellipsometer readings, the plot can be used to give directly the

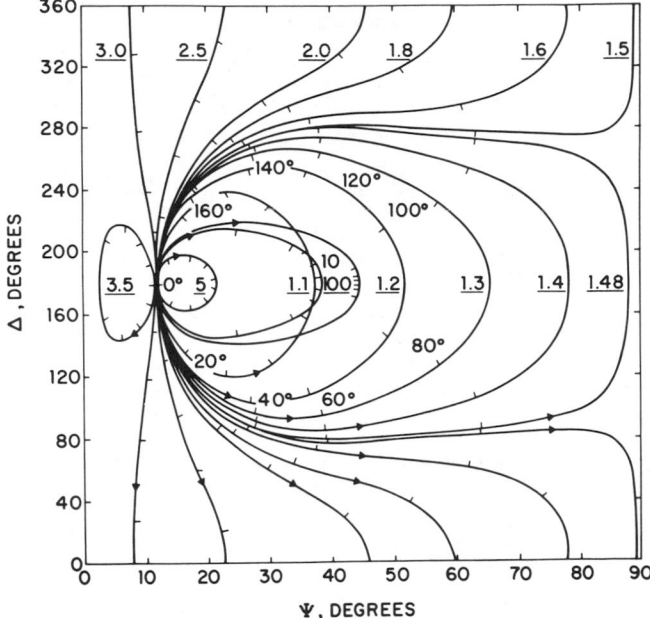

Figure 9. Variation of Δ and ψ as a function of the index of refraction and thickness (in terms of δ) of transparent films on silicon with $n_3 = 4.05$, $k_3 = 0.028$, $\lambda = 5461$ Å, $\theta_1 = 70.00°$. The underlined numbers are indexes of refraction [Archer [59,60]].

rcfractive index, n_2, of the film and δ, from which the thickness can be determined by Eq. (46) providing the order N or approximate thickness is known. The difficulty in the technique is that a new plot is needed for any change in λ, θ_1, n_3, or k_3.

A typical ellipsometer representation is shown in Fig. 10. The collimated, monochromatic light is linearly polarized by the polarizer. The linearly polarized light is made elliptically polarized by the compensator, which can be a mica quarter-wave plate or a Babinet–Soleil compensator. Although the compensator can be set at any azimuth, for simplicity it is usually oriented so that its fast axis is at $\pm 45°$ with the plane of incidence. After reflection from the sample the light is transmitted through a second polarizer which is the analyzer. Finally the light intensity is determined by eye, or preferably by a photomultiplier detector. The polarizer and analyzer are rotated until extinction is obtained. Under these conditions, the ellipticity caused by the polarizer, compensator, and analyzer combination is the opposite of that formed by reflection from the film and substrate. There are 32 possible sets of polarizer (P) and analyzer (A)

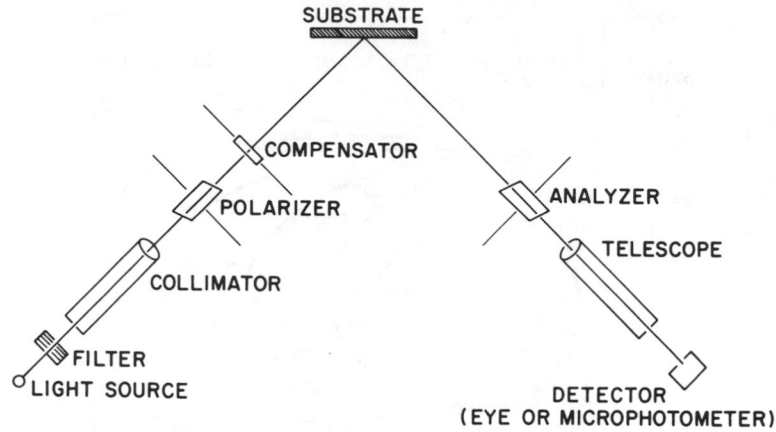

Figure 10. Schematic representation of the ellipsometer [Archer ([59,60])].

readings which will give extinction. However only four of them are independent. From these extinction readings of P and A the phase difference, Δ, and amplitude ratio, $\tan\psi$, can be determined from the following relations:

$$\tan \Delta = \sin \epsilon \tan (90° - 2P) \tag{47}$$

$$\tan \psi = \cot L \tan (-A) \tag{48}$$

where

$$\cos 2L = -\cos \epsilon \cos 2P \tag{49}$$

and ϵ is the actual relative retardation of the compensator. A detailed discussion on the various possible polarizer, compensator, and analyzer settings and the relationship between them and the Δ and ψ values can be found in the work of Winterbottom ([53]) and McCrackin et al. ([69]). The latter authors also cover detailed alignment procedures in setting up the apparatus.

The most accurate readings of P and A can be obtained using a technique suggested by Archer ([59]). After obtaining a preliminary minimal detector signal by the proper adjustment of P and A, the analyzer is kept at the same orientation while readings are taken of the polarizer set on either side of the minimum to give detector signals of equal intensity. The average of the two polarizer settings gives a more accurate value of P. With the polarizer then set at this value of P, the same procedure is repeated with the analyzer, obtaining those settings of A on either side of the minimum which give equal detector signals. The average of these two settings gives an accurate value for A.

In principle the ellipsometer technique is exact; however, near the origin ($\delta = 0°$), where the lines of constant refractive index merge, the refractive indexes cannot be determined.

The exact techniques of ellipsometry have been used in recent years for the study of various transparent films on reflective substrates. Archer ([59,60]) and Claussen and Flower ([70]) have studied a variety of silicon dioxides formed or deposited on silicon substrates. McCrackin et al. ([69]) studied BaF_2 films evaporated on chromium surfaces. Zaininger and Revesz ([71]) studied the oxide films formed in the oxidation of gallium arsenide. Bockris et al. ([72]) made in situ investigations of the passivation of nickel in acid solutions. These are only a few of the many investigations which have been done using ellipsometry. Its use has become so widespread that the investigator has a choice of good commercial ellipsometers available to him.

REFERENCES

1. A. R. Rollet, Über die Farben, welche in dem Newton'schen Ringsystem aufeinanderfolgen, *Sitzber. Akad. Wiss. Wien III*, **77**, 177–261 (1878).
2. H. Mayer, *Physik dünner Schichten, Wissenschaftliche Verlagsgesellschaft*, Stuttgart (1950).
3. U. R. Evans, *The Corrosion and Oxidation of Metals*, Arnold Ltd., London (1960), pp. 787–790.
4. K. Blodgett, Films Built by Depositing Successive Monomolecular Layers on a Solid Surface, *J. Am. Chem. Soc.* **57**, 1007–1022 (1935).
5. K. Blodgett and I. Langmuir, Built-up Films of Ba Stearate and Their Optical Properties, *Phys. Rev.* **51**, 964–982 (1937).
6. W. A. Pliskin and E. E. Conrad, Nondestructive Determination of Thickness and Refractive Index of Transparent Films, *IBM J. Res. and Develop.* **8**, 43–51 (1964).
7. A. Charlesby and J. J. Polling, The Optical Properties of Thin Oxide Films on Tantalum, *Proc. Roy. Soc.* **A227**, 434–447 (1955).
8. F. H. Constable, The Cause of the Colours Shown During the Oxidation of Metallic Copper, *Proc. Roy. Soc.* **A115**, 570–588 (1927).
9. E. Q. Adams and L. S. Ickis, Jr., Determining Film Thickness with the Recording Spectrophotometer, *Gen. Elec. Rev.* **42**, 450–451 (1939).
10. M. F. Bechtold, Coating Thickness Measurement by Interferometry, *J. Opt. Soc. Am.* **37**, 873–878 (1947).
11. J. T. Waber, G. E. Sturdy, E. M. Wise, and C. R. Tipton, Jr., A Spectrophotometric Study of the Oxidation of Tantalum, *J. Electrochem. Soc.* **99**, 121–129 (1952).
12. K. M. Greenland, Measurement and Control of the Thickness of Thin Films, *Vacuum* **2**, 216–230 (1952).
13. P. Bousquet, Structure Study of Thin Transparent Films from their Optical Properties, *Ann. Phys.* **2**, 163–213 (1957); also, *Optica Acta.* **3**, 153–160 (1956).
14. C. D. Miller, A New Technique for Studying Photooxidation Erosion of Polymer Films, *J. Appl. Polymer Sci.* **24**, 311–314 (1957).

15. E. P. Brightwell, High Precision Nondestructive Thickness Measurements of Coatings, *ASTM Bull.* **237**, 67–69 (April 1959).

16. A-F. Bogenschutz, F. Bergmann, and J. Jentsch, Optische Methode zur Dickenmessung dünner Schichten, *Z. Angew, Phys.* **14**, 469–481 (1962).

17. W. P. Ellis, Immersion Spectrophotometry of Interference Films: Refractive Indices of Fluoride Films on Uranium Dioxide and Anodic Oxide Film on Uranium Metal, *J. Opt. Soc. Am.* **53**, 613–619 (1963).

18. W. A. Pliskin and E. E. Conrad, Une Technique Simple Pour Mesurer L'Épaisseur et L'Indice de Réfraction de Couches Transparentes Sans Les Altéres, *J. Phys. Radium* **25**, 17–20, 1964.

19. E. A. Corl and H. Wimpfheimer, Thickness Measurement of Silicon Dioxide Layers by Ultraviolet-Visible Interference Method, *Solid-State Electron.* **7**, 755–761 (1964).

20. W. A. Pliskin and R. P. Esch, Refractive Index of SiO_2 Films Grown on Silicon, *J. Appl. Phys.* **36**, 2011–2013 (1965).

21. F. Reizmann, Optical Thickness Measurement of Thin Transparent Films on Silicon, *J. Appl. Phys.* **36**, 3804–3807 (1965).

22. W. A. Pliskin and H. S. Lehman, in *Proceedings of the Symposium on Manufacturing In-Process Control and Measuring Techniques for Semiconductors*, at Phoenix, Arizona, March 1966, Vol. 1, pp. 11-1 to 11-28. (Also available as IBM Technical Report TR 22.279, *Non-destructive Optical and Spectroscopic Measurements of Oxide and Glass Films*.)

23. W. A. Pliskin, Am. Ceram. Soc. Meeting, Washington, D.C., May 1966. (Also available as IBM preprint MP22.0078, *The Effect of Moisture on R.F. Sputtered and Fused Glass Films*.)

24. N. Goldsmith and L. A. Murray, Determination of Silicon Oxide Thickness, *Solid-State Electron.* **9**, 331–332 (1966).

25. R. K. Iler, Multilayers of Colloidal Particles, *J. Colloid Sci.* **21**, 569–594 (1966).

26. R. I. Hughes, Extension of the Spectrophotometric Method for Measuring Thin Films on Solid Substrates, *Nature* **212**, 1350–1351 (1966).

27. E. A. Corl and K. Kosanke, Non-destructive Measurement of Glass on Silicon Oxide Through Near Infrared (NIR) Interference, *Solid-State Electron.* **9**, 943–948 (1966).

28. L. A. Murray, N. Goldsmith, and E. L. Jordan, Measurement of Photoresist Thickness, *Electrochem. Technol.* **4**, 508–509 (1966).

29. W. A. Pliskin, Fused Glass Penetration into Thermally Grown Silicon Dioxide Films, *J. Electrochem. Soc.* **114**, 620–623 (1967).

30. R. A. Wesson, R. P. Phillips, and W. A. Pliskin, Phase-Shift-Corrected Thickness Determination of Silicon Dioxide on Silicon by Ultraviolet Interference, *J. Appl. Phys.* **38**, 2455–2460 (1967).

31. F. Lukeš and E. Schmidt, Another Method for the Determination of Silicon Oxide Thickness, *Solid-State Electron.* **10**, 264–266 (1967).

32. F. Reizmann and W. Van Gelder, Optical Thickness Measurement of SiO_2–Si_3N_4 Films on Silicon, *Solid-State Electron.* **10**, 625–632 (1967).

33. R. A. Wesson, H. W. Young, and W. A. Pliskin, Reflectivity Thickness Corrections for Silicon Dioxide Films on Silicon, *Appl. Phys. Letters* **11**, 105–106 (1967).

34. W. A. Pliskin and R. A. Wesson, Reflectivity Thickness Corrections for Silicon Dioxide Films on Silicon for Vamfo, *IBM J. Res. and Develop.*, **12**, 192–194 (1968).

35. W. A. Pliskin, Phase-Shift Corrections in Determining the Thickness of Transparent Films on Reflective Substrates, to be published in *Solid-State Electron.* **11**.

36. M. Born and E. Wolf, *Principles of Optics*, Pergamon Press Ltd., Oxford (1965) 3rd revised ed.
37. A. Vašíček, *Optics of Thin Films*, North-Holland Publishing Co., Amsterdam (1960).
38. W. A. Pliskin and E. E. Conrad, Techniques for Obtaining Uniform Thin Glass Films on Substrates, *Electrochem. Technol.* **2**, 196–200 (1964).
39. W. A. Pliskin and R. P. Esch, unpublished work.
40. D. R. Kerr, J. S. Logan, P. J. Burkhardt, and W. A. Pliskin, Stabilization of SiO_2 Passivation Layers with P_2O_5, *IBM J. Res. and Develop.* **8**, 376–384 (1964).
41. G. C. Schwartz, in *Kodak Seminar on Microminiaturization*, at Rochester, N.Y. June 1965.
42. W. A. Pliskin, The Stability of Glazed Silicon Surfaces to Water Attack, *Proc. IEEE* **52**, 1468–1471 (1964).
43. W. A. Pliskin and H. S. Lehman, Structural Evaluation of Silicon Oxide Films, *J. Electrochem. Soc.* **112**, 1013–1019 (1965).
44. J. C. Banter, Determination of the Refractive Index and Thickness of Oxide Films on Anodized Zirconium from Transmission Interference Measurements, *J. Electrochem. Soc.* **112**, 388–390 (1965).
45. W. S. Rodney and R. J. Spindler, Index of Refraction of Fused Quartz Glass for Ultraviolet, Visible, and Infrared Wavelengths, *J. Opt. Soc. Am.* **44**, 677–679 (1954).
46. W. A. Pliskin, unpublished work.
47. A. Rothen, The Ellipsometer, an Apparatus to Measure Thicknesses of Thin Surface Films, *Rev. Sci. Instr.* **16**, 26–30 (1945).
48. P. Drude, Über Oberflächenschichten, I und II, *Ann. Physik u. Chem.* **36**, 532–566, and 865–897 (1889); Bestimmung der optischen Konstanten der Metalle, *Ann. Physik u. Chem.* **39**, 481–554 (1890).
49. L. Tronstad, Some Optical Observation on the Protective Films on Aluminum in Nitric, Chromic, and Sulphuric Acids, *Trans. Faraday Soc.* **30**, 362–366 (1934).
50. L. Tronstad, The Investigation of Thin Surface Films on Metals by Means of Reflected Polarized Light, *Trans. Faraday Soc.* **29**, 502–514 (1933); The Validity of Drude's Optical Method of Investigating Transparent Films on Metals, *Trans. Faraday Soc.* **31**, 1151–1158 (1935).
51. A. B. Winterbottom, A Polarization Spectrometer for Investigation of Surface Films on Metals, *J. Sci. Instr.* **14**, 203–208 (1937).
52. A. B. Winterbottom, Polarimetric Studies of Oxide Film Formation on Metals, *Nature*, **140**, 364–365 (1937).
53. A. B. Winterbottom, *Optical Studies of Metal Surfaces*, The Royal Norwegian Scientific Society, Report No. 1, F. Brun, Trondheim, Norway (1955).
54. A. B. Winterbottom, Optical Methods of Studying Films on Reflecting Bases Depending on Polarisation and Interference Phenomena, *Trans. Faraday Soc.* **42**, 487–495 (1946).
55. A. Vašíček, The Chemical Action of Dilute Sulfuric Acid on Some Lead Glasses, *Glastech. Ber.* **18**, 45–49 (1940).
56. A. Vašíček, Polarimetric Methods for the Determination of the Refractive Index and the Thickness of Thin Films on Glass, *J. Opt. Soc. Am.* **37**, 145–153 (1947).
57. A. Rothen and M. Hanson, Optical Measurements of Surface Films, *Rev. Sci. Instr.* **19**, 839–841 (1948) and Optical Properties of Surface Films II, *Rev. Sci. Instr.* **20**, 66–72 (1949).
58. A. Rothen, Improved Method to Measure the Thickness of Thin Films with a Photoelectric Ellipsometer, *Rev. Sci. Instr.* **28**, 283–285 (1957).

59. R. J. Archer, Determination of the Properties of Films on Silicon by the Method of Ellipsometry, *J. Opt. Soc. Am.* **52**, 970–977 (1962).
60. R. J. Archer, in *Symposium on Manufacturing In-Process Control and Measuring Techniques for Semiconductors*, at Phoenix, Arizona (March 1966) pp. 17-1 to 17-19.
61. F. L. McCrackin and J. P. Colson, in *Ellipsometry in the Measurement of Surfaces and Thin Films* (E. Passaglia, R. R. Stromberg, and J. Kruger, eds.) pp. 61–82, Natl. Bur. Std. Misc. Publ. 256, U.S. Govt. Printing Office, Washington, D.C., (1964). Also NBS Tech. Note 242 (1964), A Fortran Program for Analysis of Ellipsometer Measurements and Calculation of Reflection Coefficients from Thin Films.
62. E. Passaglia, R. R. Stromberg, and J. Kruger, eds. *Ellipsometry in the Measurement of Surfaces and Thin Films*, Natl. Bur. Std. Misc. Publ. 256, U.S. Govt. Printing Office, Washington, D.C. (1964).
63. O. S. Heavens, *Optical Properties of Thin Solid Films*, Butterworths Scientific Publications, Ltd., London (1955).
64. R. J. Archer, Optical Measurement of Film Growth on Silicon and Germanium Surfaces in Room Air, *J. Electrochem. Soc.* **104**, 619–622 (1957).
65. R. J. Archer, in *Ellipsometry in the Measurement of Surfaces and Thin Films*, (E. Passaglia, R. R. Stromberg, and J. Kruger, eds.), pp. 255–279, Natl. Bur. Std. Misc. Publ. 256, U.S. Govt. Printing Office, Washington, D.C., 1964.
66. R. J. Archer and G. W. Gobeli, Measurement of Oxygen Adsorption on Silicon by Ellipsometry, *J. Phys. Chem. Solids* **26**, 343–351 (1965).
67. D. K. Burge and H. E. Bennett, Effect of a Thin Surface Film on the Ellipsometric Determination of Optical Constants, *J. Opt. Soc. Am.* **54**, 1428–1433 (1964).
68. A. N. Saxena, Changes in the Phase and Amplitude of Polarized Light Reflected from a Film-Covered Surface and Their Relations with the Film Thickness, *J. Opt. Soc. Am.* **55**, 1061–1067 (1965).
69. F. L. McCrackin, E. Passaglia, R. R. Stromberg, and H. L. Steinberg, Measurement of the Thickness and Refractive Index of Very Thin Films and the Optical Properties of Surfaces by Ellipsometry, *J. Res. Natl. Bur. Std.* **67A**, 363–377 (1963).
70. B. H. Claussen and M. Flower, An Investigation of the Optical Properties and the Growth of Oxide Films on Silicon, *J. Electrochem. Soc.* **110**, 983–987 (1963).
71. K. H. Zaininger and A. G. Revesz, Ellipsometric Investigations of Oxide Films on GaAs, *J. Phys. Radium* **25**, 208–211 (1964).
72. J. O'M. Bockris, A. K. N. Reddy, and B. Rao, An Ellipsometric Determination of the Mechanism of Passivity of Nickel, *J. Electrochem. Soc.* **113**, 1133–1144 (1966).

II. A REVIEW OF X-RAY METHODS FOR INVESTIGATING THIN FILMS AND PLATINGS

Eugene P. Bertin

Radio Corporation of America
Electronic Components and Devices
Harrison, New Jersey

X-ray investigation of films may provide the following information: thickness; surface smoothness; chemical composition; amorphous, single-crystalline, or polycrystalline state; crystallographic orientation; lattice parameter; crystallite size; stress; and dislocation and stacking-fault density. A noncritical review is given of X-ray methods for nondestructive investigation of true thin films, oxide and corrosion layers, epitaxial layers, and platings. Six X-ray methods are included: total specular reflection, diffraction, divergent-beam (Kossel) photography, diffraction topography, secondary-emission (fluorescence) spectrometry, and absorption-edge spectrometry. For each of these methods, the paper considers principles, special instrumentation and techniques required for application to films, the nature of the experimental measurements and data, film properties that can be evaluated, and scope and applications. The emphasis is on experimental techniques and treatment of data, rather than on specific materials and results.

1. INTRODUCTION

Investigations of thin superficial layers usually have one of two objectives. One is to infer the properties of the bulk material. Specimens in bulk form may not be suitable for the measurement of certain properties or applicable to certain instruments and methods. Use of films may circumvent these limitations. For example, transmission electron microscopy may be used to observe individual dislocations and other lattice defects. Also, dispersion of bulk specimens into films minimizes matrix effects in X-ray secondary-emission (fluorescence) analysis.

The other objective is to investigate the properties of thin films *per se*. Examples of such specimens include evaporated films, sublimates, oxide films, corrosion layers, semiconductor films and epitaxial layers, and platings and other protective or decorative coatings. It is also of interest to investigate the interface between layer and substrate, and to observe progressive changes in properties as a film grows in thickness and approaches the nature of bulk material.

At least six distinct X-ray methods have been applied to the characterization of films and platings, and it is fair to state that a more nearly complete characterization is possible by X-ray methods than by any other group of related methods. The methods are total specular reflection, diffraction, divergent-beam (Kossel) photography, diffraction topography, secondary-emission (fluorescence) spectrometry, and absorption-edge spectrometry. Electron-probe primary-emission X-ray spectrometry has also been applied to film and plating studies, but is not considered here.

The film properties that can be evaluated by these X-ray methods are: (1) thickness; (2) surface smoothness; (3) analysis for chemical species; (4) analysis for chemical elements; (5) amorphous, single-crystalline, or polycrystalline state; (6) crystallographic orientation; (7) lattice parameter; (8) crystallite size; (9) preferred orientation; (10) stress; (11) dislocation density; and (12) stacking fault density. The information may be qualitative or quantitative.

This paper is a noncritical review of these X-ray methods for non-destructive investigation of true thin films, oxide and corrosion layers, epitaxial layers, and platings. For each of the six methods listed above, a discussion is given of: (1) principles; (2) special instrumentation and techniques required for application to films; (3) nature of the experimental measurements and data; (4) film properties that can be evaluated; and (5) scope and limitations.

The emphasis is on experimental techniques and treatment of data, rather than on specific materials and results.

2. X-RAY REFLECTION

2.1. Principle

In Fig. 1, consider a highly collimated monochromatic X-ray beam O directed at a very small glancing angle $\phi < 1°$ on a highly polished plane surface. As ϕ is made progressively smaller, three phenomena occur which may permit the investigation of surfaces and/or of films having thickness of 10 to several thousand angstroms.

1. At some critical glancing angle ϕ_C, substantially total specular reflection occurs, giving reflected beam R_1.

2. If the reflecting surface is a thin film up to a few thousand angstroms

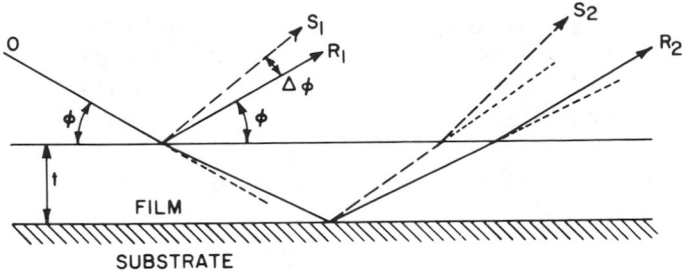

Figure 1. Origin of interference fringes from reflection and scatter of X-rays. O, incident beam; R_1, R_2, specularly reflected rays; S_1, S_2, scattered rays; ϕ, glancing angle; t, film thickness.

thick, interference fringes may appear due to the interference of the beams reflected from the film–air and film–substrate interfaces (R_1 and R_2).

3. A second set of fringes may appear due to interference of the beams scattered from the film–air and film–substrate interfaces (S_1 and S_2) ([60]).

The two types of fringe occur on both the high-ϕ (+ orders) and low-ϕ (− orders) sides of the specularly reflected beam, but the low-ϕ fringes are weaker and often undetected. The scatter fringes are weaker than the reflection fringes. It can be demonstrated in several ways that the second set of fringes arises from scattered X-rays, one being that their angular separation is twice that of the reflection fringes. This is to be expected since the scattered part of the radiation originating at the film–substrate interface makes only one traversal through the film, while the specularly reflected part makes two traversals.

2.2. Theory

The index of refraction n for X-rays is given by

$$n = 1 - \left(\frac{Ne^2\lambda^2}{2\pi mc^2}\right) - i\left(\frac{\mu\rho\lambda}{4\pi}\right) = 1 - \delta - i\beta \tag{1}$$

where N is electron density (cm^{-3}), e is electron charge (esu), m is electron mass, λ is X-ray wavelength, c is velocity of light, μ is X-ray mass absorption coefficient, and ρ is density. The quantities δ and β are real and positive, and their values are determined substantially by the electron density and electron binding energies of the refracting medium. Such factors as physical or chemical state, amorphous or crystalline state, crystallite size and orientation, etc., are important only insofar as they affect electron density.

The quantity δ is of the order 10^{-6} to 10^{-5}, except where λ is close to an absorption edge, when it may assume anomalous values as high as

10^{-4}. For a completely X-ray-transparent medium β would be 0, and true total reflection would occur; that is, the intensities of the reflected I_R and incident I_0 beams would be equal. However, since X-ray reflection involves some penetration, β is finite, and $I_R/I_0 < 1$. The value of β is usually $< 0.1\ \delta$.

Thus the index of refraction for X-rays is < 1 by $\sim 10^{-6}$ to 10^{-5}, and X-rays in vacuum or air are totally reflected from any medium if incident upon it at a very small glancing angle $\phi < \phi_C$, the critical glancing angle. By Snell's law

$$1 - \delta = \cos\phi_C = 1 - (\phi_C{}^2/2) \tag{2}$$

from which

$$\phi_C = \sqrt{2\delta} \tag{3}$$

As a typical example, values of δ, β, and ϕ_C for Al and Cu $K\alpha$ X-rays are, respectively, 8.32×10^{-6}, 1.6×10^{-7}, and 4.08 mrad (13.0 min of arc).

2.3. Instrumentation

Duncan and Parratt ([22]) built the X-ray reflectometer shown schematically in Fig. 2 by modifying a two-crystal X-ray spectrometer. X-rays from the X-ray tube A pass through a narrow slit B to a calcite monochromator C, which may be rotated about axis D to present angle θ to the X-ray beam to diffract the selected wavelength. The monochromatic beam passes through a second narrow slit E to the specimen surface F and detector G. The E–F–G assembly is mounted on a common arm pivoted on axis D to permit the assembly to present angle θ to the monochromator C. The slit E may be used to exclude the $K\alpha_2$ component from the X-ray beam.

Provision is made to: (1) vary the glancing angle ϕ by rotation of the specimen about axis H using a manually operated tangent screw; (2) manually rotate the detector about axis H independently of the setting of ϕ; and (3) expose a fine-grain photographic plate at I. A detailed description of the instrument and its alignment and operation are given in ([22]).

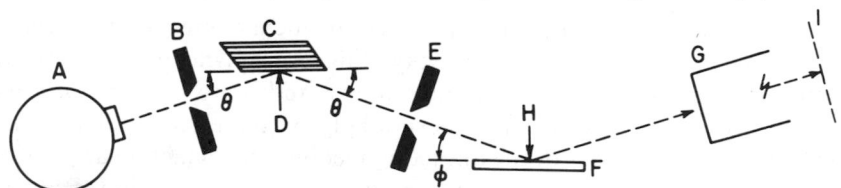

Figure 2. X-ray reflectometer built on a two-crystal X-ray spectrometer [Duncan and Parratt ([22])]. *A*, X-ray tube; *B*, slit; *C*, CaCO$_3$ monochromator; *D*, rotation axis; *E*, slit; *F*, specimen; *G*, detector; *H*, rotation axis; *I*, photographic plate.

Mozzi and Guentert ([55]) built an X-ray reflectometer by modifying a standard commercial X-ray diffractometer. A reflectometer requires two features not provided by a conventional diffractometer: a source of strictly monochromatic X-radiation having narrow angular divergence, and a specimen holder permitting precise alignment of the specimen surface with the incident beam.

The first requirement was met by use of a perfect germanium single crystal aligned for Borrmann anomalous transmission ([14]). This type of monochromator has two advantages over a conventional Bragg reflecting-crystal monochromator: (1) The anomalously transmitted beam is parallel to, and nearly coincident with, the direction of the incident beam, precluding the need to relocate the diffractometer or adjust it to a new take-off angle. (2) The anomalously transmitted beam has a very narrow angular divergence.

The second requirement was met by mounting the specimen on a goniometer head on a single-crystal goniostat. This arrangement permits: (1) translation of the specimen along its face normal; (2) tilting of the specimen about a horizontal axis perpendicular to the face normal χ; and (3) rotation about a vertical axis ϕ.

The reflectometer is shown in Fig. 3. X-rays from the line focus of the X-ray tube A pass through the diffractometer divergence and soller slit B to the germanium monochromator crystal C mounted in frame D on a goniometer head E. The goniometer permits alignment of the germanium crystal for anomalous transmission from the (220) planes. Edge F on the soller slit and edge G on the crystal limit the divergence of the monochromatic beam and exclude the $K\alpha_2$ line; G also intercepts the direct beam. The monochromatic beam passes to the specimen H mounted on another goniometer head I on a single-crystal goniostat J. This arrangement permits alignment of the specimen surface with the monochromatic beam as already described. Once the specimen surface has been aligned, operation of the θ–2θ drive of the diffractometer in the usual manner varies ϕ–2ϕ (Fig. 3). Alternatively, the θ–2θ mechanism may be decoupled so that only the detector is driven with the specimen surface fixed at any ϕ as set by the goniometer head. Procedures are given by Mozzi and Guentert ([55]) for selecting the germanium monochromator and for aligning the instrument.

2.4. Measurements and Patterns

The X-ray reflectometer may be used in three ways to record specularly reflected X-radiation and any associated reflection or scatter interference fringes:

1. Reflectance curves of I_R (or I_R/I_0) vs. ϕ (or ϕ/ϕ_C) may be established.

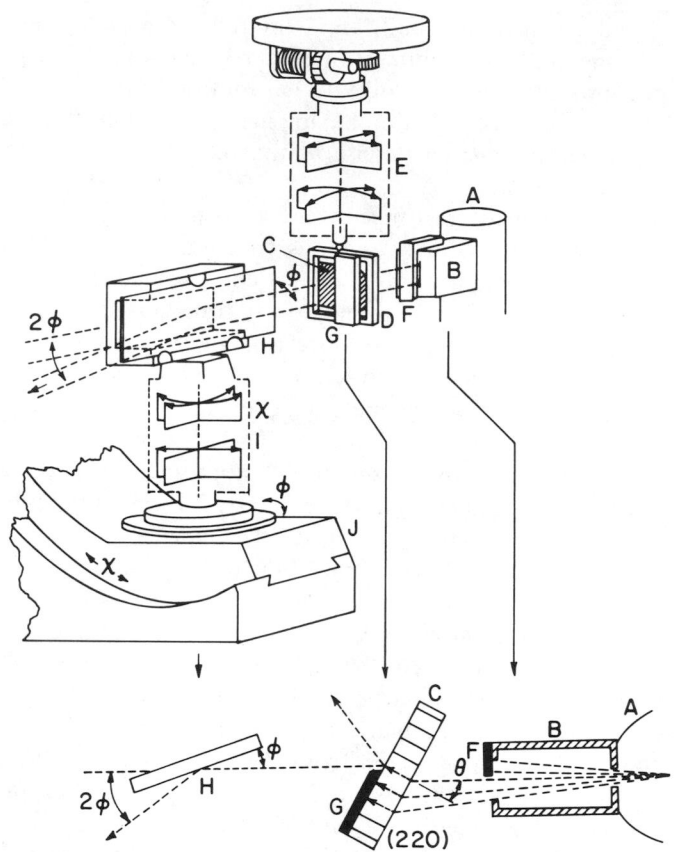

Figure 3. X-ray reflectometer built on an X-ray diffractometer equipped with a single-crystal goniostat [Mozzi and Guentert ([55])]. *A*, X-ray tube; *B*, soller and divergence slit; *C*, Ge monochromator; *D*, frame; *E*, goniometer head; *F*, edge; *G*, edge; *H*, specimen; *I*, goniometer head; *J*, single-crystal goniostat.

I_0 is measured at $\phi = 0°$. In the Duncan–Parratt reflectometer, ϕ is then increased manually in small increments, I_R scaled at each position, and the curve plotted. In the Mozzi–Guentert instrument, ϕ may be motor-driven continuously as I_R is recorded on the ratemeter-recorder.

2. The reflection profile at any fixed ϕ may be established. In the Duncan–Parratt instrument, this is done by moving the detector manually in small increments and scaling I_R at each position. In the Mozzi–Guentert instrument, it may be done by decoupling the θ–2θ mechanism and allowing

the motor drive to move only the detector as I_R is recorded. In both cases, the detector is fitted with a narrow slit.

3. In both instruments, the reflection profile at fixed ϕ may be recorded on a photographic film or plate placed 50 cm or more from the specimen. Exposures of a few minutes are sufficient to record the specularly reflected beam and its interference fringes. Exposures of several hours may be required to record the weaker scatter interference fringes.

Figure 4 ([78]) shows reflectance curves from a 1190-Å germanium film on Pyrex glass and the associated interference fringes. Figure 5 ([63]) is a photograph of scatter interference fringes near the specularly reflected beam from a copper film on Pyrex glass.

2.5. Film Properties

2.5.1. *Nature of the Film*

The critical angles and shapes of reflectance curves may be used for thin-film investigations in two ways. Experimental curves may be compared with theoretical curves (Fig. 6). Experimental curves from films prepared in various ways under various conditions on various substrates, and subjected to various treatments may be compared (Fig. 7).

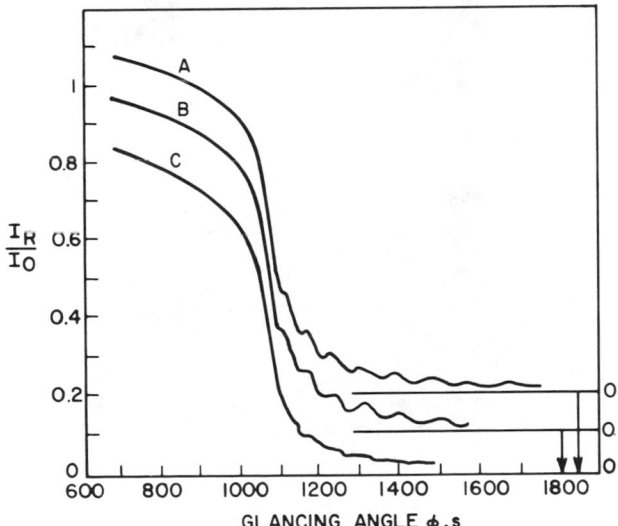

Figure 4. Typical X-ray reflection curves showing interference fringes; 1190-Å Ge films on Pyrex glass. To avoid confusion, the curves have been displaced vertically [Wainfan and Parratt ([78])]. *A*, newly deposited film; *B*, *A* after annealing in vacuum at 380°C; *C*, *B* after heating in air at 420°C.

The critical angle ϕ_C and shape of the reflectance curve are determined essentially by the electron density of the reflecting surface. Theoretical curves may be calculated for various models of the reflecting surface.

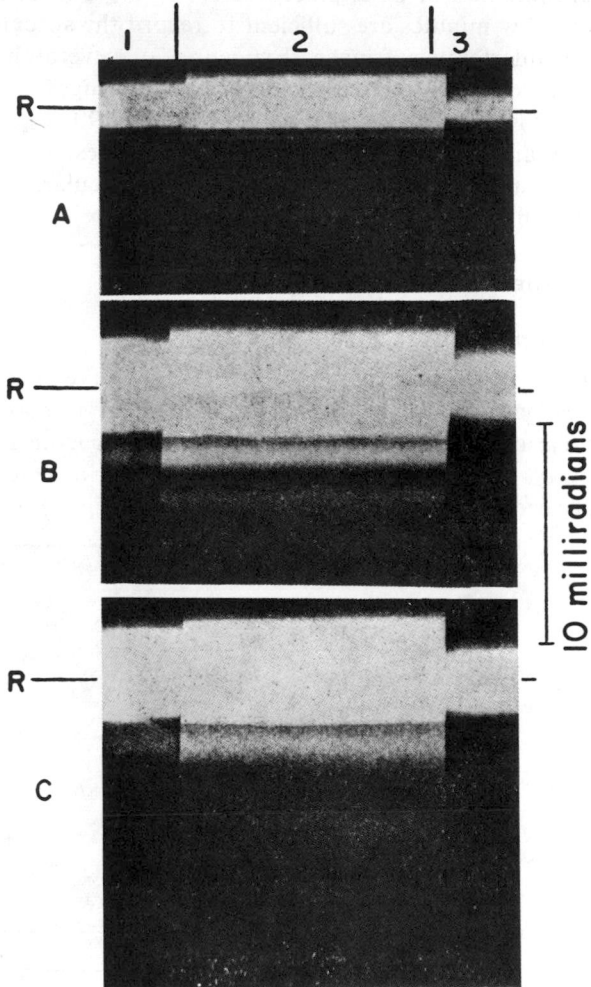

Figure 5. Photographs (positive prints) of the reflected beam from Cu films of different thickness on glass, showing interference fringes due to scattered X-rays. Each photograph was taken at a glancing angle corresponding to an interference maximum R in the specularly reflected beam. [Sauro, Fankuchen, and Wainfan [63]]. (A), 985 Å; (B), 398 Å; (C), 252 Å; 1, 0.001-inch Ni filter over photographic plate; 2, no filter; 3, 0.001-inch Fe filter over photographic plate.

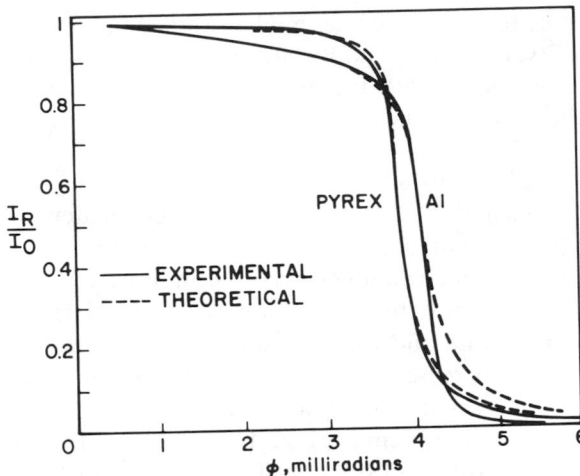

Figure 6. Experimental and theoretical X-ray reflection curves for Pyrex glass and aluminum [Duncan and Parratt ([22])].

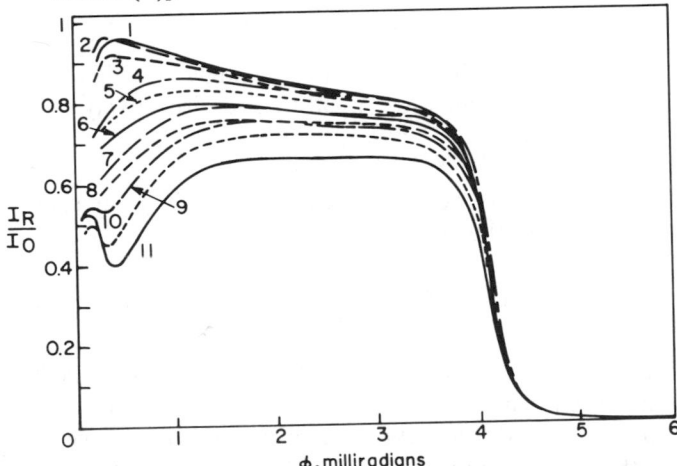

Figure 7. Experimental X-ray reflection curves of Al films subjected to various successive treatments [Duncan and Parratt ([22])]. *1*, newly deposited film; *2*, 2 weeks at room temperature; *3*, 3 h at 200°C; *4*, 3 h at 235°C; *5*, 3 h at 250°C; *6*, 2.5 h at 300°C; *7*, 2.5 h at 300°C; *8*, 2.5 h at 300°C; *9*, 2.5 h at 320°C; *10*, 2 h at 360°C; *11*, 3.5 h at 380°C.

Parratt ([57]) has extended dispersion theory to deal with reflecting surfaces consisting of different numbers of plane-parallel layers, each having its own thickness, δ, and β [Eq. (1)]. The experimental curve is compared with

theoretical curves based on various models involving various degrees and
depths of porosity, oxidation, etc. By choice of a model to give a theoretical
curve in close agreement with the experimental curve, inferences may be
made about the nature of the film.

2.5.2. Surface Smoothness

If the experimental reflectance curve does not match the theoretical
curve in the region of maximum slope, and if nonuniform electron density
can be ruled out, surface roughness may be indicated.

Another test for smoothness is comparison of enlarged photographs
of the direct X-ray beam and the specularly reflected beam. A substantial
change in shape or increase in width may indicate roughness.

If the range of variation of film thickness is such as to displace the
order number of an interference fringe by 1/2 order, that fringe and all
higher-order fringes will be destroyed. The variation in thickness Δt that
would thus smear out the first-order fringe is

$$\Delta t = \frac{\lambda}{4(\phi_1^2 - \phi_C^2)^{1/2}} \tag{4}$$

where λ is wavelength, and ϕ_1 and ϕ_C are the angle at which the first-order
fringe maximum occurs and the critical angle, respectively [78].

2.5.3. Thickness

Film thickness t may be calculated from the angular spacing of the
reflection fringes using the equation [79]

$$N = R + \left(\frac{2t}{\lambda}\right)(\phi_N^2 - \phi_C^2)^{1/2} \tag{5}$$

where R is an unknown phase constant, λ is wavelength, ϕ_N is the glancing
angle at which the intensity maximum (or minimum) occurs, and ϕ_C is the
critical angle. The quantity N is the order number of the fringe; $N = N_i$ (an
integer) for the ith maximum, and $N = N_i + \frac{1}{2}$ for the next successive
minimum. Since absolute values of N and R are often not known, the
fringes may be numbered from the first that can be measured near ϕ_C, and
thickness calculated from the slope of a plot of N vs. $(\phi_N^2 = \phi_C^2)^{1/2}$.

Thickness may also be calculated from the angular separation of the
scatter fringes by use of the equation [63]

$$N = R + \left(\frac{t}{\lambda}\right)[(\phi + \Delta\phi)^2 - \phi_C^2]^{1/2} \tag{6}$$

where N, R, t, λ, and ϕ_C have the same significance as in Eq. (5); ϕ is the glancing angle of the incident X-ray beam; $\Delta\phi$ is the angle between the specularly reflected beam and the observed scatter interference fringe (see Fig. 1). The precision of the thickness calculated from Eq. (6) is claimed to be greater than that calculated from Eq. (5) because scatter fringes are more widely spaced and more numerous than reflection fringes.

2.5.4. Density

The average film density ρ may be calculated from the equation ([79])

$$\rho = \rho_B(\phi_{CM}/\phi_C)^2 \tag{7}$$

where ρ_B is the bulk density, and ϕ_C is the critical angle. The quantity ϕ_{CM} is the experimentally measured critical angle for total reflectance. The quantity ϕ_{CM} may be difficult to measure, but $\phi_{1/2}$, the angle at which $I_R/I_O = 0.5$, is readily measured and is usually within 2% of ϕ_C. Thus $\phi_{1/2}$ may be substituted for ϕ_{CM} with little error.

Another way to derive the density is to determine t with Eq. (5) or (6), then determine the area density by chemical or X-ray spectrometric methods.

2.6. Scope and Application

X-ray reflectance techniques are applicable to films as thin as 10 Å and as thick as several thousand angstroms, depending on the absorption coefficient of the film. Reflectance studies have been reported of films of copper ([57,63,78,79]), aluminum ([22]), titanium ([55]), and nickel, germanium, and selenium ([78]), all on glass substrates.

3. X-RAY DIFFRACTION

3.1. Conventional Diffraction Methods

Conventional diffractometric or flat-film transmission and back-reflection methods are applicable to films and platings thick enough to give diffracted beams of sufficient intensity. This thickness threshold is usually $\lesssim 500$ Å and depends on the atomic number of the material. However, this threshold may be reduced to as low as ~ 40 Å if the film is single crystalline or highly oriented polycrystalline, or if focusing techniques are used. Another technique that aids in obtaining data on thinner films is to set the detector at a diffraction peak and record diffracted intensity as the film is deposited or treated.

Selection of the method may depend on the X-ray transparency of the film and substrate. These methods provide the following kinds of information: (1) single-crystalline, polycrystalline, or amorphous state; (2) chemical species; (3) crystallographic orientation; (4) lattice parameter; (5) qualitative and quantitative evaluation of solid solution, crystallite size, preferred orientation, and stress. These techniques are all well-known and require no comment here.

X-ray diffraction has been applied to the measurement of thickness of metal platings. The intensity of a diffraction line from the plating or the substrate may be measured, or both may be measured and their ratio taken. By use of standards, a calibration curve is established of either of the individual intensities or their ratio vs. plate thickness.

Clark, Pish, and Weeg [17] photographed diffraction patterns of films as thin as 5×10^{-6} cm, and Gerold [30] made diffractometric measurements of chromium platings $<1 \mu$m thick. Clark [16] reports measurement of the intensity ratio of two substrate diffraction lines with the incident beam normal to the specimen surface. Friedman and Birks [28] used a diffractometer to determine coating thickness from the intensity ratio of a diffraction line of the substrate with and without plate, and the X-ray absorption coefficient of the plate. Keating and Kammerer [39] used a diffractometer to measure thickness from the intensity ratio of two orders of the same substrate line, or from the ratio of the intensities of the same line recorded with two different X-ray wavelengths. Gray [32] gives an equation for plate thickness from the intensity ratio of back-reflection lines from the plate and base metal. Eisenstein [25] gives equations for coating thickness of plane and cylindrical specimens as a function of the intensity ratio of diffraction lines from plate and substrate. Gray and Eisenstein both used microphotometer tracings of film patterns.

Diffraction methods for determining plate thickness have serious limitations. The measured intensities are affected markedly by crystallite size, preferred orientation, and stress in the specimen, and therefore by position and orientation in the X-ray instrument. Moreover, diffracted intensities are much lower than the emitted intensities in X-ray spectrometric methods (see below). However, diffraction methods are particularly useful for platings containing elements present in the substrate; spectrometric methods are of little value in such cases.

3.2. Instrumentation

Sophisticated work with true thin films may require provision to prepare the film in the X-ray camera or diffractometer accessory in vacuum at selected substrate temperatures, and later to subject the film to various physical or chemical treatments in place.

3.2.1. *Film Cameras*

Figure 8 shows a cylindrical metal continuously pumped vacuum camera used by Ruhl ([62]) for photographing Debye–Scherrer patterns of 3000–5000-Å films of tin and tin–copper alloy evaporated in place in the camera. The film substrate holder is thermally coupled to a liquid reservoir. By use of various liquid charges, the substrate holder may be maintained for several hours at any temperature between 20 and 450°K. The former temperature is obtained by use of liquid hydrogen surrounded by liquid oxygen; other temperatures are obtained with appropriate liquefied gases or freezing mixtures, or with high-boiling liquids heated with an immersion heater.

The camera is built in a metal cylinder *A* approximately 8 cm in diameter and 35 cm long fitted with four side tubes as follows: (1) *B* is the

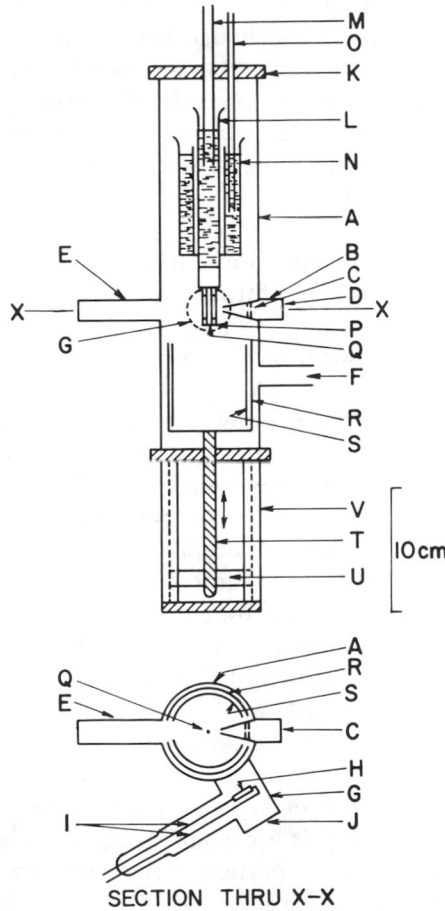

Figure 8. Debye–Scherrer camera for investigation of thin films [Ruhl ([62])]. *A*, cylindrical metal body; *B*, X-ray beam entrance port; *C*, entrance slit; *D*, Ni foil; *E*, X-ray beam exit port; *F*, evacuation tube; *G*, evaporation tube; *H*, W channel; *I*, current leads; *J*, window; *K*, top cap; *L*, inner liquid reservoir; *M*, filling tube for *L*; *N*, outer liquid reservoir; *O*, filling tube for *N*; *P*, substrate holder; *Q*, Al-foil substrate; *R*, camera body; *S*, photographic film; *T*, push-rod for *R*; *U*, guides; *V*, guide channels.

SECTION THRU X–X

X-ray beam entrance port, fitted with a 0.8 × 0.1-mm entrance slit C and sealed with nickel foil D which also serves as a Cu $K\beta$ filter. (2) E is the X-ray beam exit port. (3) F is the evacuation tube. A pressure of 5×10^{-6} mm Hg (torr) can be maintained. (4) G is the evaporation tube and is provided with a tungsten channel H, electric current leads I, and window J for observing the progress of the evaporation.

The top cap K is cemented to the cylindrical body A and holds an inner liquid reservoir L and filling tube M and an outer liquid reservoir N and filling tube O. For a 20°K substrate temperature, the inner and outer reservoirs are filled with liquid hydrogen and oxygen, respectively. In thermal contact with the bottom of the inner reservoir is the bowed copper substrate holder P, across which is stretched the aluminum foil substrate Q, 3 mm wide and 10 μm thick.

The lower portion of the cylinder holds the camera body R, which consists of a cylinder having slots to clear the entrance slit and direct X-ray beam when the camera is later advanced into position to photograph the pattern. The photographic film S is placed inside the camera body and consists of one or two semicylindrical pieces. The proximity of the camera body to the evacuation tube F is beneficial for outgassing the photographic emulsion.

After evacuation of the camera and evaporation of the film, the camera body is advanced into position to photograph the pattern by means of the rod T, which is fitted with guides U which slide in channels V. Five Debye–Scherrer patterns may be photographed on the same film by stepwise advancement of the camera body. Exposure times were ~4 h for Cu $K\alpha$ at 35 kV, 30 mA.

Figure 9 shows an all-glass sealed-off vacuum camera used by Keith [41] for photographing diffraction patterns of 2000-Å polycrystalline copper films evaporated in place in the camera. Provision is made to cool the substrate to the temperature of liquid nitrogen and later to oxidize the film in place. A Seeman–Bohlin focusing arrangement was adopted in order to achieve diffracted intensities sufficient for reasonable exposure times with a narrow entrance slit. The Cu $K\alpha$ radiation, monochromatized with a curved quartz crystal, was used to photograph the diffracted beams from the (200) and (311) planes at 22.5 and 45° θ, respectively. Exposure times at 35 kV were ~160 and ~240 mA-h for annealed and highly disordered films, respectively.

The camera body B constitutes the cylindrical lower portion of the outer jacket of a dewar vessel A approximately 10 cm in diameter. The film substrate C is a cylindrical glass surface having a 6-cm radius and sealed into the lower portion of the inner vessel of A. The cylindrical camera body B is fitted with seven side tubes as follows.

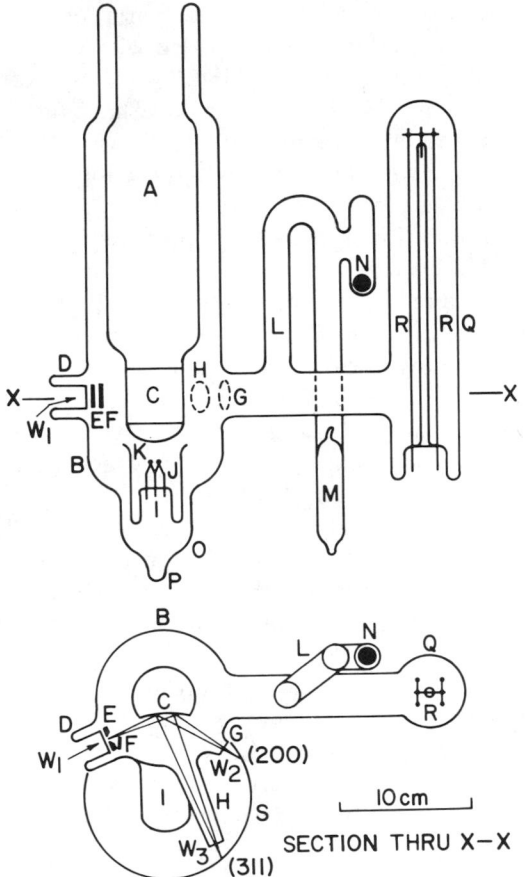

Figure 9. Seeman–Bohlin camera for investigation of thin films [Keith ([41])]. A, dewar vessel; B, camera body; C, substrate surface; D, X-ray beam entrance port; E, entrance slit; F, scatter shield; G, diffracted beam exit port; H, diffracted beam exit port; I, evaporation tube; J, Mo filament; K, Cu beads; L, oxygen tube; M, oxygen ampule; N, steel ball; O, evacuation tube; P, tip-off constriction; Q, getter tube; R, Mo getter filament; S, photographic film; W_1, W_2, W_3, X-ray windows.

1. D is the X-ray beam entrance port. It is a re-entrant tube sealed with an X-ray window W_1 and provided with a 10 × 0.2-mm entrance slit E and a scatter shield F to intercept direct-beam scatter toward window W_2. The incident beam is directed on the substrate at 20°.

2. G and H are the diffracted beam exit ports for the (200) and (311) diffracted beams, respectively. They are sealed with windows W_2 and W_3. All windows (W_1, W_2, and W_3) are of thin blown borosilicate glass capable of withstanding vacuum even during the 400°C bakeout and having 70% transmittance for Cu $K\alpha$ at normal incidence. Obviously, the construction limits use of the camera to (200) and (311) "reflections" from copper with Cu $K\alpha$ X-radiation.

3. I is the evaporation tube and is provided with a molybdenum filament J to which are welded beads of spectroscopically pure Cu K. The copper sublimate is directed on the substrate at an angle of 45° from a distance of 7 cm. The effective film area is ~ 3 cm^2.

4. L is a tube holding a sealed ampule of oxygen M, whose tip may be broken by means of the steel ball N dropped by an external magnet.

5. O is the evacuation tube and has a constriction for tip-off P after repeated bakeout at 400°C under continuous evacuation. At tip-off the pressure was always $< 10^{-7}$ mm Hg (torr).

6. Q is a getter tube having molybdenum filaments R which may be heated electrically to evaporate a molybdenum getter mirror on the tube wall after tip-off. The getter reduces the pressure to $\ll 10^{-7}$ mm Hg (torr).

After tip-off the camera is aligned with the X-ray beam, and the cylindrical photographic film S is placed as shown. The camera is now ready for preparation of the film and recording of the pattern. After the pattern is photographed, a new photographic film may be placed, the specimen film subjected to treatment, and a new pattern recorded, etc.

Both Ruhl and Keith made microdensitometer traces of the lines on their photographic patterns; measurements were then made on the densitometer charts.

3.2.2. Diffractometer Accessories

Figure 10 shows a continuously pumped vacuum accessory for X-ray investigation of thin films on a commercial horizontal diffractometer. The accessory was designed by Vook and Schoening [75], and the unit shown in Fig. 11 is available commercially from Materials Research Corp. Films of any suitable substance may be evaporated at temperatures up to 2600°C and pressures down to 10^{-9} mm Hg (torr) on any suitable substrate at temperatures from -180 to $+300$°C. Vook and Schoening's accessory was of monel, the MRC model of stainless steel.

The central component is a semicylindrical compartment A having two 1-inch ID vacuum flanges B, C and a 180° slot D. The slot is fitted with a thin beryllium X-ray window and permits a useful 2θ range of 0–160°.

The radial flange B is fitted with the evaporator assembly. The evaporator is a tungsten basket E surrounded on all sides but one by a

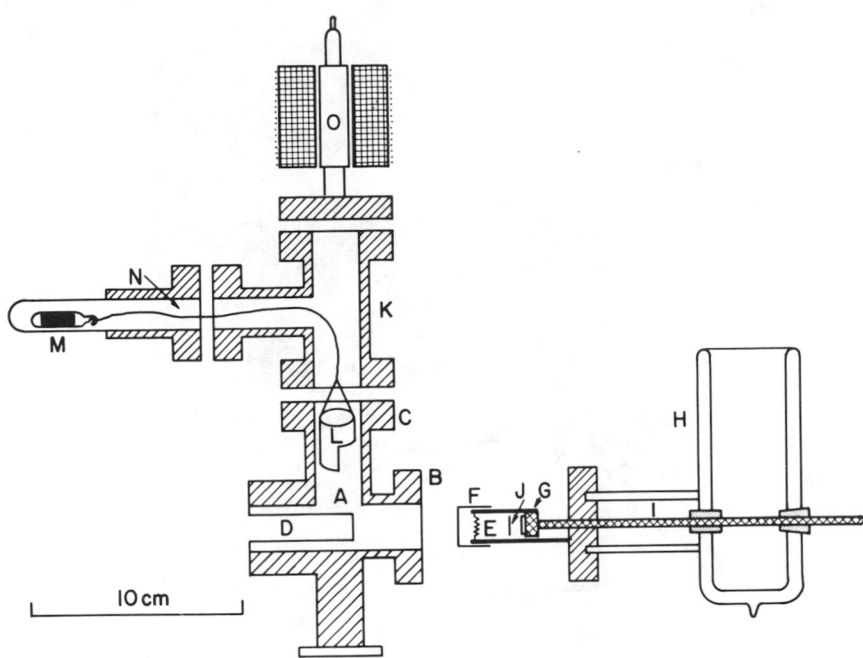

Figure 10. Diffractometer accessory for investigation of thin films [Vook and Schoening ([75])]. *A*, central compartment; *B*, vacuum flange; *C*, vacuum flange; *D*, slot for X-ray window; *E*, W basket; *F*, Ta shield; *G*, Cu substrate holder; *H*, dewar vessel; *I*, Cu thermal conductivity rod; *J*, sublimation shutter; *K*, vacuum T joint; *L*, X-ray shutter; *M*, Fe bar for operating *M*; *N*, wire for operating *M*; *O*, vacuum ion pump.

tantalum shield *F* to confine the sublimate to the direction of the substrate. An electron-beam evaporation accessory is available for the MRC unit. The copper substrate holder *G* is $\frac{1}{2}$ in. high and $\frac{3}{4}$ in. long. Various substrates may be affixed to its face. The holder may be rotated and translated by external adjustments. The holder may be cooled down to $-180°C$ by placing various liquefied gases or freezing mixtures in the dewar vessel *H*. The holder may be heated up to $\sim 300°C$ by a cartridge heater, not shown. The $\frac{1}{8}$-in. copper rod *I* conducts heat between the substrate holder and the charge in the dewar vessel. An externally operated shutter *J* is provided between the evaporator and substrate. A window, not shown, permits observation of the progress of the evaporation.

The axial flange *C* is fitted with a vacuum T joint *K* having a semicylindrical X-ray shutter *L* magnetically manipulated by means of the iron bar *M* and wire *N*. The top of the T joint is fitted with an ion pump *O*, or with fittings to a diffusion pump. Two commercial models are available.

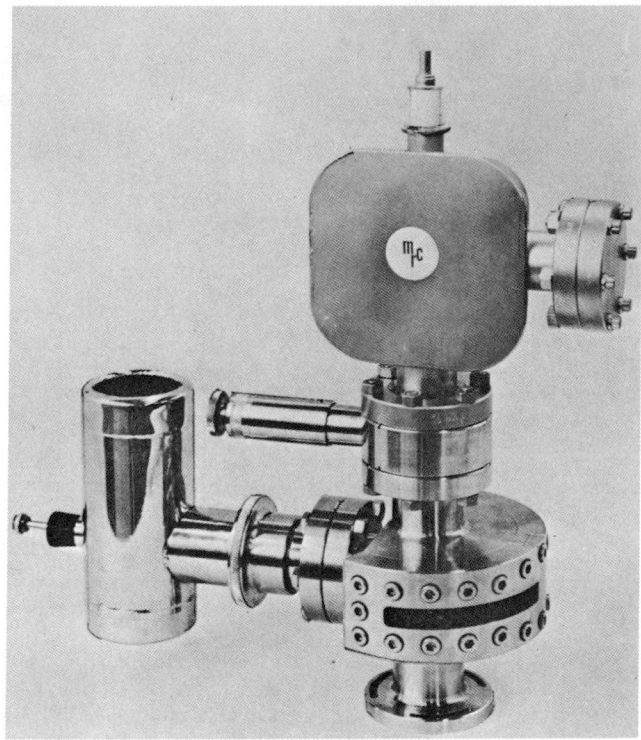

Figure 11. Commercial diffractometer accessory for investigation
of thin films [Materials Research Corp.].

One has Viton vacuum seals, cannot be baked, and is intended for use with diffusion pumps at pressures down to 10^{-6} mm Hg (torr). The other has copper and gold vacuum seals, can be baked up to 200°C, and is intended for use with an ion pump at pressures down to 10^{-8} or 10^{-9} mm Hg (torr).

Diffractometric studies of thin films may be made on a conventional diffractometer, either with an accessory like that just described, or with previously prepared films mounted on the conventional diffractometer specimen stage. However, the diffractometer is usually fitted with a monochromator, preferably one capable of excluding the $K\alpha_2$ component and providing a beam of very low divergence.

The diffractometer may be operated in any of several modes: (1) A θ scan may be made of a wide 2θ region using the θ–2θ drive and ratemeter-recorder. (2) Profiles of individual (hkl) peaks may be made with the step scanner and scaler. (3) Rocking curves of individual peaks may be made with 2θ fixed at the (hkl) peak by rocking the crystal over a small angular interval using the ω-drive and ratemeter-recorder. (4) Integrated intensities of individual peaks may be made by scaling diffracted intensity while making a continuous or stepwise θ scan, or while making a rocking curve.

Borie and Sparks ([11,12]) made useful measurements on Cu_2O films as thin as 40 Å by using a doubly-curved LiF crystal ~ 1 in. square. In this way an intense horizontal linear monochromatic incident beam is focused on the specimen and a vertical linear diffracted beam on the detector. Their arrangement is shown in Fig. 12.

3.3. Measurements and Film Properties

3.3.1. *Polycrystalline Films*

For polycrystalline film specimens, four types of measurement may be made on each diffractometer peak or on each microdensitometer tracing of a photographically recorded line: (1) line position or shift, (2) line profile or symmetry, (3) line width or broadening, and (4) line area or integrated intensity; integrated intensity may also be measured directly on the diffractometer, as already described.

From these measurements, the film may be characterized with respect to the following properties: (1) lattice parameter; (2) crystallite size;

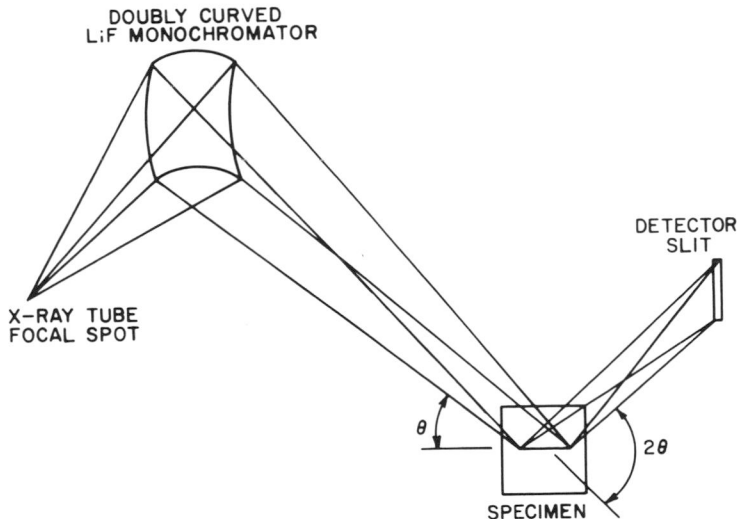

Figure 12. Diffractometer arrangement for investigation of films having thickness down to ~ 40 Å [Borie and Sparks ([11,12])].

(3) preferred orientation; (4) presence and density of intrinsic and extrinsic stacking faults; (5) presence and density of twin stacking faults; and (6) uniform, nonuniform, and thermal stress.

Unfortunately, each of the diffraction line parameters is affected by more than one of the film properties to be evaluated. However, methods are available to "sort out" these effects so that the film may be characterized. Following is a summary of the effects of various film properties on each of the four types of measurement.

3.3.1.1. *Line Position*

1. Lattice parameter of the specimen a_0. In the absence of other influences, a plot of a_0 calculated from each (hkl) peak vs. some function of θ would be linear and could be extrapolated to the true value of a_0 at $\theta = 90°$. Figure 13 (A) shows such a plot for several copper films. The individual values of a_0 could be plotted against θ or $\cos^2 \theta$. However, in the figure the Nelson–Riley function ([56]) is used

$$\frac{1}{2}\left(\frac{\cos^2 \theta}{\sin \theta} + \frac{\cos^2 \theta}{\theta}\right)$$

This function corrects for errors due to absorption and eccentricity of the specimen from the diffractometer axis.

2. Intrinsic stacking fault density α. The quantity α is the number of ISF's per 111 plane for (hkl)-oriented crystallites, (hkl) being the plane of origin of the peak on which the measurement is made. Figure 13 (C) shows the effect of α on $(\Delta d/d)_{hkl}$, the relative change in interplanar spacing d of the diffracting plane. Note that $(\Delta d/d)$ is of opposite direction and different magnitude for different orders of the same (hkl): (111), (222) and (200), (400).

3. Uniform stress. $(\Delta d/d)$ is the same for all (hkl).
4. Nonuniform stress. $(\Delta d/d)$ is not the same for all (hkl).
5. Thermal stress. $(\Delta d/d)$ is the same for different orders of the same (hkl). This is shown in Fig. 13 (B), where $(\Delta L/L)$ is the relative stress in the plane of the film due to different thermal expansion coefficients of film and substrate. The calculations involve the assumptions that: (1) the film adheres firmly to the substrate; (2) the thermal expansion coefficient of the substrate is isotropic in the plane of the substrate; (3) the stress on the film in the direction normal to the film plane is zero; and (4) shear strain in the film plane is zero. Compare the values for (111), (222) and (200), (400) in Figs. 13 (B) and 13 (C).

3.3.1.2. *Line Width*

1. Nonuniform stress. This is evaluated by the Warren–Averbach technique ([81]), which involves Fourier analysis.

2. Intrinsic stacking fault density α.

3. Twin-fault density β.

4. True crystallite size D_{hkl}.

Calculation of β and D_{hkl} is discussed below.

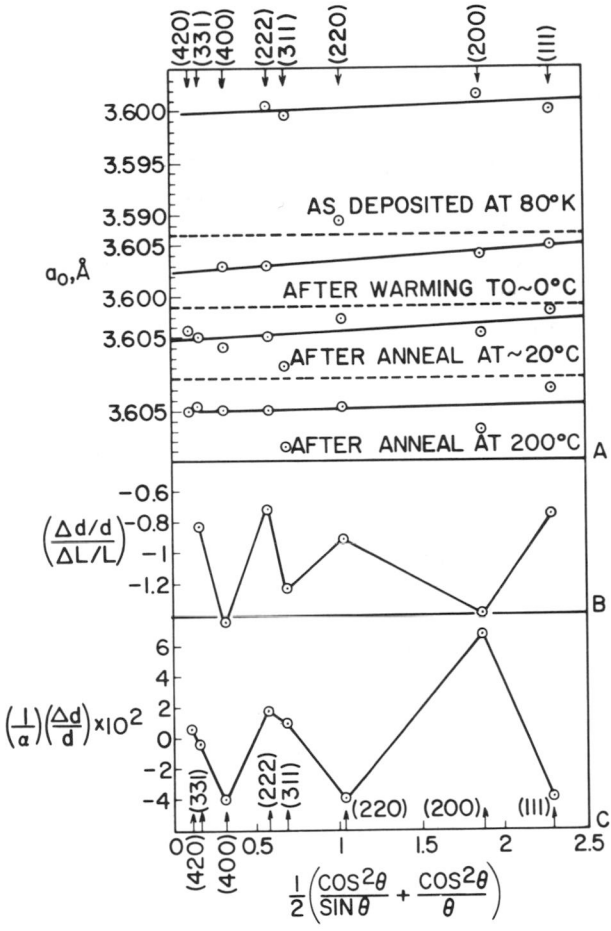

Figure 13. Effect of annealing (A), thermal stress (B), and intrinsic stacking fault density (C) on lattice parameter of Cu films [Vook and Witt ([76])].

3.3.1.3. *Line Profile*

1. Intrinsic stacking faults give peak shift and symmetrical broadening.

2. Extrinsic stacking faults give peak shifts of the same magnitude but opposite sign, and asymmetrical broadening.

3. Twin stacking faults give no peak shift and asymmetrical broadening. For example, in face-centered cubic films, twin faults increase the diffracted intensity on the high-2θ side of (111) peaks and on the low-2θ side of (200) peaks.

3.3.1.4. *Line Area*

Line area is proportional to the total volume of the material in the (*hkl*) orientation. However, observed X-ray line intensity must be corrected for the condition that the X-irradiated area of the specimen decreases as θ increases. This is done by dividing the line area or integrated intensity by $\sin \theta_{111}/\sin \theta_{hkl}$. These corrected values represent integrated line intensities from equal volumes of specimen irradiated by the X-ray beam. Integrated intensity, or line area, is affected principally by preferred orientation.

3.3.1.5. *Dynamic Investigations*

Valuable information is derived from *in situ* dynamic studies of films subjected to various treatments. Line position, profile, width, and area may change during annealing, indicating a change in crystallite size, preferred orientation, stress, and imperfection density. The effect of residual gas, introduced during or after evaporation of the film, on the properties of the film and on the annealing may be observed.

3.3.1.6. *Evaluation of Diffraction Data*

The techniques used by Vook and Witt ([76,77]) to determine twin-fault density β and true crystallite size D_{hkl} in copper and gold films on glass provide excellent examples of how the various film parameters may be isolated.

Twin-fault density was determined from the asymmetry of the (111) and (200) peaks in three ways.

1. The quantity β was derived from the unresolved $K\alpha_1\alpha_2$ peaks disregarding α_1–α_2 asymmetry: The $K\alpha_1\alpha_2$ diffraction line was plotted on an intensity vs. $\sin \theta$ scale. The profile was divided into 240 equal intervals i along the $\sin \theta$ scale with the midpoint at the peak: $-120 \ldots 0 \ldots +120$.

Then:

$$\beta_{111} = \left(\frac{2}{\sqrt{3}}\right)\left(\frac{P_i\Delta I_i - P_{-i}\Delta I_{-i}}{(PA_0)_{111}}\right) \tan\left(\frac{\pi i}{240}\right) \tag{8}$$

$$\beta_{200} = \left(\frac{\sqrt{3}}{2}\right)\left(\frac{P_{-i}\Delta I_{-i} - P_i\Delta I_i}{(PA_0)_{200}}\right) \tan\left(\frac{\pi i}{240}\right) \tag{9}$$

$$P = (\sin\theta \sin 2\theta)/f^2(1 + \cos^2 2\theta) \tag{10}$$

where ΔI_i is X-ray intensity above background at the ith interval; P_{111} and P_{200} are P for $i = 0$; $(A_0)_{111}$ and $(A_0)_{200}$ are the measured areas of the (111) or (200) peak divided by the length of the diffraction line; and f is the atomic scattering factor.

2. The Rachinger method ([59]) was used to separate the $K\alpha_1\alpha_2$ lines, and the method just described was used to determine β from the $K\alpha_2$ line.

3. The Warren double-line method ([80]) was applied to the $K\alpha_1\alpha_2$ diffraction peaks of (111) and (200).

The true crystallite size D_{hkl} was determined as follows.

1. The nominal crystallite size D_N, which contains contributions from crystallite size, stress, intrinsic stacking faults, and twinning, was derived from the Scherrer equation

$$D_N = K\lambda/(B' \cos\theta) \tag{11}$$

where K varies with (hkl) and crystallite shape and usually has a value ~ 1; B' is the true line half-width; and λ and θ are the wavelength and Bragg angle, respectively.

2. Line broadening due to average nonuniform strain $(\Delta d/d)$ was separated from the broadening due to effective crystallite size D_E by assuming that the diffraction peaks had either Cauchy or Gauss profiles, with the most probable situation lying somewhere between the two extremes:

$$\text{Cauchy:} \quad B = [(\lambda/D_E)/\cos\theta] + 2(\Delta d/d)\tan\theta \tag{12}$$

$$\text{Gauss:} \quad B^2 = [(\lambda/D_E)/\cos\theta]^2 + [2(\Delta d/d)\tan\theta]^2 \tag{13}$$

For a Cauchy profile, $(B \cos\theta)$ was plotted against $\sin\theta$ for each (hkl); for a Gauss profile, $(B \cos\theta)^2$ was plotted against $\sin^2\theta$ for each (hkl). Straight lines were drawn through the various orders of a given (hkl), e.g., (111), (222). The intercept of the line at $\sin\theta = 0$ gives the effective crystallite size D_E.

3. The effective crystallite size due to intrinsic stacking faults D_α, and the effective crystallite size due to twinning D_β were calculated from values of α and β.

4. True crystallite size was then determined in four ways by combining the D_E's from the Cauchy and Gauss analysis with two D_β's derived in two different ways.

5. Crystallite sizes were also estimated from the sizes of diffraction spots on conventional flat-film diffraction patterns corrected for incident beam size and collimation ([71]).

3.3.2. Single-Crystalline Films

Much the same information is obtained from diffractometric studies of single-crystalline films. The lattice parameter is obtained from line position. The thickness ("crystallite size" in the direction normal to the film surface) and stress are obtained by Warren–Averbach ([81]) treatment of line broadening.

Sometimes valuable inferences may be drawn from the thickness and stress data. For example, Borie and Sparks ([11,12]) determined the lattice parameter as a function of distance from surface to substrate of Cu_2O films on copper on the basis of the following assumptions: (1) The film is strained because conditions at its two interfaces are different. At the oxide–metal interface the film is constrained by the smaller metal lattice, while at the oxide–air interface it is unconstrained. (2) The interplanar spacing d is different at the two interfaces. (3) This difference Δd is distributed linearly from top to bottom of the film. (4) The film has uniform thickness t. Then the Fourier coefficients in the Warren–Averbach treatment may be computed in terms of Δd and t, and d may be obtained as a function of distance from top to bottom of the film.

Several types of information are provided by rocking curves. If the monochromatic X-ray beam has a cross-sectional area A, the X-irradiated area of the film is $A/\sin\theta$, and the irradiated volume V is $At/\sin\theta$, where t is thickness. Then:

$$I_0 V = I_0 At/\sin\theta \tag{14}$$

$I_0 A$ is the total power of the incident beam and can be measured, permitting a determination of t independent of line broadening. The calculation may be made on as many orders of (hkl) as can be recorded.

Holloway ([37]) used X-ray rocking curves to assess the degree of perfection of epitaxial layers. He showed that a direct correlation existed between rocking curve half-width and certain photoelectric performance for gallium arsenide layers prepared for evaluation in solar cells. The X-ray method provides information more rapidly than device fabrication and testing and also provides information as to the nature of the deficiencies.

Sometimes special information may be derived from such data. For example, for Cu_2O, (110) planes contain only Cu atoms, while (220) planes contain both Cu and O atoms. Thus thickness calculated from these two planes provides a means of evaluating the stoichiometry. The more nearly true stoichiometry is approached, the better is the agreement of the two calculated thicknesses ([12]).

A comparison of the observed rocking curve with that calculated for a perfect crystal permits calculation of dislocation density.

3.4. X-Ray Interference

In certain cases, interference fringes may be observed beside the diffracted beam of a certain (hkl) plane in a thin film. This may occur in a single-crystalline film having a certain plane (hkl) parallel to the substrate. It may occur in a polycrystalline film having crystallites so highly oriented that a certain plane (hkl) lies parallel to the substrate and is extremely well aligned from the top to the bottom of the film.

Croce and his co-workers ([20,21]) recorded such fringes from (111) planes of polycrystalline gold films diffractometrically by making a stepwise θ scan using a narrow detector slit. Their results are shown in Fig. 14 (A). Croce ([20,21]) and Vook and Witt ([77]) recorded polycrystalline gold (111) fringes photographically by setting the diffractometer at 2θ for gold (111) planes and exposing a fine-grain photographic plate to the diffracted beam. The photograph in Fig. 14 (B) is from Vook and Witt.

Film thickness may be calculated from these fringes. Croce and his co-workers give the equation

$$t = \lambda/(2\Delta\theta \cos \theta) = (d/\Delta\theta) \tan \theta \tag{15}$$

where t, λ, θ, and d are thickness, wavelength, Bragg angle, and interplanar spacing; $2\Delta\theta$ is the angle between the diffraction maximum and the first minimum, or between two consecutive minima.

Vook and Witt give the equation

$$t = L\lambda/(L' \cos \theta) \tag{16}$$

where L is the distance between the specimen film and photographic plate, and L' is the fringe spacing.

3.5. Scope and Application

X-ray diffraction methods provide more kinds of information about films than any of the other X-ray methods, and the literature on X-ray diffraction investigations of films is too large to summarize here. Detailed descriptions of treatment of X-ray diffraction data are given by Borie and Sparks for Cu_2O films ([11-13]), Light and Wagner for silver ([49]), Segmueller for nickel ([66]), and Vook and Witt for copper ([76]) and gold ([77]).

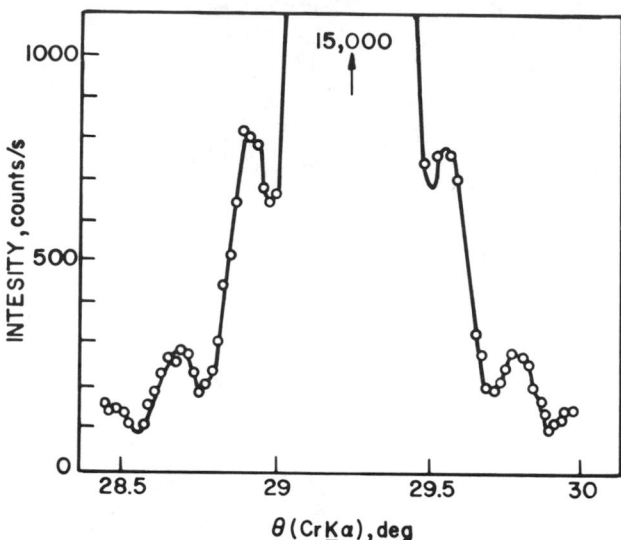

Figure 14 (A). Interface fringes in diffracted beams from (111) planes in highly oriented Au films, diffractometric recording [Croce, Devant, Gandais, and Marraud ([21])].

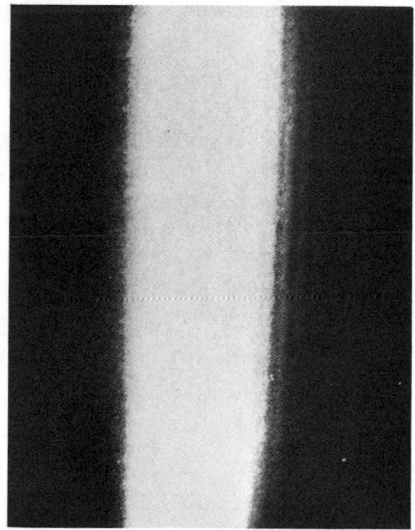

Figure 14 (B). Photographic recording (positive print) of interference fringes (see Fig. 14A) [Vook and Witt ([77])].

4. X-RAY DIVERGENT-BEAM (KOSSEL) PHOTOGRAPHY

4.1. Principle

In Fig. 15, a point source of spherically divergent, substantially monochromatic X-rays S irradiates a single crystal C. Flat films are placed in the transmission F_T and back-reflection F_B positions. If no diffraction occurred, the transmission film would be uniformly exposed by the transmitted X-rays, while the back-reflection film would receive only X-rays scattered by the crystal and remain substantially unexposed.

Figure 15 (A) shows a set of crystallographic planes inclined at a relatively small angle to the axis of the incident cone of X-rays SA. Certain rays 1, 2 in the divergent beam strike these planes at the Bragg angle θ for the wavelength used, giving diffracted rays D_1, D_2 and decreasing the intensity of rays L_1, L_2. Thus the exposure of the transmission film F_T is greater at D_1 and D_2 and smaller at L_1 and L_2, giving rise to dark and light lines, respectively. These planes give no response on the back-reflection film F_B.

Similarly, Fig. 15 (B) shows a set of planes inclined at a relatively large angle to the axis of the incident rays. Rays 1 and 2 fall on these planes at the Bragg angle θ, giving diffracted rays D_1, D_2 and decreasing the intensity of rays L_1, L_2. Thus film F_B will show only dark lines, F_T only light lines.

The diffracted and depleted beams have the form of cones and record on the flat films as light and dark circular, elliptical, parabolic, or hyperbolic Kossel lines.

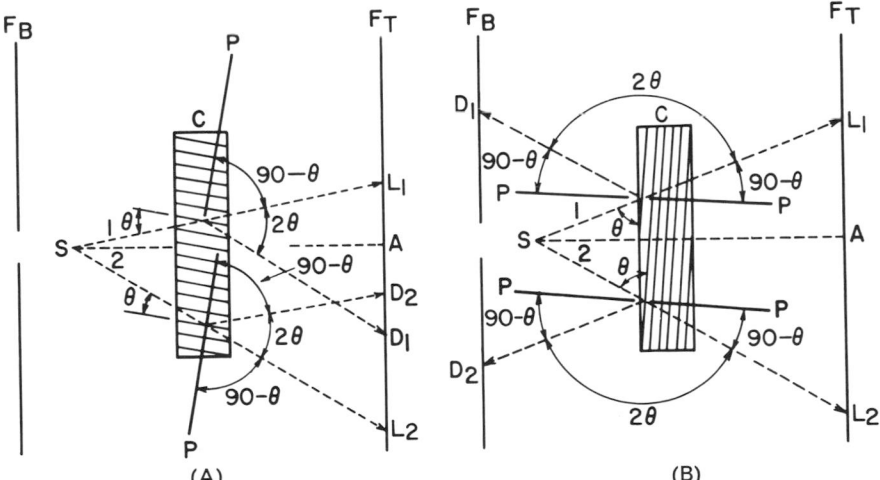

Figure 15. Principle of X-ray divergent-beam photography for the transmission (A) and back-reflection (B) cases.

4.2. Instrumentation

The divergent X-ray beam may be generated in three ways: (1) A point-focus X-ray tube may be used having a thin foil target which also serves as the X-ray window ([38]). (2) An end-focus beam from a conventional diffraction tube may be pinhole-collimated and directed on a thin foil of an element having an absorption edge on the long-wavelength side of the principal spectral line of the X-ray tube target ([29]). The secondary line emission from the foil is spherically divergent. The foil may be placed at S (Fig. 15) to give transmission divergent-beam patterns, or, if the crystal is sufficiently X-ray-transparent, it may be placed on the opposite side of the crystal to give back-reflection patterns. (3) If the specimen contains a heavy element, it may act as its own secondary source when irradiated by a pinhole-collimated primary X-ray beam.

In the last two methods, the primary beam also generates transmission and back-reflection Laue patterns, which appear superposed on the divergent-beam patterns.

For unsupported films or films and platings on X-ray-transparent substrates, the transmission and back-reflection methods using any of the three sources are applicable. For films and platings on opaque substrates, only the back-reflection method using the point-focus X-ray tube is feasible.

4.3. Film Properties

Certain types of information are obtained by inspection of the patterns. Polygonization and crystallographic imperfections are revealed by local irregularities of intensity, width, or continuity of the dark and light lines. Figure 16 is a back-reflection divergent-beam pattern showing several such imperfections ([50]).

Divergent-beam patterns also provide a means for accurate measurement of the lattice parameter and thereby of stress. Relative changes in the lattice constant of one part in 10^5 are detectable. The measurements are based on the location of points of intersection of cones relative to each other and to other cones lying close to such points of intersection.

The dark and light lines on the pattern may be identified by comparison with a stereographic projection plotted as follows. On the patterns in Fig. 15, both the dark (D) and light (L) lines form cones of half vertex angle $90° - \theta$ about the pole P of the reflecting plane. Thus, the D and L cones are represented on a stereographic projection by circles of radius $r = 90° - \theta$ about the poles of the diffracting planes. For a divergent-beam pattern of a cubic crystal having unit cell dimension a_0, photographed with

X-rays of wavelength λ, r is given by

$$r_{hkl} = 90° - \theta = \cos^{-1} \lambda \left(\frac{h^2 + k^2 + l^2}{2a_0} \right)^{1/2} \tag{17}$$

Circles having radius r are drawn about the pole of each plane (hkl) on a standard cubic stereographic projection.

4.4. Scope and Applications

The back-reflection divergent-beam technique has been applied to single-crystal copper electroplatings 3–15 μm thick on single-crystal copper substrates [50]. Application to thinner specimens is feasible, but has not yet been reported.

5. X-RAY DIFFRACTION TOPOGRAPHY

The various techniques of X-ray diffraction topography (also known as diffraction micrography, diffraction contrast, and extinction contrast)

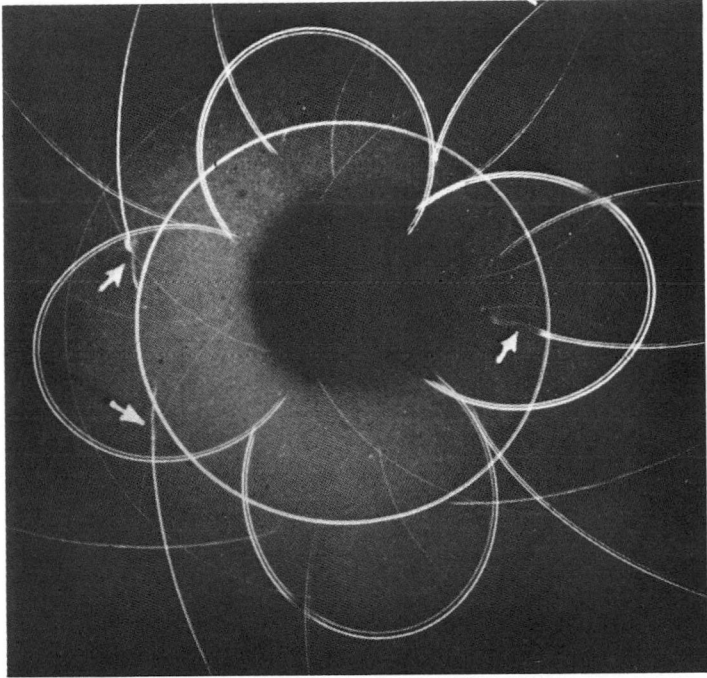

Figure 16. Back-reflection divergent-beam pattern (positive print) of epitaxial electrodeposited single-crystal Cu on single-crystal Cu substrate. Arrows indicate local displacements of the elliptical pattern due to polygonization [Lighty, Shanefield, Weissmann, and Shrier [50]].

provide means for photographing dislocations and other imperfections in single crystals. Although a wide variety of topographic techniques have been described ([45]), they may be classified in three categories: (1) Bragg (reflection) diffraction geometry, typified by the Berg–Barratt technique; (2) Laue (transmission) diffraction geometry, typified by the Lang technique; and (3) Borrmann anomalous transmission geometry. Only the first two of these are applicable to film studies.

Figure 17 (A) shows the arrangement for the Lang method. Slits AA provide a strictly monochromatic beam having very small divergence and directed on a single crystal B having an epitaxial layer C. The crystal is

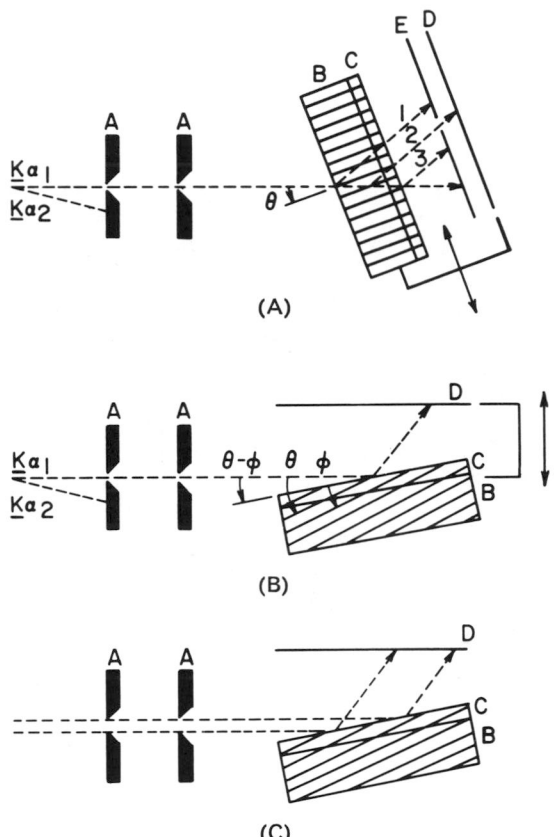

Figure 17. Arrangements for X-ray diffraction topography by Lang (A) and Berg–Barratt (B, C) techniques. A, slit; B, single-crystal substrate; C, epitaxial film; D, photographic film or plate; E, shield; θ, Bragg angle; ϕ, (hkl) ∧ crystal surface.

oriented so that the crystallographic planes shown are at the Bragg angle θ to the incident beam, thereby diffracting rays *1, 2, 3*. A photographic film *D* is placed behind shield *E* having a slit aperture and placed to pass ray *2*. The crystal and film are translated together as indicated by the arrow so that the film receives diffracted radiation from all parts of the crystal.

If the crystal were perfect, the film would be uniformly exposed, but if dislocations or other imperfections are present, they will show as variations in exposure on the film. Stereo film pairs may be made for three-dimensional analysis.

The Lang technique has disadvantages for the observation of imperfections in epitaxial layers on substrates having high X-ray absorption. In homoepitaxial films, all dislocations in both substrate and film are recorded, giving a confused picture.

In heteroepitaxial films, most semiconducting substances have absorption coefficients so high that anomalous transmission must be used to get sufficient intensity through the crystal unless the substrate is very thin. (Silicon is an exception to this.) Even if the specimen is arranged for anomalous transmission through the substrate, the epitaxial layer would be out of Bragg orientation so that its defects would show little or no contrast. The first of these disadvantages may be minimized by placing the shield *E* in position to pass diffracted ray *3* [Fig. 17 (A)] instead of ray *2*.

A more favorable arrangement for X-ray topography of films is the Berg–Barratt method shown in Figure 17 (B), where the X-ray beam is "reflected" from the specimen surface. The specimen and film are translated as shown to record diffraction from the entire surface, and no shield is required. For minimum distortion of the image, the Bragg angle θ should be $\sim 45°$, and ϕ, the angle between the diffracting planes and the crystal surface, should be a few degrees less than θ.

An alternative Berg–Barratt arrangement is shown in Fig. 17 (C) where the entire specimen surface is irradiated at once, and no translation is required.

Figure 18 shows some typical X-ray diffraction topographs of epitaxial layers.

6. X-RAY SECONDARY-EMISSION (FLUORESCENCE) SPECTROMETRY

6.1. Principle and Instrumentation

In Fig. 19, X-rays from the X-ray tube *A* irradiate the specimen *B*, usually held in some type of specimen drawer *C* in a specimen compartment *D*. The primary X-rays excite each chemical element in the specimen to

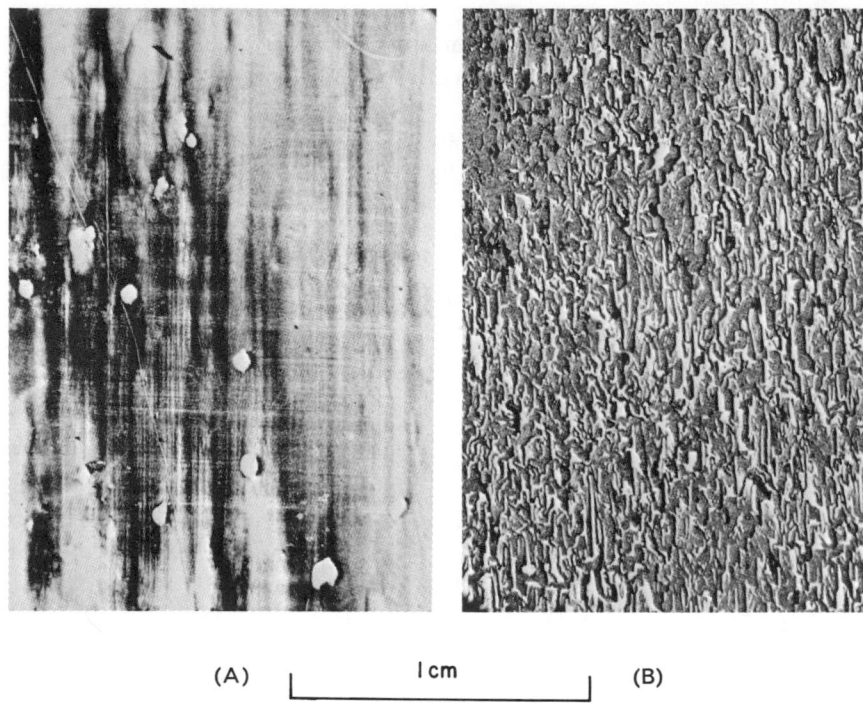

(A) |_____ l cm _____| (B)

Figure 18. Typical reflection X-ray diffraction topographs (positive prints) of epitaxial layers on (100) planes of GaAs. Jarrell–Ash microfocus X-ray generator, $CuK\alpha_1$ radiation, Ilford G5 plates (emulsion 25 μm thick). The diffracting planes are (422), for which θ and $\theta - \phi$ (see Fig. 17) are 41.9° and 6.6°, respectively [unpublished work, S. H. McFarlane, RCA Laboratories, Princeton, N.J. 08540]. (A) Ga(As,P) layer grown from vapor phase. The white spots are pits in the layer. The crossed lines lie along [011] and [0$\bar{1}$1] directions and are probably mismatch dislocations caused by variation in P concentration during growth of the layer. (B) Zn-doped GaAs grown from solution. The crystallographic nature of the layer is entirely different from the vapor-phase layer shown in (A).

emit its secondary X-ray spectrum having wavelengths characteristic of that element and intensities related to its concentration, or, for thin films and platings, to its area density or thickness. The secondary X-rays pass through a soller collimator E to the dispersion crystal F. The X-rays diffracted by the crystal pass through a second collimator G to the detector H. There is a helium or vacuum enclosure I for work at wavelengths $\geqslant 2.5$ Å. The selected-area apertures J and K will be discussed later. The detector output passes in turn to a preamplifier, amplifier, and pulse-height selector, then to a ratemeter and recorder or to a scaler and timer.

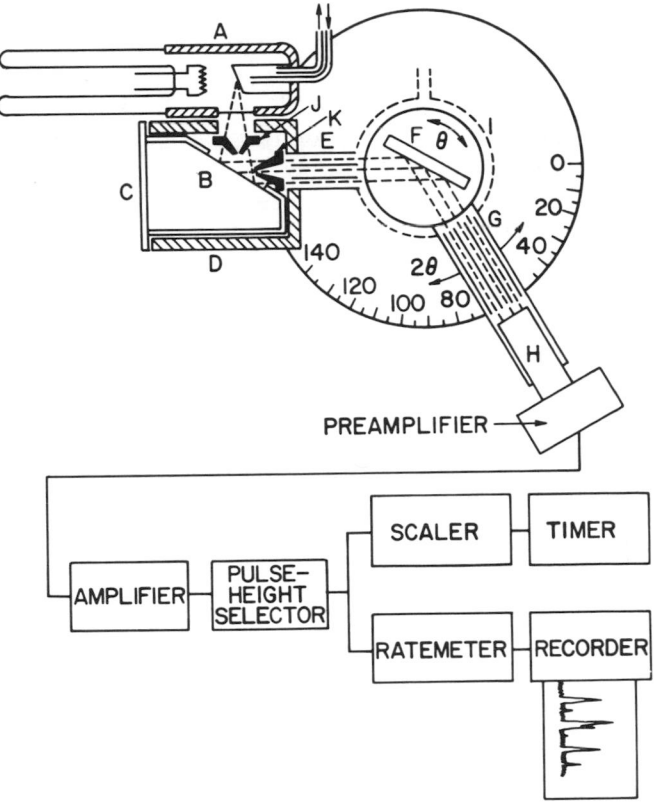

Figure 19. X-ray secondary-emission (fluorescence) spectrometer. *A*, X-ray tube; *B*, specimen; *C*, specimen drawer; *D*, specimen compartment; *E*, source soller collimator; *F*, dispersion crystal; *G*, detector soller collimator; *H*, detector; *I*, He or vacuum enclosure; *J*, primary aperture; *K*, secondary aperture.

6.2. Techniques

The X-ray spectrometer provides only three types of information about films and platings: composition, area density, and thickness. The film may be presented to the instrument in any of three ways: (1) after removal from the substrate without regard to preservation of film integrity; (2) after removal from the substrate intact; and (3) nondestructively, that is, in place on the substrate. Unsupported films and films on thin X-ray-transparent substrates belong by their nature in the second group. Bertin and Longobucco ([7]) have reviewed these methods, particularly as applied to the measurement of thickness of platings.

The first technique mentioned is not considered here. The work of Rhodin ([50]) is an outstanding example of the second technique. He studied films prepared in three ways: (1) chromium, iron, nickel, and stainless steel films up to 300 Å thick were evaporated on 0.00025-in. Mylar. (2) Oxide films were prepared by vacuum-evaporating chromium, iron, nickel, and stainless steel on Formvar and floating the Formvar-backed films on a HNO_3–$K_2Cr_2O_7$ solution for various times to form oxide films of various thicknesses. Unoxidized metal was removed in bromine–methanol in an inert atmosphere, and the Formvar was removed in ethylene chloride. The oxide films were scooped up on Mylar. (3) Oxide films were removed from bulk metals by chemical stripping in bromine–methanol, then scooped up on Mylar. Rhodin obtained sensitivities for Cr, Fe, and Ni of 8.5, 16.5, and 27 counts/sec per $\mu g/cm^2$, respectively.

The remainder of this section is devoted to consideration of X-ray spectrometric analysis of films and platings in place on the substrate. Such analyses may be based on: (1) the intensity of a film or plate line; (2) the attenuation of the intensity of a substrate line; or (3) the intensity ratio of a film and substrate line.

6.2.1. Film Emission Method

Koh and Caugherty ([43]) were the first to show the practicability of this method, and Rhodin ([60]) has made a comprehensive study of it. Zimmerman ([85]) evaluated three plate-metal intensity functions: (1) plate $K\alpha/K\beta$ intensity ratio vs. thickness, for plate metals of relatively low atomic number; (2) plate $L\alpha/L\beta$ intensity ratio vs. thickness, for heavier elements; and (3) $(I_\infty - I_P)/I_\infty$ vs. thickness, where I_P and I_∞ are plate-metal line intensities from, respectively, the plating and an infinitely thick layer of plate metal. A function similar to this last one was used by Sellers and Carroll ([67]): $\log_e [I_\infty/(I_\infty - I_P)]$ vs. thickness. Goodwin and Winchester ([31]) and Keesaer ([40]) applied the background-ratio method ([2]) to minimize variations in X-ray tube output, sample position, condition of the plate surface, etc. Keesaer also describes some modifications of a commercial flat-crystal spectrometer to increase its utility for determining plate thickness.

6.2.2. Substrate Attenuation Method

This method has been applied more widely than the film emission method ([10,16,31,46–48,64]). Zemany and Liebhafsky ([84]) have made a comprehensive study of the technique. Lambert ([44]), Lowe, Sierer, and Ogilvie ([52]), and Lublin ([53]) have applied this method to determination of the thickness of aluminum, stainless steel, and zirconium claddings on uranium and plutonium nuclear reactor fuel elements. Zimmerman ([85]) evaluated two substrate intensity functions: the intensity ratio from the plated and unplated substrate vs. plate thickness, and the $K\alpha/K\beta$ intensity ratio vs. plate thickness. Cline and Schwartz ([18]) determined the thickness of 0–4-μm Al films on Si by both Al $K\alpha$ emission and Si $K\alpha$ attenuation. The emission method gave the best results, with ultimate thickness sensitivity of ± 6 Å in very thin layers. Smuts, Plug, and van Niekerk ([70]) determined the thickness of Sn plate on steel by four methods: Sn $K\alpha$ emission, Fe $K\alpha$ attenuation, Fe $K\alpha$/Fe $K\beta$ attenuation, and Sn $K\alpha$/Fe $K\alpha$ intensity ratio.

The plate/substrate line intensity ratio was used by Bertin and Longobucco ([6]) to determine plate thickness on fine wires; this work is discussed below.

6.2.3. *Multiple-Layer Platings*

Birks, Brooks, and Friedman ([10]) determined the thickness of both platings in Ni–Cu-plated steel. Nickel thickness was obtained from Ni $K\alpha$ intensity. Copper thickness was obtained from a set of curves of Fe $K\alpha$ intensity vs. copper thickness, each curve for a different nickel thickness. Keesaer ([40]) determined the thickness of chromium and nickel in "triplate" (Cr–Ni–Cu-plated steel). Chromium thickness was obtained from Cr $K\alpha$ intensity, nickel thickness from Ni $K\alpha$ intensity corrected for absorption in the overlying chromium plate. Gerold ([30]) combined X-ray diffraction and spectrometry to determine chromium and nickel thickness in Cr–Ni-plated brass. Chromium was determined by diffractometry, nickel by spectrometry of the Ni $K\alpha$ line.

Ebel and Klugel ([24]) calculated film thickness from equations based on the variation of emitted spectral line intensity as a function of take-off angle from the film and from infinitely thick element. Calibration with films of known thickness is not required. Under certain conditions the method is useful for multiple layers and was applied to double layers of ~ 940 Å Cu and ~ 5570 Å Sn.

6.2.4. *Alloy Coatings*

Bertin ([4]) determined niobium and tin thickness in cryogenic Nb_3Sn coatings on metal and ceramic substrates from a $\log_{10}$–$\log_{10}$ plot of Nb $K\alpha$/Sn $K\alpha$ intensity ratio vs. Nb/Sn concentration ratio established from standards having coatings of known composition. The method is applicable to any binary system and to any ternary or higher-order system in which only two elements vary in concentration in an otherwise constant matrix. The calibration curve is always linear and is insensitive to reasonable variations in specimen area, position, and surface condition.

Many methods have been reported for simultaneous determination of both composition and thickness of films. All these methods were developed for analysis of Ni–Fe (Permalloy) films.

Schindler, Month, and Antalec ([65]) report solution and nondestructive methods for the determination of the composition and thickness of Ni–Fe films on gold in the ranges 0–40 % Fe, 10^2–10^5 Å. Five stock solutions were prepared having concentration 10 mg Ni + Fe per ml and Ni:Fe weight ratios 10:0, 9:1, 8:2, 7:3, and 6:4. Aliquots of each of these five solutions were diluted to give five solutions having concentrations 1, 2, 3, 4, and 5 mg Ni + Fe per ml for each Ni:Fe ratio. The Ni $K\alpha$ and Fe $K\alpha$ intensities were measured from all 25 solutions, and the data was plotted on a graph of Fe $K\alpha$ intensity vs. Ni $K\alpha$ intensity. A grid consisting of two sets of lines was drawn on the plot. One set represented the same nickel concentration for different total weights of Ni–Fe. The other set represented the same total weight of Ni–Fe for different nickel concentrations.

Next, Ni $K\alpha$ and Fe $K\alpha$ intensities were measured on 150 Ni–Fe films having various compositions and thicknesses on gold disks. The films were then dissolved quantitatively and Ni $K\alpha$ and Fe $K\alpha$ intensities measured on the solutions. Composition (Ni:Fe) of each film was derived from the grid. Thickness was derived from the film weight (obtained by weighing the gold disks before and after dissolution of the film), area, and composition, and the densities of nickel and iron. A plot of Fe $K\alpha$ vs. Ni $K\alpha$ intensity was made of the data from the *films*. A grid consisting of two sets of lines was drawn on the plot. One set represented the same nickel concentration for different thicknesses. The other set represented the same thickness for different nickel concentrations. Finally, the grid on the plot of *solution* data was redrawn in terms of thickness rather than total weight of Ni–Fe so that thickness could be derived directly either nondestructively or by the solution technique. The form of the calibration grid is shown in Fig. 20.

Hirokawa, Shimanuki, and Goto ([35]) prepared a series of Ni, Fe, and 80Ni–20Fe films having thickness up to $\sim 3\,\mu$m. The intensities of Ni $K\alpha$ and Fe $K\alpha$ were measured on all the standards (I_t) and on infinitely thick nickel and iron (I_∞). Four curves were plotted on a log $[1 - (I_t/I_\infty)]$ vs. t graph: Ni $K\alpha$ intensity from Ni and from Ni–Fe, and Fe $K\alpha$ intensity from Fe and from Ni–Fe. All the curves were linear. From these curves, two pairs of simultaneous equations were derived for determination of thickness and composition near 80Ni–20Fe. The two pairs of equations are for thickness $> 0.1\,\mu$m and $< 0.1\,\mu$m, respectively.

Verderber ([72]) developed a method for determination of composition and thickness of Ni–Fe films on magnetic tapes in the ranges ~ 81Ni–19Fe and 1000–4000 Å. Three stock solutions were prepared having concentration 3 mg Ni + Fe per ml and Ni:Fe weight ratios 85:15, 80:20, and

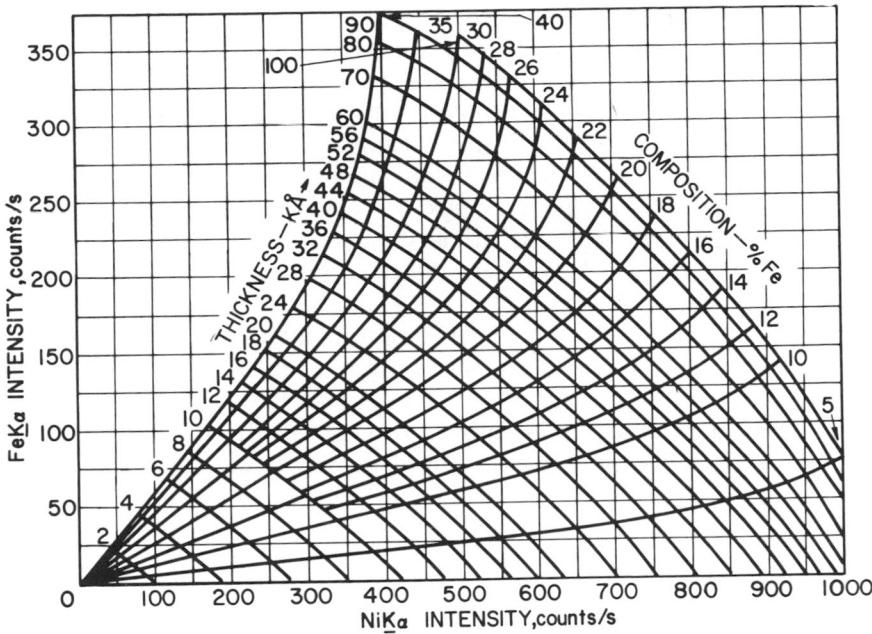

Figure 20. Calibration plot for determination of composition and thickness of Ni–Fe films [Schindler, Month, and Antalec ([65])].

75:25. Aliquots of each of these three solutions were diluted to give seven solutions of different concentration for each Ni:Fe ratio, the most dilute having 0.4 mg Ni + Fe per ml. The intensities of Ni $K\alpha$ and Fe $K\alpha$ were measured from all 21 solutions, and two calibration curves were established: Ni $K\alpha$ intensity vs. mg Ni/ml and Fe $K\alpha$ intensity vs. mg Fe/ml.

Next, 21 evaporated Ni–Fe films were selected, all having nominal 81Ni–19Fe composition, but varying in thickness from 1000–4000 Å. Approximately 100 cm² of each film was dissolved quantitatively, and Ni $K\alpha$ and Fe $K\alpha$ intensities were measured from each solution. Nickel and iron concentrations were derived from the calibration curves and used to calculate film composition.

On an unused portion of each film, thickness was measured by a physical method, and Ni $K\alpha$ and Fe $K\alpha$ intensities were measured. Two new calibration curves were now established from the data from the films (thickness, composition, and Ni $K\alpha$ and Fe $K\alpha$ intensity): Ni $K\alpha$ intensity vs. (thickness × %Ni) and Fe $K\alpha$ intensity vs. (thickness × %Fe). Thereafter, these curves were used for nondestructive analysis of films.

Weyl ([82]) and Pluchery ([58]) developed absolute mathematical methods for determining the thickness and composition of thin alloy films without calibration standards other than the pure constituent elements. Their equations correct for spectral intensity distribution in the primary beam, fluorescent yields of the constituent elements, secondary excitation of low atomic number elements by high atomic number elements, and attenuation of the spectral emission on its way to the detector. Pluchery used filters to remove target lines from the primary beam and corrected for scattered continuous background. Weyl and Pluchery evaluated their equations for simple Ni–Fe films, but Dunn ([23]) has greatly extended their applicability.

Silver and Chow ([68]) compared optical interferometric, stylus, and X-ray spectrometric methods for determining thickness of Ni–Fe films having composition 81–82% Ni and thickness 400–3500 Å. Thickness of several standard films was established by chemical determination of nickel and iron and physical determination of density by measurement of mass and area

$$t_S = \frac{100\rho_A}{(W\rho)_{\mathrm{Ni}} + (W\rho)_{\mathrm{Fe}}} \tag{18}$$

where t_S is thickness of the standard in angstroms, ρ_A is area density in $\mu g/cm^2$, ρ is bulk density in g/cm^3, and W is weight fraction. An X-ray spectrometric thickness measurement consisted of measuring the Ni $K\alpha$ and Fe $K\alpha$ intensities from the samples and one of the standards. Then

$$t_X = t_S \left[\frac{(kI_{\mathrm{Ni}} + I_{\mathrm{Fe}})_X}{(kI_{\mathrm{Ni}} + I_{\mathrm{Fe}})_S} \right] \tag{19}$$

where t is thickness, I is net intensity in counts/sec, $k = (I_{\mathrm{Fe}}/I_{\mathrm{Ni}})/(\%\mathrm{Ni}/\%\mathrm{Fe})$ calculated from the standard, and S and X refer to the standard and specimen, respectively. Agreement between X-ray and interferometric methods was very good; the stylus method was the least accurate.

6.2.5. *Special Specimen Forms*

Zimmerman ([85]) applied three techniques to the determination of plate thickness on a wide variety of small, irregularly shaped, plated parts, such as washers, solder lugs, connectors, etc.: selected-area apertures (see below), masks, and impression molds in sealing wax to permit reproducible positioning of irregularly shaped parts in the spectrometer specimen drawer.

Bertin and Longobucco ([6]) developed two methods for determining plate thickness on wires having a diameter of 0.0004–0.010 in. One method is applicable to large numbers of specimens consisting of infinitely thick layers of wire ($\geqslant 3$ to 5 layers) wound on identical spools that fit the spectrometer specimen compartment. With the instrument set at a plate-metal line, each spool is placed in turn in the specimen drawer and the ratemeter allowed to trace plate-metal intensity for 15 sec or more. A set of spools wound with standard wires is treated the same way. As many as four specimens can be analyzed each minute.

For more accurate analysis, a few meters of wire is wound on a small open frame, card, or spool. The intensities of a plate and substrate line are measured and their ratio calculated. A calibration curve of plate/substrate intensity ratio vs. plate thickness is established from wires of known plate thickness on the same type of support.

6.2.6. *Special Techniques*

6.2.6.1. *Selected-Area Analysis*

In Fig. 19, pinhole or slit apertures may be placed in the primary J or secondary K X-ray beam. In the former case, only the specimen area under the aperture receives primary irradiation; in the latter case, although the entire specimen is irradiated, only secondary emission from the specimen area lying in the projection of the secondary aperture is measured.

When such apertures are used, the flat crystal F should be replaced with a curved crystal. For optimum performance, provision should be made to continuously change either the radius of curvature of the crystal or the specimen–crystal–detector distances as θ is changed. However, useful work can be done with one crystal of fixed radius, and two or three crystals of different radii give entirely satisfactory performance. Collimators E and G are removed, and G should be replaced with a single slit at the detector window.

By using such accessories, the analysis of small selected areas and a point-by-point measurement of uniformity of composition and/or thickness of films are feasible. With the spectrometer set at the spectral line of an element in the film, the specimen may be translated continuously with a motor drive while intensity is recorded as a function of distance in a line across the specimen. Alternatively, the specimen may be moved manually in small increments and intensity measured at each position with the scaler. Successive scans can be made at different places and/or at the same place for different elements.

General descriptions of selected-area accessories and techniques have been reported by Loomis ([51]) and Bertin ([5]). Using such techniques, Zimmerman ([85]) measured variation in plate thickness over plated surfaces; he also investigated wear of gold-plated nickel by scanning (longitudinally and laterally) a wear track and recording Ni $K\alpha$ intensity along or across the track. Bertin and Longobucco ([8]) analyzed and mapped the distribution of sublimates on bulbs, stems, micas, grids, and plates of electron tubes. Sloan ([69]) evaluated point-to-point variation of composition and thickness of ~ 1500-Å Nichrome films with a 0.5-mm secondary-beam pinhole aperture. Ni $K\alpha$ and Cr $K\alpha$ intensities were measured at 1-mm intervals over the film. The Ni $K\alpha$ and Cr $K\alpha$ intensities were used to indicate film thickness, Ni $K\alpha$/Cr $K\alpha$ intensity ratios to indicate composition.

6.2.6.2. Selective Excitation

Beeghley ([3]) measured tin plate thickness by operating the X-ray tube below the K-excitation potential of tin (28 kV) so as to excite only Fe $K\alpha$ (K-excitation potential 7 kV) from the base metal. The selective excitation method has since been applied by others ([10,48]).

6.2.6.3. Enhancement

If the specimen is an unsupported film or a film on a highly X-ray-transparent substrate, most of the primary radiation passes through the specimen and is lost. Hirokawa, Suzuki, and Goto ([36]) placed under such specimens a secondary radiator having a strong spectral line of wavelength just shorter than that of the absorption edge of the element to be excited in the film. The primary X-rays transmitted by the film excite the radiator spectrum, which in turn excites additional emission from the film. Enhancements up to 50% were obtained for chromium and nickel films.

Alternatively, for X-ray-opaque film–substrate systems, the radiator may be placed in the primary beam ([34]). However, this technique reduces the total primary intensity incident on the specimen and therefore reduces the measured intensity by $\sim 50\%$. The only advantage is improved line:background ratio.

6.2.6.4. Excitation by Radioactive Sources

Cook, Mellish, and Payne ([19]) used radioactive isotopes to excite, and a nondispersive spectrometer to measure plate-metal emission. Excitation of base-metal emission by radioactive isotopes is described by the same workers, by Cameron and Rhodes ([15]), and by Zemany ([83]).

Cameron and Rhodes ([15]) report the use of tritium sources for excitation of Fe K radiation in galvanized (zinc-coated) steel and in copper-plated steel, Ti $K\alpha$ radiation in platinum-clad titanium, and CuK radiation in silver-plated copper wire. Their work was done on a nondispersive instrument.

Zemany's work ([83]) is particularly noteworthy because it combines the techniques of excitation by radioactive sources, selective excitation, and nondispersive detection. He used Fe-55, a K-capture isotope emitting only

Mn K X-rays, which can excite only K spectra of elements *below* atomic number 25 (manganese), and L spectra of elements *below* 61 (promethium). If the measurements are made in air, absorption eliminates the K spectra of elements below 19 (potassium) and L spectra of elements below 47 (silver). If the method is to be applicable to one element plated on another, it is necessary that the plate be among the elements K through Cr, or Ag through Nd, but that the base metal not be among these elements. Zemany applied the method to Ti-plated Kovar (Fe–Co–Ni), using a gas-flow proportional counter as detector. He suggests that other K-capture isotopes might extend the utility of the technique.

6.2.6.5. *Nondispersive Operation*

Use of specially built nondispersive spectrometers has been mentioned above in connection with radioactive sources. Standard commercial X-ray spectrometers can be operated in nondispersive mode by setting the goniometer to $0°$ 2θ, removing the crystal, and using a pulse-height selector. Elimination of the crystal increases the measured intensity by two orders or more. Further increase in sensitivity may be realized by moving the detector closer to the specimen compartment. Achey and Serfass ([1]) used balanced (Ross) filters ([42,61]) to isolate the spectral line to be measured.

6.2.6.6. *Decoration*

Lundquist ([54]) evaluated porosity of nickel electroplatings in uranium as follows. The Ni-plated uranium was anodized in a solution containing potassium ferrocyanide, $K_4Fe(CN)_6$, under conditions that minimize attack of nickel, but precipitate uranyl ferrocyanide, $(UO_2)_2Fe(CN)_6$, wherever uranium is exposed. The Fe $K\alpha$ intensity is then measured. This technique should be valuable for investigating porosity and discontinuity of films.

6.3. Image Spectrography

Von Hamos ([73,74]) describes an X-ray image spectrograph or X-ray emission micrograph which permits photography of the area distribution of chemical elements over a flat specimen surface. The method would be useful for mapping variations in composition and/or thickness of thin films and platings on flat substrates. The instrumental arrangement is shown in Fig. 21. The specimen is irradiated by the primary beam from the X-ray tube, and each chemical element in the specimen surface is excited to emit its characteristic X-ray spectrum, just as in a conventional X-ray spectrometer. For each secondary wavelength λ_1, λ_2, λ_3, ... emitted by the specimen, the intensity distribution over the specimen surface corres-

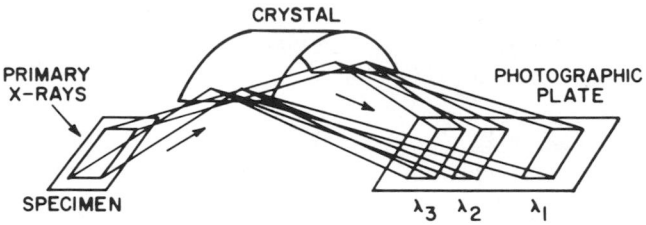

Figure 21. Principle of the Von Hamos image spectrograph.

ponds to the concentration distribution of the element producing it. In thin films and platings, the intensity distribution would also correspond to the point-to-point thickness. A cylindrically curved crystal is arranged to form a series of separate true monochromatic images of the specimen surface on a plane fine-grain photographic plate. Each image shows the intensity distribution of a certain spectral line over the specimen surface—and thereby the concentration or thickness distribution of the element emitting that line. Figure 22 (A) shows a conventional light photograph of the surface of a copper-bearing mineral, and Fig. 22 (B) shows the corresponding Cu $K\alpha$ image spectrum.

Estimations of surface concentrations or film thickness are made by comparing the image spectrum of the sample with spectra of standards having known composition or thickness. Determinations of surface concentrations or film thickness are made by measuring photographic densities of the image spectra of samples and standards with a microdensitometer. A photographic emulsion calibration curve is prepared to permit conversion of densities to intensities.

The useful specimen area may be as much as ~ 1 cm^2 and the spacial resolution $\leqslant 0.1$ mm. An idea of the sensitivity may be derived from the following datum: $0.02\,\mu$g Co in 0.01 mm^2 gave a useful photographic density (0.12) in a 1-hr exposure.

6.4. Scope and Application

X-ray secondary-emission spectrometry has been applied most widely to platings, but the method is sufficiently sensitive to be applicable to true thin films. For most elements, a monolayer having an area of ~ 1 cm^2 is readily measurable.

The method actually measures only area concentration, and thickness is derived only by making assumptions about the densities of the constituent elements. However, the great sensitivity, convenience, and

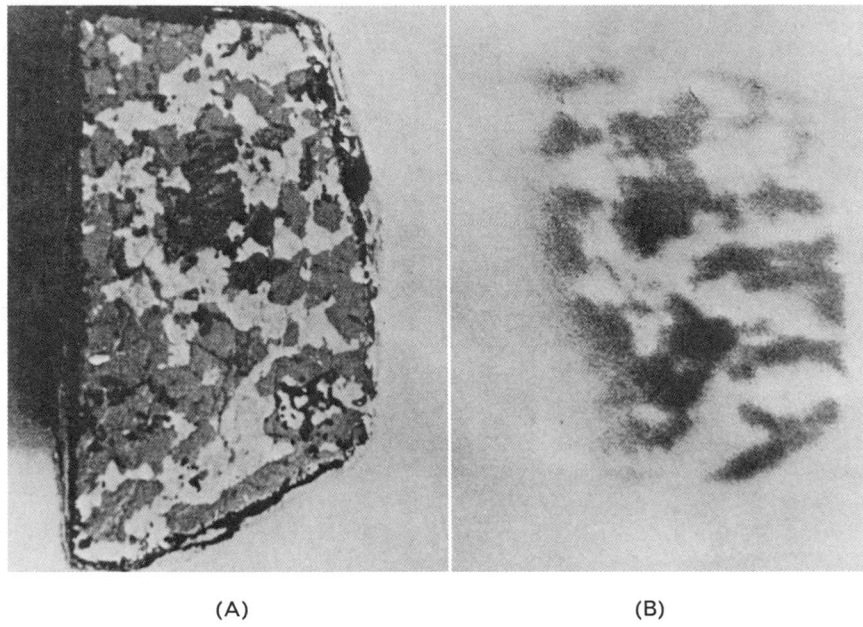

(A)   (B)

Figure 22. Light photograph of surface of Cu-bearing mineral (A) and the corresponding Cu$K\alpha$ image spectrum (B). The long dimension of the mineral is ~ 1.5 cm [Von Hamos, *Trans. Roy. Inst. Technol.* (Stockholm)].

versatility of the method and the ease of evaluating uniformity make it very useful for film work.

Several workers ([26,27,33]) have found it advantageous to disperse bulk specimens into films to reduce matrix effects in X-ray spectrometric analysis. Finnegan ([27]) describes a technique for preparing films by grinding the specimen to a fine powder, suspending it with an organic binder in an organic vehicle, and casting the slurry on a glass plate with a casting knife. Bertin and Longobucco ([8]) used this technique to calibrate their sublimate determinations.

7. X-RAY ABSORPTION-EDGE SPECTROMETRY

Bertin, Longobucco, and Carver ([9]) applied the method of absorption-edge spectrometry to films of $(Ba,Sr,Ca)CO_3$ and Nb_3Sn made by casting slurries of these substances in an organic vehicle and binder ([27]). In this method, one or more wavelengths on each side of the absorption edge of the analyte are passed in turn through each specimen and through an empty specimen support or clean substrate. Only the analyte undergoes any substantial change in absorption coefficient between the bracketing wavelengths; the absorption coefficients of the matrix elements remain substantially unchanged. Analyte concentration is calculated from these transmitted intensities using an equation having form similar to the following:

$$C = \frac{2303}{(\mu - k\mu')} [\log_{10}(I_0/I) - k \log_{10}(I_0'/I')] \tag{20}$$

where I_0 and I_0' are intensities transmitted by the clean substrate or empty specimen support, I and I' are intensities transmitted by the film–substrate system, and μ and μ' are the analyte mass absorption coefficients at the two bracketing wavelengths. The quantity k is an experimentally evaluated correction factor. C is the area density in mg/cm^2. Calibration standards are not required.

The bracketing wavelengths are obtained in either of two ways: (1) The primary X-ray beam may be directed through the specimen, and the crystal-detector system set to measure the two wavelengths in turn. (2) The primary beam may be directed on a secondary target having spectral lines bracketing the analyte absorption edge. Both lines may be derived from the same target; otherwise two targets are used in succession. Again the crystal-detector system is set to measure the two wavelengths in turn.

REFERENCES

1. F. A. Achey and E. J. Serfass, A New Approach to Coating Thickness by Fluorescent X-Ray Absorption, *J. Electrochem. Soc.* **105**, 204–205 (1958).
2. G. Andermann and J. W. Kemp, Scattered X-Rays as Internal Standards in X-Ray Emission Spectroscopy, *Anal. Chem.* **30**, 1306–1309 (1958).
3. H. F. Beeghley, X-Ray Method for Determining Tin Coating Thickness, *J. Electrochem. Soc.* **97**, 152–157 (1950).
4. E. P. Bertin, Intensity-Ratio Technique for X-Ray Spectrometric Analysis of Binary Samples, *Anal. Chem.* **36**, 826–832 (1964).
5. E. P. Bertin, Evaluation and Application of an Improved Slit Probe for the X-Ray Secondary-Emission Spectrometer, *Advan. X-Ray Anal.* **8**, 231–247 (1965).
6. E. P. Bertin and R. J. Longobucco, X-Ray Spectrometric Determination of Plate Metals on Plated Wires, *Anal. Chem.* **34**, 804–811 (1962).
7. E. P. Bertin and R. J. Longobucco, X-Ray Methods for Determination of Plate Thickness, *Metal Finishing* **60**(8) 42–44 (1962).
8. E. P. Bertin and R. J. Longobucco, X-Ray Spectrometric Determination of Composition and Distribution of Sublimates in Receiving-Type Electron Tubes, *Advan. X-Ray Anal.* **7**, 566–583 (1964).

9. E. P. Bertin, R. J. Longobucco, and R. J. Carver, A Simplified Routine Method for X-Ray Absorption-Edge Spectrometric Analysis, *Anal. Chem.* **36**, 641–655 (1964).

10. L. S. Birks, E. J. Brooks, and H. Friedman, Fluorescent X-Ray Spectroscopy, *Anal. Chem.* **25**, 692–697 (1953).

11. B. Borie and C. J. Sparks, Jr., Special Methods for the Structural Investigation of Thin Films; in *Thin Films*, Am. Soc. Metals, Metals Park, Ohio; ch. 2, pp. 45–58 (1964).

12. B. Borie and C. J. Sparks, Jr., Analysis of Thin Films; in *Local Atomic Arrangements Studied by X-Ray Diffraction* (J. B. Cohen and J. B. Hilliard, eds.), *Metallurgical Society Conference*, Vol. 36, 341–349, Gordon C. Breach, New York (1966).

13. B. Borie, C. J. Sparks, Jr., and J. V. Cathcart, Epitaxially Induced Strains in Cu_2O Films on Copper Single Crystals. I. X-Ray Diffraction Effects, *Acta Met.* **10**, 691–697 (1962).

14. G. Borrmann, The Extinction Diagram of Quartz, *Physik. Z.* **42**, 157–162 (1941).

15. J. F. Cameron and J. R. Rhodes, Measurement of Tinplate Thickness Using Fluorescent X-Rays Excited by a Radioactive Source, *Brit. J. Appl. Phys.* **11**, 49–52 (1960).

16. G. L. Clark, X-Ray and Gamma-Ray Absorption Photometry (Absorptiometry); in *Encyclopedia of Spectroscopy* (G. L. Clark, ed.), Reinhold Publishing Corp., New York (1960) pp. 705–706.

17. G. L. Clark, G. Pish, and L. E. Weeg, Bonding and Structural Variations of Commercial Electroplatings 2–55 × 10^{-6} inch Thick, *J. Appl. Phys.* **15**, 193–200 (1944).

18. J. E. Cline and S. Schwartz, Determination of the Thickness of Aluminum on Silicon by X-Ray Fluorescence, *J. Electrochem. Soc.* **114**, 605–608 (1967).

19. G. B. Cook, C. E. Mellish, and J. A. Payne, Measurement of Thin Metal Layers; Fluorescent X-Ray Production by Radioisotope Sources, *Anal. Chem.* **32**, 590–593 (1960).

20. P. Croce, M. Gandais, and A. Marraud, Study of the Structure of Thin Films of Gold and Indium, *Rev. d'Optique* **40**, 555–562 (1961).

21. P. Croce, G. Devant, M. Gandais, and A. Marraud, Study of the Structure of X-Ray Diffraction Lines for Thin Gold Layers, *Acta Cryst.* **15**, 424 (1962).

22. R. C. Duncan and L. G. Parratt, *A Study of Evaporated Aluminum Films by X-Ray Total Reflection*, U.S. Air Force, Office of Scientific Research, Rept. AFOSR-TN-58-680, ASTIA No. AD-162-212, 105 p. (21 Aug. 1958).

23. H. M. Dunn, International Business Machines Corp., Yorktown Heights, N.Y. 10598; unpublished work.

24. H. Ebel and J. Klugel, Determination of Thickness of Thin Planar Multilayers by X-Ray Fluorescence, *Z. Naturforsch.* **21**, 2108–2109 (1966).

25. A. Eisenstein, X-Ray Methods for Measuring the Thickness of Thin Crystalline Films, *J. Appl. Phys.* **17**, 874–878 (1946).

26. E. J. Felten, I. Fankuchen, and J. Steigman, A Possible Solution of the Matrix Problem in X-Ray Fluorescence Spectroscopy, *Anal. Chem.* **31**, 1771–1776 (1959).

27. J. J. Finnegan, Thin-Film X-Ray Spectroscopy, *Advan. X-Ray Anal.* **5**, 500–511 (1962).

28. H. Friedman and L. S. Birks, Thickness Measurement of Thin Coatings by X-Ray Absorption, *Rev. Sci. Instr.* **17**, 99–101 (1946).

29. A. H. Geisler, J. K. Hill, and J. B. Newkirk, Divergent-Beam X-Ray Photography with Standard Diffraction Equipment, *J. Appl. Phys.* **19**, 1041–1049 (1948).

30. V. Gerold, X-Ray Thickness Gaging of Galvanized Layers with a Counter-Tube Diffractometer, *Z. Angew. Phys.* **4**, 247–254 (1952).

31. P. S. Goodwin and C. L. Winchester, Continuous Measurement of Plating Thickness, *Plating* **46**, 41–44 (1959).
32. R. B. Gray, X-Ray Measurement of the Thickness of Silver Plating, *Phys. Rev.* **69**, 49 (1946).
33. E. L. Gunn, X-Ray Fluorescent Intensity of Elements Evaporated from Solution onto Thin Film, *Anal. Chem.* **33**, 921–927 (1961).
34. E. L. Gunn, Problems of Direct Determination of Trace Nickel in Oil by X-Ray Emission Spectrography, *Anal. Chem.* **36**, 2086–2090 (1964).
35. K. Hirokawa, T. Shimanuki, and H. Goto, Simultaneous Determination of Alloy Film Thickness and Its Composition with X-Ray Fluorescent Spectroscopy. Determination of the Composition and Thickness of Nickel-Iron Alloy Films on Copper, *Z. Anal. Chem.* **190**, 309–315 (1962).
36. K. Hirokawa, M. Suzuki, and H. Goto, Effect of Backing Metals in the X-Ray Fluorescence Spectral Analysis of Metal Films and Its Application. Absorption-Edge Effect, *Z. Anal. Chem.* **199**, 89–94 (1964).
37. H. Holloway, Some Diffraction Methods for the Study of Epitaxial Layers; in *Use of Thin Films in Physical Investigations* (J. C. Anderson, ed.), Academic Press, New York (1966).
38. T. Imura, S. Weissmann, and J. J. Slade, Jr., A Study of Age-Hardening of Al-3.5%Cu by the Divergent X-Ray-Beam Method, *Acta Cryst.* **15**, 786–793 (1962).
39. D. T. Keating and O. F. Kammerer, Film Thickness Determination from Substrate X-Ray Reflections, *Rev. Sci. Instr.* **29**, 34–36 (1958).
40. W. C. Keesaer, Establishment of Q Rating Factor for Decorative Chromium Plate by X-Ray Fluorescence, *Advan. X-Ray Anal.* **3**, 77–94 (1959).
41. H. D. Keith, An X-Ray Study in High Vacuum of the Structure of Evaporated Copper Films, *Proc. Phys. Soc. (London)* **69B**, 180–192 (1956).
42. P. Kirkpatrick, Theory and Use of Ross Filters, *Rev. Sci. Instr.* **10**, 186–191 (1939); **15**, 223–229 (1944).
43. P. K. Koh and B. Caugherty, Metallurgical Applications of X-Ray Fluorescent Analysis, *J. Appl. Phys.* **23**, 427–433 (1952).
44. M. C. Lambert, X-Ray Spectrographic Determination of Uranium and Plutonium in Aluminum and Other Reactor Fuel Materials, *Advan. X-Ray Anal.* **2**, 193–213 (1959).
45. A. R. Lang, X-Ray Diffraction Topography; in *Encyclopedia of X-Rays and Gamma-Rays* (G. L. Clark, ed), Reinhold Publishing Corp., New York (1963) pp. 1053–1058.
46. C. Legrand, Measurement of the Thickness of Thin Layers by X-Ray Fluorescence, *J. Chim. Phys.* **53**, 587–592 (1956).
47. C. Legrand and J. J. Trillat, Investigation of Surface Films by X-Ray Fluorescence, *Rev. Met.* **53**, 645–648 (1956).
48. H. A. Liebhafsky and P. D. Zemany, Film Thickness by X-Ray Emission Spectrography, *Anal. Chem.* **28**, 455–459 (1956).
49. T. B. Light and N. J. Wagner, X-Ray Diffraction Study of Vacuum-Evaporated Silver Films, *J. Vacuum Sci. Technol.* **3**, 1–5 (1966).
50. P. E. Lighty, D. Shanefield, S. Weissmann, and A. Shrier, X-Ray Studies of Epitaxial Copper Electrocrystallization, *J. Appl. Phys.* **34**, 2233–2239 (1963).
51. T. C. Loomis, X-Ray Spectroscopy as an Analytical Tool, *Ann. N. Y. Acad. Sci.* **137**, 284–296 (1966).
52. B. J. Lowe, P. D. Sierer, and R. B. Ogilvie, Cladding Thickness of Fuel Elements by X-Rays, *Advan. X-Ray Anal.* **2**, 275–281 (1958).

53. P. Lublin, Determination of Cladding Thickness of Nuclear Fuel Elements by X-Rays, *Norelco Reptr.* **6**, 57–59 (1959).

54. L. R. Lundquist, Porosity Test for Thin Electrodeposits on Uranium by X-Ray Fluorescence, *Plating* **52**, 1316 (1965).

55. R. L. Mozzi and O. J. Guentert, Adaptation of an X-Ray Diffractometer for Thin Film Studies by Total Reflection of X-Rays, *Rev. Sci. Instr.* **35**, 75–79 (1964).

56. J. B. Nelson and D. P. Riley, An Experimental Investigation of Extrapolation Methods in the Derivation of Accurate Unit-Cell Dimensions of Crystals, *Proc. Phys. Soc. (London)* **57**, 160–177 (1945).

57. L. G. Parratt, Surface Studies of Solids by Total Reflection of X-Rays, *Phys. Rev.* **95**, 359–369 (1954).

58. M. Pluchery, Absolute Method for X-Ray Fluorescence Analysis Applicable to the Films Obtained by Vacuum Evaporation of Iron–Nickel Alloys, *Spectrochim. Acta* **19**, 533–540 (1963).

59. W. A. Rachinger, A Correction for the α_1–α_2 Doublet in the Measurement of Widths of X-Ray Diffraction Lines, *J. Sci. Instr.* **25**, 254–255 (1948).

60. T. N. Rhodin, Chemical Analysis of Thin Films by X-Ray Emission Spectrography, *Anal. Chem.* **27**, 1857–1861 (1955).

61. P. A. Ross, New Method of Spectroscopy for Faint X-Radiations, *J. Opt. Soc. Am.* **16**, 433–438 (1928).

62. W. Ruhl, X-Ray Investigations on Condensed Tin Films at Low Temperatures, *Z. Phys.* **138**, 121–135 (1954).

63. J. Sauro, I. Fankuchen, and N. Wainfan, X-Ray Interference Structure in the Specularly Reflected Radiation from Thin Films, *Phys. Rev.* **132**, 1544–1546 (1963).

64. D. Schenk, Methods for Measuring the Thickness of Corrosion-Protective Coatings, *Korrosion u. Metallschutz* **19**, 1–5 (1943).

65. M. J. Schindler, A. Month, and J. Antalec, *An X-Ray Fluorescence Technique for Analysis of Iron–Nickel Films over an Extremely Wide Range of Composition and Thickness*, Pittsburgh Conf. Anal. Chem. Appl. Spectry. (1961).

66. A. Segmueller, Study of X-Ray Structures for the Determination of Crystallite Size and Average Value of the Internal Stress of Thin Metal Layers, *Z. Metallk.* **54**, 247–251 (1963).

67. W. W. Sellers, Jr. and K. G. Carroll, Gaging of Thin Nickel Coatings by X-Ray Fluorescence, *Proc. Am. Electroplaters Soc.* **43**, 97–100 (1956).

68. M. D. Silver and E. T.-K. Chow, Thickness Measurements of Thin Permalloy Films; Comparison of X-Ray Emission Spectroscopy, Interferometry, and Stylus Methods, *J. Vacuum Sci. Technol.* **2**, 203–207 (1965).

69. R. D. Sloan, X-Ray Spectrographic Analysis of Thin Films by the Milliprobe Technique, *Advan. X-Ray Anal.* **5**, 512–515 (1962).

70. J. Smuts, C. Plug, and J. N. van Niekerk, Coating Thickness Determination of Tin Plate by X-Ray Methods, *J. S. African Inst. Mining Met.* **67**, 462–472 (1967); *C. A.* **67**, 75624 (1967).

71. A. Taylor, *X-Ray Metallography*, John Wiley and Sons, New York (1961) ch. 14, pp. 656–723.

72. R. R. Verderber, X-Ray Fluorescence Analysis of the Composition of Ni–Fe Thin Films, *Norelco Reptr.* **10**, 30–34 (1963).

73. L. Von Hamos, X-Ray Image Method of Chemical Analysis, *Am. Mineralogist* **23**, 215–226 (1938).

74. L. Von Hamos, X-Ray Micro-Analyzer, *J. Sci. Instr.* **15**, 87–94 (1938).

75. R. W. Vook and F. R. L. Schoening, X-Ray Diffractometer Attachment for Direct Observation of Evaporated Thin Films, *Rev. Sci. Instr.* **34**, 792–793 (1963).

76. R. W. Vook and F. Witt, Structure and Annealing Behavior of Metal Films Deposited on Substrates near 80°K. I. Copper Films on Glass, *J. Vacuum Sci. Technol.* **2**, 49–57 (1965).

77. R. W. Vook and F. Witt, Structure and Annealing Behavior of Metal Films Deposited on Substrates near 80°K. II. Gold Films on Glass, *J. Vacuum Sci. Technol.* **2**, 243–249 (1965).

78. N. Wainfan and L. G. Parratt, X-Ray Reflection Studies of the Anneal and Oxidation of Some Thin Solid Films, *J. Appl. Phys.* **31**, 1331–1337 (1960).

79. N. Wainfan, N. J. Scott, and L. G. Parratt, Density Measurements of Some Thin Copper Films, *J. Appl. Phys.* **30**, 1604–1609 (1959).

80. B. E. Warren, Presence and Density of Faults and Twins by Measurement of Diffraction Peak Shifts and Line Symmetries, *Prog. Metal Phys.* **8**, 147 (1959).

81. B. E. Warren and B. L. Averbach, Effect of Cold Work Distortion on X-Ray Patterns, *J. Appl. Phys.* **21**, 595–598 (1950).

82. R. Weyl, Nondestructive Measurement of Composition and Layer Thickness of Thin Films by X-Ray Fluorescence, *Z. Angew. Phys.* **13**, 283–288 (1961).

83. P. D. Zemany, Use of Fe[55] for Measuring Titanium Coating Thickness, *Rev. Sci. Instr.* **30**, 292–293 (1959).

84. P. D. Zemany and H. A. Liebhafsky, Plating Thickness by the Attenuation of Characteristic X-Rays, *J. Electrochem. Soc.* **103**, 157–159 (1956).

85. R. H. Zimmerman, Measuring Plating Thickness; Industrial Applications of X-Ray Methods, *Metal Finishing* **59**(5) 67–73 (1961).

III. X-RAY FLUORESCENCE AND ELECTRON MICROPROBE TECHNIQUES FOR DETERMINATION OF THIN-FILM THICKNESSES

James E. Cline

Electronics Research Center
National Aeronautics and Space Administration
Cambridge, Massachusetts

This paper discusses two methods for determining the thickness of thin films: X-ray fluorescence and electron microprobe techniques. For X-ray fluorescence, a linear relationship is obtained between the function $-\log (1 - I_t/I_0)$ and the mass thickness of the thin film, where I_t is the intensity of the characteristic X-rays from the thin film and I_0 is the limiting intensity from thick layers.

For electron microprobe techniques a more complex relationship is found due to the variation of the effective electron excitation function, which reaches a maximum at a penetration depth depending on the electron beam voltage of the characteristic X-rays emitted. A method is described for the simultaneous determination of both gold and molybdenum thicknesses in a laminated metallization system used for integrated circuits.

1. INTRODUCTION

This paper covers the basic relationships which govern the X-ray emission from thin films and the underlying substrates when they are subjected to either X-ray photons or to energetic electrons. Either technique can be used to give more precise thickness, or surface density, measurements than are obtained by optical interference methods on very thin films.

2. X-RAY FLUORESCENCE TECHNIQUES

An example of the application of X-ray fluorescence for a typical determination of thin-film thickness is here described ([1]) for the case of aluminum films on silicon substrates. X-ray fluorescence can be applied only to those thin films which emit characteristic X-rays in the detectable

83

range. With our equipment, the elements from aluminum to uranium could be detected; special analyzing crystals can be used to extend the range toward the lighter elements.

Two basic methods were involved in the utilization of X-ray fluorescence for determination of the thickness of the aluminum film. In one technique, emission of the characteristic Al $K\alpha$ radiation by the aluminum film was measured and found to increase with film thickness. In the other, measurements were made of the Si $K\alpha$ X-rays emitted by the substrate; this radiation decreased with aluminum thickness due to absorption.

In both cases the aluminum and silicon fluorescence lines were activated by X-rays from a tungsten-target tube in a Norelco vacuum X-ray fluorescence spectrometer. Tube voltages from 15 to 50 kV were used, with currents up to 50 mA. A flat EDDT crystal with a 2d-spacing of 8.76 Å was used with a flow proportional detector and pulse amplitude discrimination.

The samples used in this work were polished silicon wafers on which various thicknesses of aluminum were deposited by vacuum evaporation, partly masked to form steps for calibration of the thicknesses by a Zeiss interference microscope. Samples and standards could be readily compared by rotating the spectrometer sample holder. A stainless-steel mask with an opening 0.625 in. in diameter was used in each sample holder to define the area of the aluminum film under examination. Areas of smaller size could be measured with a decrease in sensitivity.

In Fig. 1, an enlarged cross section of the aluminum-coated silicon wafer is shown diagrammatically, with ϕ representing the angle of incidence of the primary radiation with the specimen surface and ψ the angle of emission of the fluorescence radiation. These angles were determined by the position of the specimen in relation to the X-ray tube target and to the collimator of the spectrometer.

The intensity I_t of the characteristic Al $K\alpha$ radiation reaches a limiting value I_0 for thick aluminum (over $40\,\mu$), and the following relationship holds:

$$I_t/I_0 = 1 - e^{-At} \tag{1}$$

where t is the thickness of aluminum in microns, assuming films of invariant porosity. The constant A is related [2,3] to μ_p and μ_s, the linear absorption coefficients of aluminum for the primary and fluorescence radiation, respectively, by the following equation:

$$A = 10^{-4}\left(\frac{\mu_p}{\sin\phi} + \frac{\mu_s}{\sin\psi}\right) \tag{2}$$

Only the second term in the parentheses can be calculated directly, since the value of μ_p is uncertain, depending on the average effective wavelength

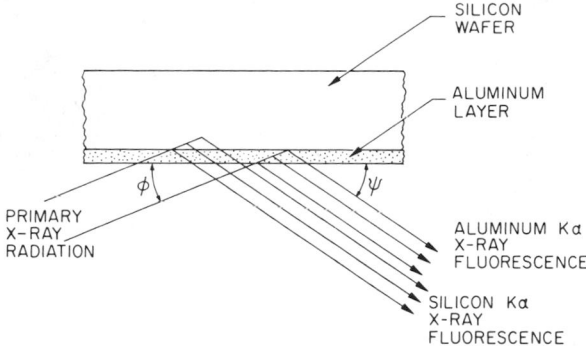

Figure 1. Paths of X-rays in aluminum film and silicon substrate, showing angles of primary and fluorescence radiation.

of the primary radiation. In our work the constant A was determined experimentally.

From Eq. (1) a linear relationship between a function of the intensity $f(I_t)$ and the thickness t can be obtained by

$$f(I_t) = -\log_{10}(1 - I_t/I_0) = At/2.3026 \tag{3}$$

Our experimental data show that a plot of $f(I_t)$ vs. thickness of aluminum is linear, as can be seen in Fig. 2. There was found to be very little variation of this function with tube voltage in the range 15 to 50 kV. From the slope of the line in Fig. 2, the constant A was found to be 0.348.

Instead of using the Al $K\alpha$ fluorescence, the thickness of the aluminum layer on silicon can also be determined by measurement of the X-ray fluorescence from the substrate. In this case the maximum Si $K\alpha$ fluorescence intensity is obtained at zero thickness of the aluminum, and the intensity decreases exponentially as the aluminum thickness increases as is shown by the equation

$$I'_t/I'_0 = e^{-Bt} \tag{4}$$

where I'_t and I'_0 are the intensities of Si $K\alpha$ fluorescence at thicknesses of t (microns) and zero, respectively. The constant B can be expressed by

$$B = 10^{-4}\left(\frac{\mu'_p}{\sin\phi} + \frac{\mu'_s}{\sin\psi}\right) \tag{5}$$

where μ'_p and μ'_s are the linear absorption coefficients of aluminum for the primary radiation and Si $K\alpha$ fluorescence, respectively.

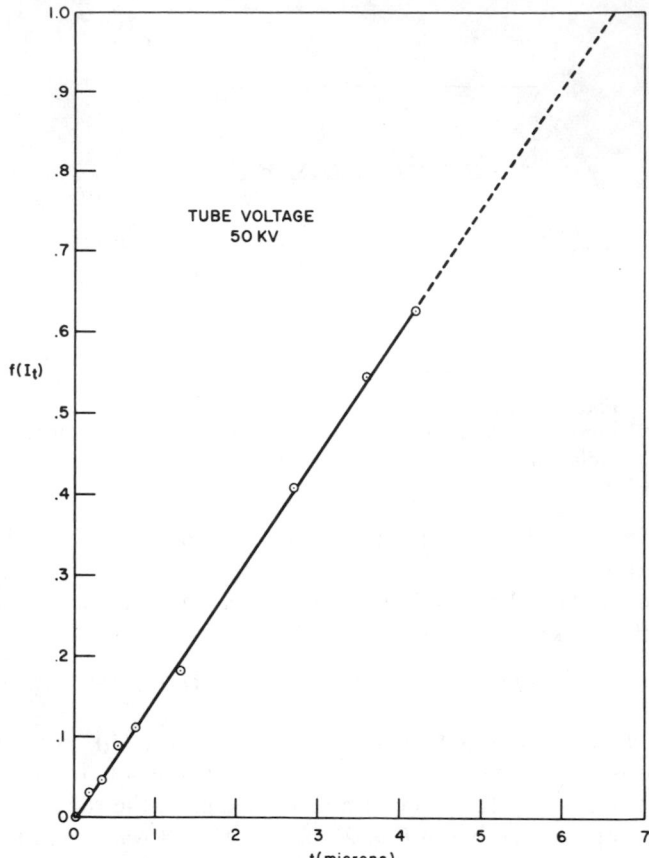

Figure 2. Plot of $f(I_t)$ vs. t using Al $K\alpha$ at 50 kV. Slope of line = 0.151, calculated from least squares fit.

From Eq. (4) a linear relationship between a function of the intensity $F(I_t')$ and t can be obtained by

$$F(I_t') = -\log_{10}(I_t'/I_0') = Bt/2.3026 \tag{6}$$

Values of $F(I_t')$ were obtained from our experimental data and plotted against t, as shown in Fig. 3. From the slope of the line the constant B was calculated to be 1.771. The constant B is greater than A because the linear absorption coefficient of aluminum for Si $K\alpha$ radiation is much greater than that for Al $K\alpha$.

From an analysis of the signal-to-noise ratios in the two X-ray fluorescence techniques, it was concluded that the direct measurement of

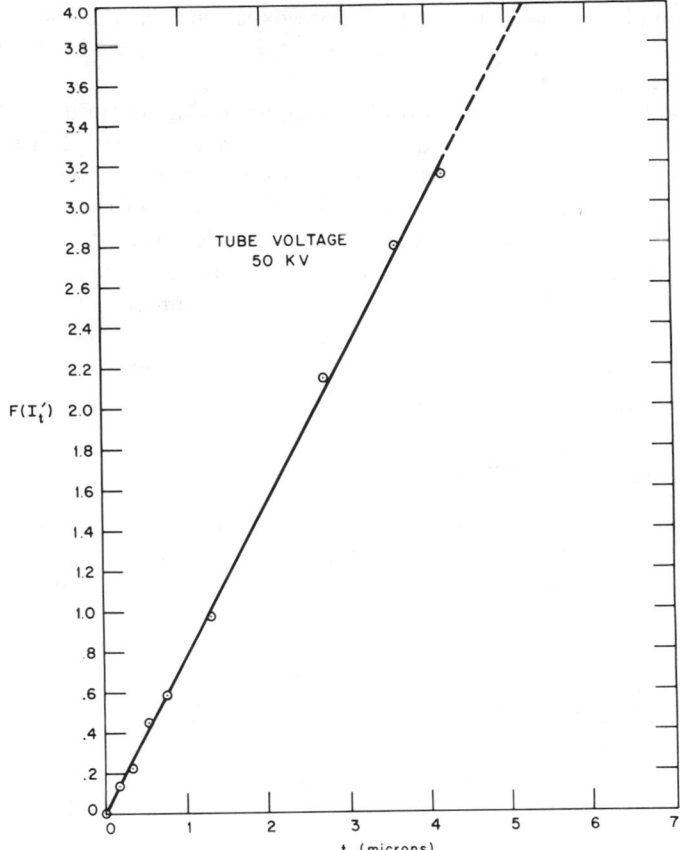

Figure 3. Plot of $F(I_t')$ vs. t using Si $K\alpha$ at 50 kV. Slope of line = 0.769, calculated from least squares fit.

the Al $K\alpha$ X-rays was better than the measurement of the silicon radiation, especially for very thin films. The ultimate sensitivity of this technique for very thin films was estimated to be $\pm 6\,\text{Å}$ of aluminum.

3. GOLD–MOLYBDENUM METALLIZATION

The gold–molybdenum metallization system for integrated circuits offers many outstanding potential advantages over the more usual aluminum metallization, such as the ease with which it bonds to gold leads, the absence of formation of brittle intermetallics, the higher temperature capability, and the lack of significant electromigration during operation.

The semiconductor industry has had more experience in the use of aluminum metallization, which is more economical to deposit and easier to etch into the interconnection pattern.

There are some serious problems in achieving optimum reliability in integrated circuits using gold–molybdenum metallization. For example, if the underlying molybdenum layer is too thin, or contains pinholes, there is a strong possibility that the gold will diffuse through the molybdenum into the silicon substrate, causing undesirable electrical effects. By using an electron microprobe analyzer, a technique was developed by which the completed gold–molybdenum metallization in an integrated circuit could be examined point by point to determine both the thickness of the gold layer and the thickness of the underlying molybdenum. The area under observation at any one point is approximately one-micron square.

4. EFFECTIVE ELECTRON PENETRATION

In the development of a technique for determining the thickness of a layer of one metal underlying another layer, it is necessary to obtain a convenient mathematical expression for the effective penetration of electrons to the underlying layer. Since the thickness determination depends on the generation of a particular characteristic X-ray wavelength from the layer, the effective electron penetration is related not only to the total number of electrons striking the underlying layer, but also to their energy and direction of movement after being scattered in the topmost layer. Highly energetic electrons become more effective for generating X-rays as they penetrate below the surface since their lower energy and longer path length due to scattering increases the probability of a collision process taking place. However, in still deeper layers the effectiveness decreases as the number of available electrons decreases and as the electron energy falls toward that of the critical excitation energy, below which the characteristic X-ray wavelength used for the determination cannot be generated.

A schematic diagram in Fig. 4 shows the electron penetration and X-ray emission from gold–molybdenum metallization, where d is the thickness of the gold layer, d' is the thickness of the underlying molybdenum layer, and ψ is the angle of the detected X-rays. For simultaneous determination of both gold and molybdenum thicknesses, the following experimental conditions must be obtained:

1. The penetration of electrons must be deep enough to generate characteristic X-rays in both gold and molybdenum layers.

2. Excess electrons with energy above the molybdenum critical excitation energy must penetrate into the substrate below the molybdenum layer.

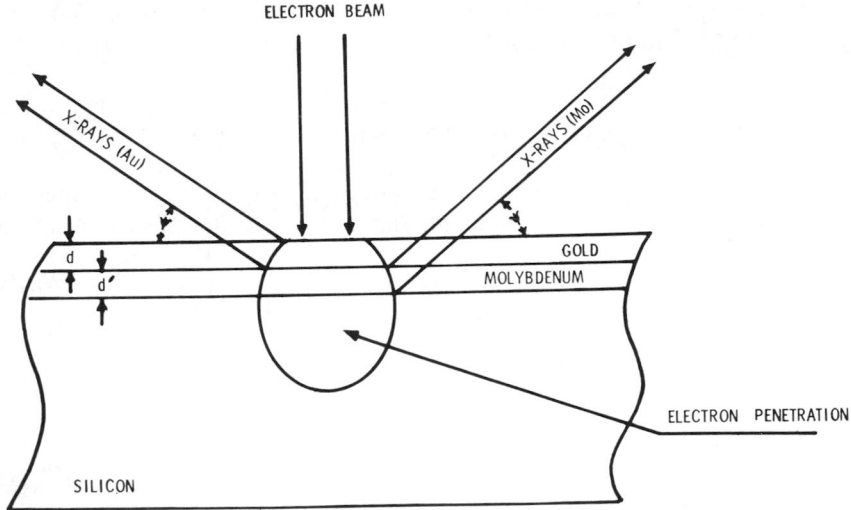

Figure 4. Schematic diagram of electron penetration into gold–molybdenum metallization and paths of emitted X-rays.

3. The generated characteristic gold X-ray wavelength must be able to emerge back through the gold layer at the angle of the X-ray detection system.

4. The generated characteristic molybdenum X-ray wavelength must be able to emerge back through both the gold and molybdenum layers at the angle of the X-ray detection system.

It was anticipated that the mass thickness of the gold layer in integrated circuit gold–molybdenum metallizations would range up to about 1 mg/cm² (0.52 μ). This thickness of gold absorbs molybdenum L characteristic X-rays almost completely, so that the determination of the thickness of the underlying molybdenum layer requires the employment of the more penetrating, shorter wavelength, molybdenum K X-rays.

Castaing and Descamps ([4]) determined experimentally the effective penetration of 29 keV electrons through a gold layer for generation of bismuth L X-rays. New correction expressions were derived in this work to take into consideration our different electron beam voltages and the difference between the critical excitation voltages for bismuth L and molybdenum K X-rays.

In order to simplify the computations, the curve of Castaing was expressed by empirical equations in which log ϕ (the logarithm to the base 10 of the effective electron penetration) was related to X (equivalent to ρx under Castaing's conditions) by a parabola for thicknesses between 0 and 0.4 mg/cm², (0 and 0.2 μ) and by a straight line between 0.4 and 1.5 mg/cm² (0.2 and 0.8 μ), as shown in Eqs. (7) and (8), respectively

$$\log \phi = 0.856766 X - 2.17633 X^2, \quad \text{when } 0 \leq X \leq 0.4 \tag{7}$$

$$\log \phi = 0.3333 - 0.847 X, \quad \text{when } 0.4 \leq X \leq 1.5 \tag{8}$$

For the general case involving a variety of electron beam voltages it was assumed, following Duncumb and Shields ([5]), that the effective electron penetration is proportional to $V_0^{1.5} - V_c^{1.5}$, where V_0 is the electron beam voltage and V_c is the critical excitation voltage for the characteristic X-ray wavelength. Thus, one obtains

$$X = k(\rho x)/(V_0^{1.5} - V_c^{1.5}) \tag{9}$$

where (ρx) is the mass thickness of gold in mg/cm², and k is the proportionality constant.

Normalizing X for Castaing's experimental conditions, $V_0 = 29$ keV and $V_c = 13.42$ keV for bismuth L_3 excitation, it is found that $k = 107.1$. For excitation of molybdenum K X-rays, $V_c = 20.003$ keV; and for the gold–molybdenum metallization,

$$X = 107.1(\rho x)/(V_0^{1.5} - 89.4) \tag{10}$$

In Fig. 5, curve B represents the data of Castaing and Descamps ([4]) for the electron excitation function, $\log \phi$, plotted against thickness of gold. Curves A, C, and D were derived from curve B and by using Eq. (10) for the function X to correspond to V_0 of 29, 35, and 41 keV, respectively.

5. RELATIVE MOLYBDENUM X-RAY INTENSITY

In order to calculate the thickness of the underlying molybdenum layer using the intensity of Mo $K\alpha$ X-rays emerging back through the gold layer, it is necessary to correct for their absorption in the gold. The relative molybdenum X-ray intensity, I_d/I_s, is given by

$$I_d/I_s = \phi \cdot f_k \tag{11}$$

where I_d is the X-ray intensity measured through a gold layer of thickness d, I_s is the intensity measured without a layer of gold, and f_k is the absorption correction due to the presence of the gold layer.

The absorption correction can be calculated by

$$f_k = e^{-\mu'(\rho x)\, \csc \psi} \tag{12}$$

where μ' is the mass absorption coefficient.

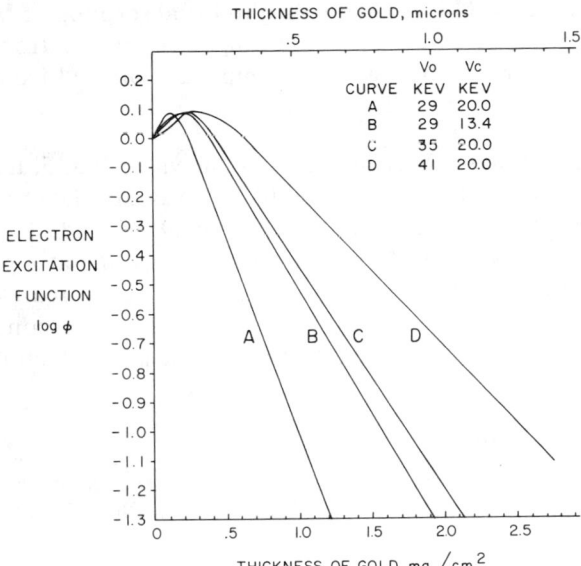

Figure 5. Plot of electron excitation function log ϕ vs. gold thickness at various electron beam voltages and critical excitation voltages.

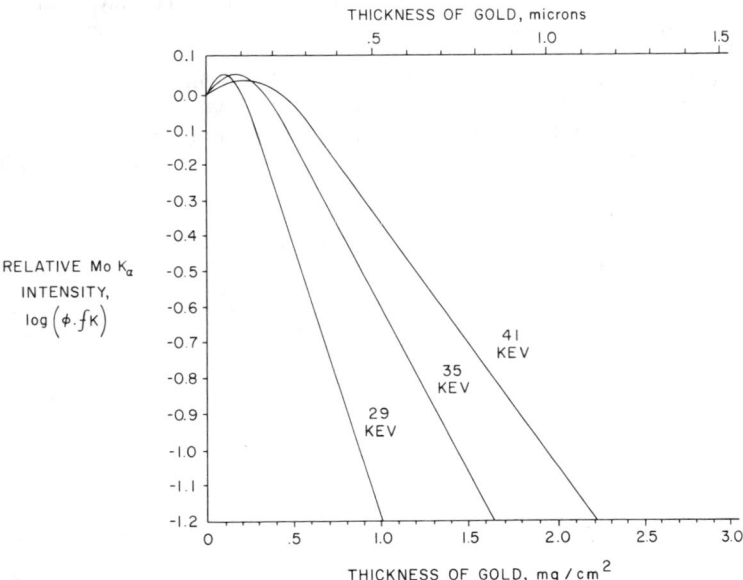

Figure 6. Relative Mo $K\alpha$ intensity log $(\phi \cdot f_k)$ plotted against gold thickness at electron beam voltages of 29, 35, and 41 keV.

By setting $\mu' = 119$, corresponding to the absorption of Mo $K\alpha$ X-rays by gold, and ψ (the X-ray detection angle of our electron microprobe analyzer) = 18° the following relationship was obtained from Eq. (12):

$$f_k = e^{-385.1(\rho x)} \tag{13}$$

Using computed values of log ϕ, as shown in Fig. 5, and the values of f_k from Eq. (13), the function log ($\phi \cdot f_k$) was calculated for a range of gold thicknesses at electron beam voltages of 29, 35, and 41 keV, as shown in the curves in Fig. 6. At 41 keV, log ($\phi \cdot f_k$) = -0.3 at a gold thickness of 0.5 μ, indicating a decrease in X-ray intensity compared to that of bare molybdenum by only a factor of 2. At 35 keV, the corresponding decrease is by a factor of 4; while at 29 keV, the decrease is by a factor of about 16.

ACKNOWLEDGMENT

I want to thank Mr. Robert L. Trent for his encouragement of this work and Mr. Seymour Schwartz, Mrs. Rosemary P. Beatty and Mr. Jon Gerhard for their contributions to the experiments in this paper.

REFERENCES

1. J. E. Cline and S. Schwartz, *J. Electrochem. Soc.* **114**, 605–608, June, 1967.
2. H. A. Liebhafsky, H. G. Pfeiffer, E. H. Winslow, and P. D. Zemany, *X-Ray Absorption and Emission in Analytical Chemistry*, John Wiley & Sons, New York (1960) p. 167.
3. N. Spielberg and G. Abowitz, *Anal. Chem.* **38**, 200 (1966).
4. R. Castaing and J. Descamps, *J. Phys. Radium* **16**, 304 (1955).
5. P. Duncumb and P. K. Shields, *The Electron Microprobe* (T. D. McKinley, K. F. J. Heinrich, and D. B. Wittry, Eds.) John Wiley & Sons, New York (1966) pp. 284–295.

IV. DENSITY DETERMINATION OF SPUTTERED TANTALUM FILMS BY A BETA-BACKSCATTER TECHNIQUE

Richard Brown*

Bell Telephone Laboratories
Murray Hill, New Jersey

Backscattered beta radiation can be used for film-thickness measurements where the response from a sample is compared to that of a standard film of known thickness and equal density. If film thickness is determined independently, the beta-backscatter response can also be used for obtaining the density of thin films. This density determination for areas as small as 0.04 cm² is accurate to ±0.5% for films 5000 Å thick and 2% for films 200 Å thick thus allowing the determination of density variations in a single sample. The usefulness of this has been illustrated for tantalum films covering a range of 40 to 97% of the density of bulk tantalum. It was found that the density of sputtered films is dependent on the purity of the vacuum atmosphere, level of reactive gas, argon pressure, sputtering voltage and electrode geometry. Films sputtered at 4.5 kV and 10–15 μ argon pressures exhibit densities about 5% less than bulk values. This difference is attributed to the large number of grain boundaries and to the level of impurities incorporated in the film.

1. INTRODUCTION

It has been recognized for some time that the apparent density of evaporated films may deviate from bulk values. The density of copper and silver [1,4], aluminum [2,4,5], chromium [3,4] and gold [4,5] have been investigated. Deviations from the bulk value were attributed to voids at the substrate–film interface, porosity, small crystallite size, and a high impurity level [1–4]. Others [5,6] suggested that discrepancies in density were due to errors incurred when indirectly measuring film thickness or surface density.

Films deposited by sputtering are produced under conditions quite different from those found in an evaporation chamber. Diode sputtered species arrive at the substrate with considerably greater energy, at lower

---

*Present address: Pyrofilm Resistor Company, Inc., Cedar Knolls, New Jersey 07927.

rates, and pass through atmospheres and potential gradients not seen by evaporated atoms.

It is not surprising then that many electrical and physical properties of most sputtered films are different from those reported for bulk material, and that the properties of these films depend on the sputtering parameters. The properties of sputtered tantalum films, for example, are sensitive to the sputtering voltage ([7,8]) and to reactive gases intentionally added to the sputtering atmosphere ([9]). Yet there are few results concerning the effect of sputtering conditions on film density. The absence is probably due to the fact that making density determinations of these films is awkward. Density can be obtained by determining the mass per unit area and the absolute thickness. The measurement of the mass per unit area generally requires precision weighing and absolute area determinations. The latter can be in considerable error due to material deposited on the substrate sides, poorly defined edges, and pinholes.

In an alternative method described here, the film density can be obtained by determining the absolute thickness, while the surface density is obtained from backscattered-beta radiation measurements.

2. PRINCIPLES OF BETA-BACKSCATTER

The beta-ray backscatter method is based on the principle that part of a high energy electron (beta-ray) beam striking a sample will be scattered.

The intensity of the scattered radiation is dependent on the atomic number (Z), density, and thickness of the scattering material; the greater these values, the greater the scattering. By holding two of these parameters constant, the third can be obtained from the backscatter response. This principle permits the measurement of a thin layer of one substance on a base material providing the atomic numbers of the materials are different by at least eight atomic units ([10]).

A typical backscatter detection arrangement is shown in Fig. 1. For this work a Microderm* beta-backscatter thickness gauge was used. The beta sources were either C^{14} (0.16 MeV) or Pm^{147} (0.22 MeV), each with a nominal strength of $50 \mu Ci$. The source was axially mounted through a hole in a pancake Geiger tube. Collimated primary radiation, β_1, was directed away from the face of the Geiger tube so that the beta-rays impinged directly on the film–substrate couple through an area-defining aperture. The rays, β_2, reflected from this couple were then directed into the Geiger tube. Nonreflected rays were dissipated through absorption.

---

*Unit Process Assemblies, Woodside, Long Island.

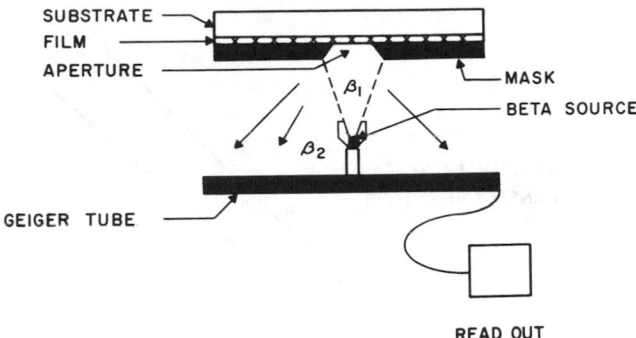

Figure 1. Schematic of beta-backscatter detection system.

The backscatter method is based on a comparison between a standard and unknown, and must be calibrated with a primary standard. The backscatter response then becomes a function of the mass per unit area

$$t_\beta = \alpha m_s \tag{1}$$

where t_β is the backscatter response corrected for the substrate response which can be as high as 95% of the total for very thin films, α is the proportionality factor related to the electron-scattering mechanism, and m_s is the surface density (mass per unit area).

Equation (1) may also be written as

$$t_\beta = \alpha d_v t_a \tag{2}$$

where d_v is the volume density and t_a the absolute thickness. It has been shown that α is independent of film thickness up to about 20% of the maximum beta-particle penetration ([10]). Beyond this point α becomes non-linear. For tantalum, a linear relation should exist between 0 to 6000 Å, using Pm^{147} as a beta source. This is shown in Fig. 2, where the scattering from tantalum and tantalum nitride films is plotted against their absolute thickness, in the range from 200 to 5000 Å. These calibration curves are the basis of the use of beta-backscatter methods for determining film thickness.

The dependence of backscattering on the effective atomic number (Z_{eff}) is also shown in Fig. 2. For the elements Z_{eff} is equal to Z. For a compound $B_n C_m$, Z_{eff} may be readily calculated ([11]) from Eq. (3)

$$Z_{\text{eff}} = \frac{n(A_B \cdot Z_B) + m(A_C \cdot Z_C)}{\text{molecular wt. } (B_n C_m)} \tag{3}$$

where A_B and A_C are the atomic weights of B and C, and Z_B and Z_C their respective atomic numbers.

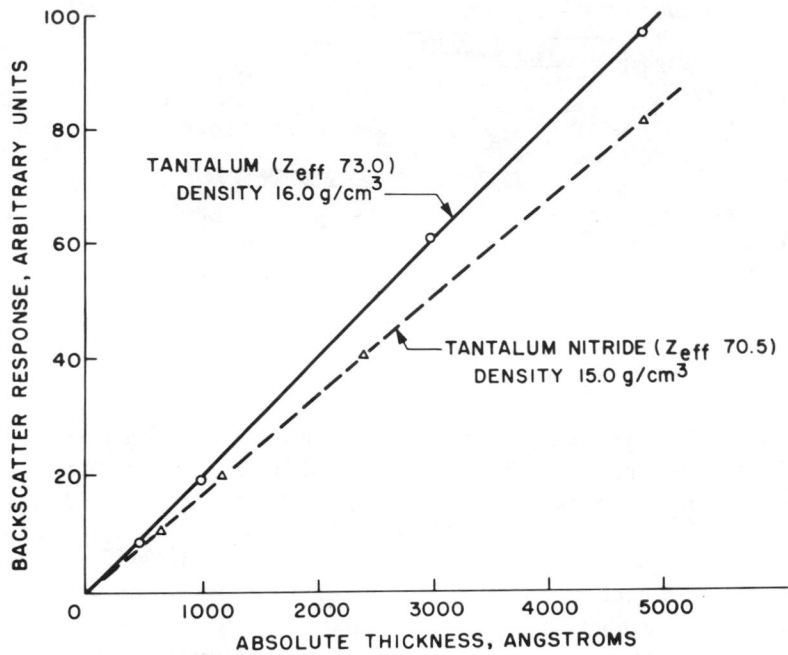

Figure 2. Effect of film composition on beta-backscatter response.

Thus defined, Z_{eff} is the sum of each atomic number multiplied by the weight fraction of that atom present in the compound. It is for this reason that the contribution of oxygen and nitrogen to the effective atomic numbers of tantalum compounds is not significant. For example, Ta_2N with 30 at. % nitrogen has an effective atomic number of 70.5 compared to tantalum with Z equal to 73.

The reason for the significant difference in scattering between two materials with relatively little difference in atomic numbers, such as is shown in Fig. 2, may be attributed to the fact that the relative increase in scattering is not linear with respect to the difference in atomic number between film and substrate, but is logarithmically dependent ([12]). At higher atomic numbers, a small increase in effective Z is reflected in a large increase in scattering.

It should also be kept in mind that backscattering is dependent on the geometry of the system. The relationship among source-to-sample distance, aperture dimension, and Geiger-tube geometry is complicated and not clearly understood. Secondary scattering from the environment is important, but the role of this phenomenon has not been clearly defined

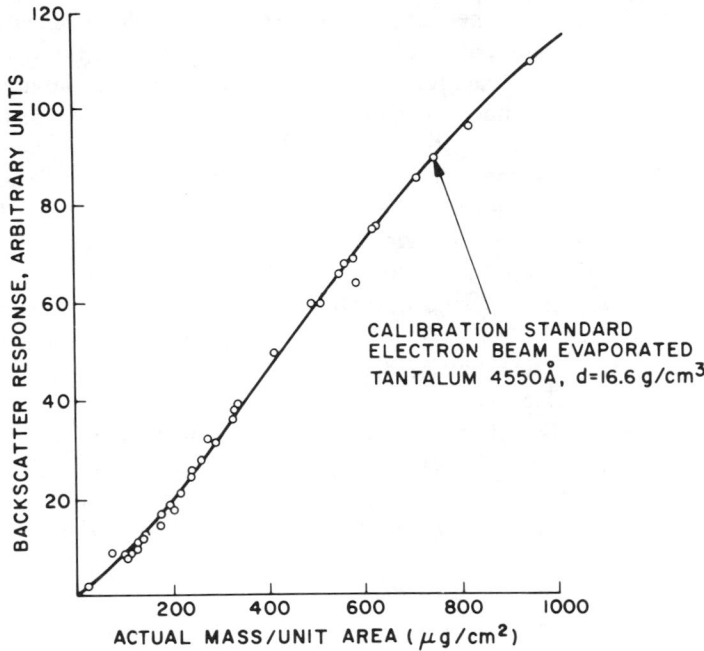

Figure 3. Backscatter response as a function of actual mass per unit area.

as yet. The data reported here, specifically Fig. 3, are characteristic of the particular experimental arrangement of the system. Thus, the shape of this curve may vary slightly from instrument to instrument depending on geometry and source strength.

3. EXPERIMENTAL

For this work a variety of tantalum films were deposited on $25 \times 25 \times 1$ mm polished, synthetic sapphire substrates. This single-crystal material is inert to the hydrofluoric acid used in etching patterns in the tantalum film. It is also less likely to have the defects associated with polycrystalline surfaces, so that sharp steps necessary for accurate film determinations, as well as reproducible film areas, are easily made. The film mass was determined by weighing the substrate before deposition and after generation of a precision pattern used for area measurements. The samples were weighed on a microbalance* with a sensitivity of $\pm 2.5\ \mu g$. The weighing error ranged from $\pm 10\%$ for a 200-Å film to $\pm 0.5\%$ for a

*Mettler Instrument Company, Hightstown, New Jersey.

film 5000 Å thick. Area measurements were made with an accuracy of $\pm 0.01\%$ on the precision pattern generated by photolithographic methods. This process eliminated measurement errors arising from material deposited on the substrate sides and dimensional variations from substrate to substrate.

The relative backscatter, corrected for the substrate, was measured for each sample and plotted against the surface density measured independently above. It is this empirical curve (see Fig. 3) which related the beta-backscatter response to the experimentally determined surface density of the film, which serves as the basis for this technique. In this curve the proportionality factor α appears to be slightly dependent on thickness and density. This dependence may be due to instrumental parameters, absorption and substrate effects.

It is then a simple matter to rapidly determine the surface density of an unknown film. Its relative backscattering is measured and from Fig. 3, the corresponding value for surface density is determined. The mass per unit area is then divided by the absolute thickness to obtain the volume density of the film.

The film thickness was determined with a stylus instrument ([13]). Improvements in instrument sensitivity and the use of a two-step average reduce the measurement error to ± 25 Å from the ± 45 Å previously reported. By using multiple readings the overall error was reduced to less than $\pm 5\%$ for films ranging in thickness from 250 to 5000 Å.

4. RESULTS

4.1. Effect of Reactively Sputtering in Oxygen and Nitrogen

It has been shown by numerous authors that sputtering of metals in the presence of a reactive gas is a versatile technique for altering the characteristics of the deposited film. By controlling the fraction of reactive gas in the inert sputtering gas, it is possible, especially with refractory metals, to obtain phases which range from a metal with dissolved gas, to mixtures of compounds and finally stoichiometric compounds. It is to be expected that films prepared under such varied conditions show wide variations in density.

The density as a function of the partial pressure of oxygen is plotted in Fig. 4. Normal glow discharge sputtering in a system with an ultimate pressure of about 2×10^{-6} torr yields films with a density of 16.0 ± 0.2 g/cm^3 in contrast to the value of 16.6 g/cm^3 exhibited by the bulk material ([14]). The 5% lower value for these sputtered films can be explained by the large number of grain boundaries associated with the

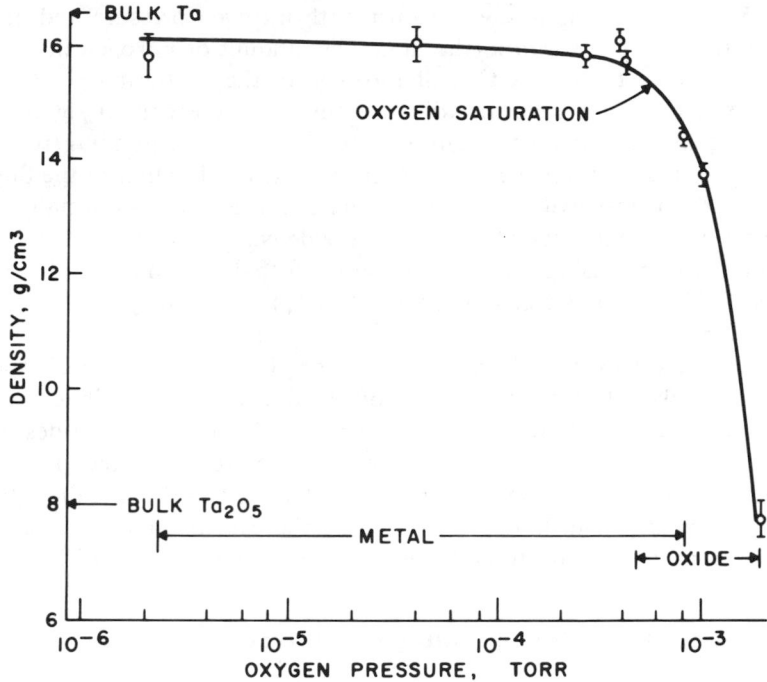

Figure 4. Effect of varying oxygen pressure during sputtering on film density. Films sputtered at 6600 V, 0.25 mA/cm², 14 μ argon.

small grain size and argon atoms which are incorporated in the film ([15]). The addition of up to 5×10^{-4} torr oxygen to the sputtering atmosphere does little to change the film density. In this pressure range the film consists of oxygen dissolved in the tantalum (indicated by region marked metal), where the oxygen markedly changes the electrical properties without detectably changing the crystal structure of the films. In the sputtering series used for this work precipitation of tantalum oxide begins at 5×10^{-4} torr oxygen (indicated by region marked oxide*) accompanied by a pronounced reduction in film density. At higher oxygen pressures, non-stoichiometric Ta_2O_5 is formed followed by insulating Ta_2O_5, with a density of 7.8 g/cm³. This is about 5% less than values of 8.2 g/cm³ previously cited for anodic Ta_2O_5 ([16]).

The addition of nitrogen to the sputtering atmosphere produces a more gradual decrease in density with increasing nitrogen pressure. In

---

*The pressure where the transition occurs from metal to oxide depends on the exact deposition conditions. An overlap region is indicated therefore in Fig. 4.

Fig. 5, film density is plotted against both nitrogen pressure and atomic concentration of nitrogen in the film. The amount of nitrogen in the film is proportional to the fraction of nitrogen in the sputtering gas ([15]). As with oxygen, the nitrogen first dissolves in the metal without significantly changing film density. At about 1×10^{-4} torr, corresponding to about 10 at. % nitrogen, Ta_2N is first detected by X-ray diffraction of the film. In contrast to the resistivity and temperature coefficient which normally reach an almost constant value at this point, the density begins to decrease more rapidly with increasing nitrogen pressure, so that at about 8×10^{-4} torr when TaN is first detected (about 40 at. %) the density of the film is 14.0 g/cm^3.

The bulk density of TaN may vary from 15.2 to 14.4 g/cm^3, while the value of Ta_2N is 15.6 g/cm^3 ([14]). All of the films in Fig. 5 exhibited density values considerably lower than those reported for the bulk nitrides where the densities of the latter are very sensitive to stoichiometry. The lower density of the sputtered samples may be attributed to the large number of grain boundaries and lattice defects as in the case of film sputtered only in argon, as well as nonstoichiometry of the nitrides.

4.2. Effect of Sputtering Voltage and Argon Pressure

Another deposition variable is the sputtering voltage and/or pressure. In diode glow discharge sputtering at constant current density and a fixed interelectrode distance, the voltage cannot be decreased without increasing

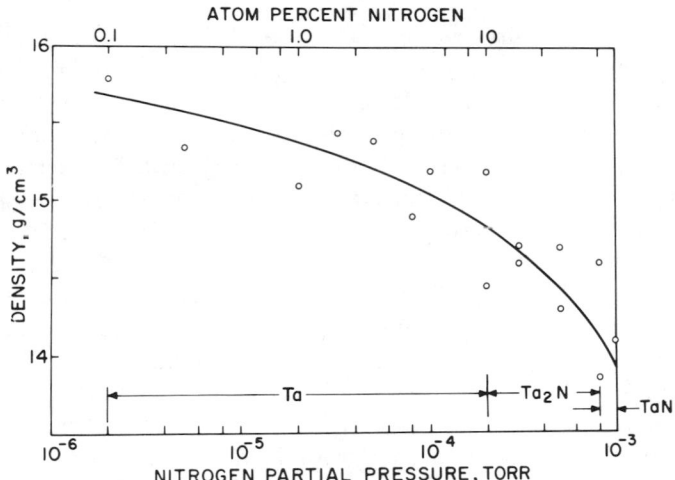

Figure 5. Effect of varying nitrogen pressure during sputtering on film density. Films sputtered at 6600 V, 0.25 mA/cm², 19 μ argon.

the pressure. For most work, films are customarily deposited at about 4–6 kV DC. Films deposited at voltages below 3 kV are characterized by markedly increased specific resistivities and lower temperature coefficients and unusually low densities. These properties were attributed to their porous structure ([7,8]).

A comparison of the texture of films sputtered at 5 and 1.5 kV is shown in Fig. 6. Figure 6 (A) is an electron micrograph of a film sputtered at 5 kV. This is coherent film with randomly oriented crystallites ranging from 50 to 100 Å in width. The electron micrograph of a 350-Å film sputtered at 1.5 kV indicates that the equal intensity exhibited by all the metallic portions of the films is due to the fact that these interconnected metal islands, about 200 Å wide, consist of crystallites perhaps two or three unit cells in size. Secondly, there are large chasms, about 50 Å wide surrounding these conductive areas. The porous structure of low voltage films is responsible for their low density.

The effect of variations in argon pressure on the film density is shown in Fig. 7; the corresponding sputtering voltages are also included. Above 4.5 kV the density is essentially independent of voltage and pressure, as are films sputtered below 1.3 kV. In between, there is a gradual decrease in density. The results plotted in Fig. 7 are specific for one pumping station. The shape of the curve will probably shift from one station to another due to variations in electrode geometry.

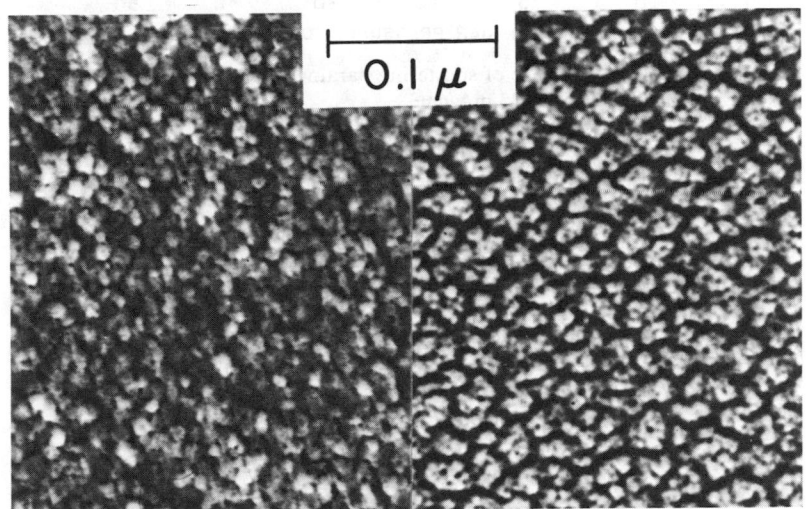

Figure 6. Transmission photomicrographs of high and low density films. (A) 350-Å film sputtered at 5000 V, 0.035 mA/cm², 18 μ argon, density = 15.9 g/cm³; (B) 350-Å film sputtered at 1500 V, 0.35 mA/cm², 80 μ argon, density = 11.2 g/cm³.

5. USE OF BETA-BACKSCATTER FOR MAPPING

A unique advantage of the beta-backscatter technique is that scattering from areas as small as 0.04 cm² can be detected. This makes the method suitable for determining the density distribution across a substrate if good film thickness uniformity of ±2% can be obtained.

In Fig. 8, the density contour of 17.5 × 17.5 cm substrate array is presented. The films were sputtered from a cathode 35 cm in diameter.

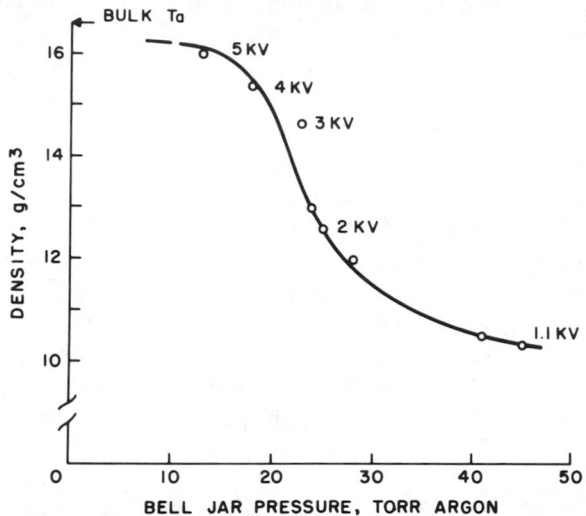

Figure 7. Influence of sputtering parameters on film density. Current density 0.35 mA/cm².

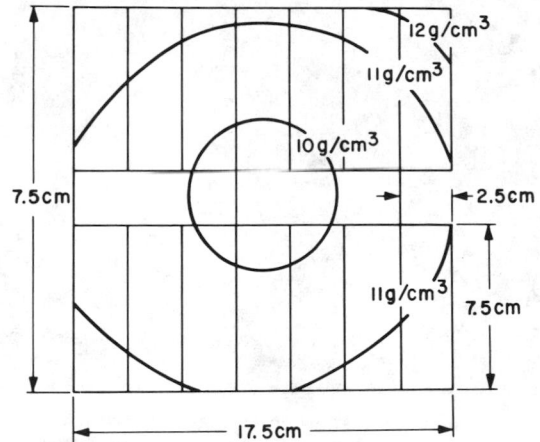

Figure 8. Density contour. Films sputtered at 1500 V, 0.25 mA/cm², 75 μ argon.

The tantalum films were deposited at a sputtering voltage of 1.5 kV onto 7.5 × 2.5 cm glass substrates on which gold tabs about 1 mm wide had been previously deposited at 2-cm intervals. After deposition of the tantalum film, the gold film was removed providing sharp steps in the tantalum film for the thickness measurements. About 125 measurements were taken on the array to obtain the density contour shown in Fig. 7.

The density appears fairly symmetrical around the center of the sputtering area, and radially increases from a value of 10 to 11 g/cm³. The 12 g/cm³ line may have been due to local perturbation of the glow discharge by the resistance monitor which is attached in that area. Although the results presented represent only one atypical run, they do show the effectiveness of this technique.

6. SUMMARY

A rapid method for determining the densities of thin films using a beta-backscattering technique has been described. Only two measurements are required, the thickness and a beta-backscatter measurement. The thickness measurement was the accuracy-limiting factor at the 200-Å level; however, multiple readings can significantly reduce this source of error.

The method is rapid and the density of films with areas as small as 0.04 cm² or with irregularly shaped periphery can be routinely determined to ±0.5% for 5000 Å films to ±2% for films as thin as 200 Å, so that variations in density may be readily observed.

The method is particularly suited to the measurement of tantalum films deposited on glass and ceramic since there is such a large difference in effective atomic number between film and substrate. The results obtained in this work indicate the density of sputtered films to be dependent on the sputtering voltage, level of the reacting gas and argon pressure, and on the electrode geometry of the sputtering station. In general, films sputtered at 4–6 kV and at argon pressures about 15 μ without additional reacting gas, exhibit densities about 5% less than bulk values. This is attributed to the large number of grain boundaries and dissolved impurities. Lowering the sputtering voltage, or adding reactive gases can reduce the film density to values less than 50% of bulk.

ACKNOWLEDGMENTS

The author would like to thank W. H. Jackson and A. J. Masessa for the use of their samples and unpublished data, and Mrs. M. H. Read for the X-ray measurements. The author wishes also to thank C. J. Calbick for his photomicrographs.

REFERENCES

1. M. S. Blois and L. M. Reiser, Apparent Density of Thin Evaporated Films, *J. Appl. Phys.* **25**, 338–340 (1964).
2. T. E. Hartman, Density of Thin Evaporated Aluminum Films, *J. Vacuum Sci. Tech.* **2**, 239–242 (1965).
3. P. A. Gould, Resistance and Structure of Chromium Films, *Brit. J. Appl. Phys.* **16**, 1457 (1966).
4. A. R. Wolter, Measurement of Metallic Film Densities by an Optical Technique, *J. Appl. Phys.* **36**, 2377–2381 (1966).
5. J. Edgecomb, Thin Film Densities, *J. Vacuum Sci. Tech.* **3**, 28–30 (1966).
6. S. Aisenberg, The Sticking Coefficient, Optical Transmission and Oxidation of Thin Metallic Films, in *1963 Transactions, Tenth National Vacuum Symposium, American Vacuum Society, Boston*, Macmillan Company, New York (1963), p. 457.
7. H. J. Scheutze, H. W. Ehlbeck and G. G. Doerbeck, Investigation of Thin Tantalum Films, in *1963 Transactions, Tenth National Vacuum Symposium, American Vacuum Society, Boston*, Macmillan Company, New York (1963), p. 434.
8. B. H. Vromen, Properties of Low Density Tantalum Films, Presented at Spring Meeting, Electrochemical Society May 2, 1966, Cleveland. Abst. #7, **113**, 58C (1966).
9. N. Schwartz, Reactive Sputtering, in *1963 Transactions, Tenth National Vacuum Symposium, American Vacuum Society, Boston*, Macmillan Company, New York (1963), pp. 325–334.
10. R. Danguy and B. Girard, Thickness Measurement of Thin Layers by the Backscattering of Beta Rays, in International Conference on the Peaceful Uses of Atomic Energy, Vol. 19, 2nd Edition United Nations (1958).
11. R. H. Muller, Interaction of Beta Particles with Matter, *Anal. Chem.* **29**, 969–975 (1957).
12. G. C. Rein, Jr., Engineering Research Center, Western Electric Company, Princeton, N.J. Personal communication.
13. N. Schwartz and R. Brown, A Stylus Method for Evaluating the Thickness of Thin Films & Substrate Surface Roughness, *1961 Transactions, Eighth National Vacuum Symposium, American Vacuum Society, Washington D.C.*, Pergamon Press, New York (1962), pp. 836–845.
14. Cited in G. L. Miller, *Tantalum and Niobium*, Butterworths Scientific Publications, London (1959).
15. W. G. Guldner and R. Brown, The Analysis of Gases in Thin Films by a Xenon Flash Technique, in *Measurement Techniques for Thin Films* (B. Schwartz and N. Schwartz, eds.), The Electrochemical Society, Inc., New York (1967), pp. 82–101.
16. J. Klerer, Determination of the Density and Dielectric Constant of Thin Ta_2O_5 Films, *J. Electrochem. Soc.* **112**, 896–899 (1965).

V. THE CHARACTERIZATION OF SOLID THIN FILMS AND SURFACES BY ELECTRON MICROSCOPY AND DIFFRACTION

R. B. Marcus

Bell Telephone Laboratories, Incorporated
Murray Hill, New Jersey

In a number of areas of solid state research an understanding of the physical structure of films and surfaces is very important. This type of analysis is particularly pertinent in technological areas relating to the growth of thin films on solids. A number of these structural properties can be obtained with the electron microscope operating in its two instrumental modes: as an instrument for high-magnification imaging of materials, and as an instrument for obtaining the diffraction patterns of these materials. A combination of the two approaches is often the most efficient method for obtaining structural information. This paper discusses the use of electron microscopy and electron diffraction techniques in determining the following three types of structural features: the texture of films and surfaces, the crystal structure, and the defect structure of materials.

1. INTRODUCTION

This paper presents a discussion of current techniques for investigating the texture, crystal structure, and defect structure of the volumes and surfaces of thin films by means of the electron microscope. There are two ways in which the electron microscope can make this information available: by providing a microscope image near 5 Å resolution of ordered or unordered material, and by forming an electron diffraction pattern of ordered structures. Since a combination of microscopy and diffraction investigations is frequently the best approach to a particular problem, this discussion therefore is organized on the basis of the nature of the problem under investigation rather than on the basis of instrumental features of the electron microscope.

It is assumed that the reader is already familiar with the basic principles of the operation of the electron microscope and only a cursory description of the instrumental features will be given in order to define some terms that are used later in the paper. Complete descriptions of the instrument appear in a number of texts, including Hirsch *et al.* ([1]), Kay ([2]), Heidenreich ([3]), Grivet ([4]), Thomas ([5]), Siegel ([6]), Hall ([7]), Zworykin *et al.* ([8]), and Cosslett ([9]).

The parts of an electron microscope in the order of their appearance along the microscope column starting with the source of electrons are:

1. The electron gun. Electrons are generated by thermionic emission and accelerated (typically to -100 kV) through an anode at ground potential.
2. The condenser lenses. The first condenser lens demagnifies the beam source; the image is projected onto the specimen by the second lens. Narrow high-intensity beams of a few microns diameter can be produced which give rise to sharp microscope images and diffraction beams.
3. The condenser aperture. This aperture is inserted below the second condenser lens. It serves to maintain a small beam diameter when the second condenser lens is defocused, to approximate axial illumination of the specimen (with a consequent loss in beam intensity).
4. The specimen. Requirements for specimen geometry are given later in this paper.
5. The objective lens. This lens produces the primary magnification.
6. The objective aperture. In addition to its role of providing contrast in a microscope image, a medium quality dark field micrograph can be obtained by moving the aperture off the optical axis of the column to a position where one diffracted beam is allowed to pass downward to the screen.
7. The selected area aperture. This aperture limits the field of view of the specimen (smallest area $\sim 1\,\mu$ diameter) and so enables a diffraction pattern to be obtained from a very small "selected" area.
8. Intermediate and projector lenses. These lenses have longer focal length than the objective and produce final magnification of the image.

2. TEXTURE

It is often necessary to carry out thin film studies on surfaces of unknown morphology. The surface texture of a given material can seldom be assumed, and suitable combinations of electron microscopy and diffraction techniques are almost mandatory appendages to the main experiment in order to determine this texture. Further, since surface phenomena often coexist with volume effects, as in the association of adsorption and chemical reactivity with mass and thermal transport, an analysis of the volume texture of the material is important. This latter analysis is also achieved through electron diffraction and microscopy, its purpose being to describe the size and shapes of the crystallites in the solid.

2.1. Texture: Surface Texture

2.1.1. Replicas

The most easily interpretable technique for obtaining information about surface texture is the electron microscope examination of shadowed replicas of surfaces. There are numerous methods for making replicas, and a recent review is given by Bradley ([10]). The basic principle of the technique involves making an impression of a surface with a thin film and examining the film in the electron microscope; this is illustrated in Fig. 1a. The variations in thickness of the replica produce corresponding gradations in intensity of the transmitted electron beam, so that hills and valleys on the original surface are made to appear as contrasting regions of light and dark on the microscope screen.

The choice of replicating material is controlled by two basic considerations: the material should possess no structure above the resolution

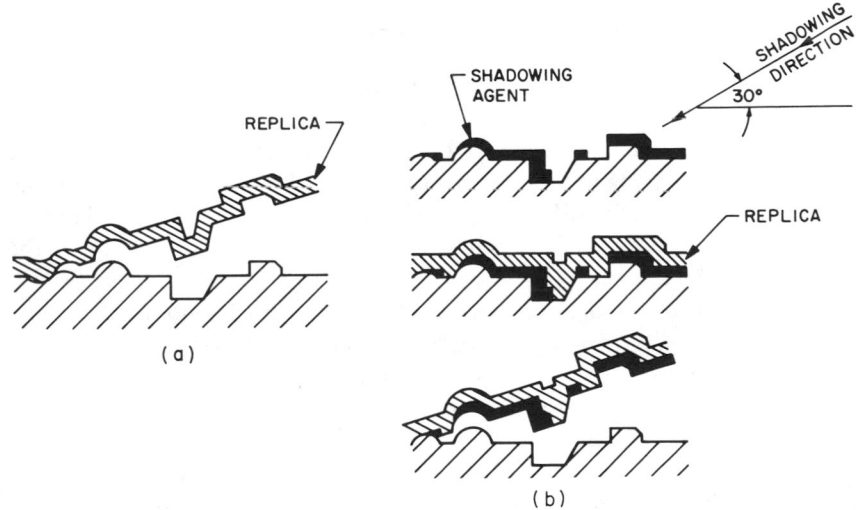

Figure 1. Diagram of replica partially removed from surface showing imprinting of surface texture on the replica (a). Illustration of three steps in the formation of a preshadowed replica (b).

limit needed by the experimenter, and the material must provide enough electron scattering to allow detection of small differences in thickness. A type of thin-film replica that has found considerable success in satisfying both these requirements consists of two phases. The minor phase provides the contrast differences in the electron micrograph that relate to the surface texture, and is supported by the film proper, which consists of a second phase. The contrast differences occur when a heavy scatterer of electrons is deposited on a surface from a point source at a large angle to the average surface normal. Surface regions of varying gradations receive different thicknesses of deposit, and certain surface regions receive no deposit because they are hidden ("shadowed") by protuberances, as illustrated in the upper drawing of Fig. 1b. A backing is deposited over the shadowed surface and the "shadowed replica" is removed for examination, as shown in the center and lower drawings of Fig. 1b.

The resolution of a shadowed replica is increased by decreasing the granularity and increasing the scattering power of the shadowing material, as described by Calbick [11]. Since scattering power increases with atomic number and density, heavy metals that deposit as fine (~ 10 Å) grains are most suitable as shadowing agents; the characteristics of a number of these metals are described by Bradley [10]. The support film needed for dimensional stability of the replica must be a poor scatterer so as not to interfere with intensity variations due to the shadowed deposit; evaporated carbon has found extensive use as this material.

Both the shadowing agent and support film can be deposited in one operation in a replicating procedure described by Bradley [10], using a carbon–platinum source. When these films are not easily removed from the replicated surface, the platinum–carbon source (commercially available as pellets) is immersed in a 10 % solution of Victawet in water and acetone (1:1) prior to mounting in the evaporator. Victawet evaporates first, coating the surface with a water-soluble layer which then acts as a parting layer in the subsequent removal of the shadowed replica from the surface in the manner of Calbick [12].

The resolution of the carbon–platinum technique is nominally 20 Å, the limit being set by the granularity of the shadowing agent. Other geometrical factors in the replica-deposition process, such as curvature of surface features and shadowing angle, are an additional limit to the resolution—these are discussed by Calbick [11].

2.1.2. Decoration of Steps

A second method of obtaining information on surface texture is particularly useful for displaying the position of terraces on cleavage faces. Under certain conditions of deposition, nuclei (~ 20 Å) of the deposit form preferentially at terrace sites on the surface even when steps are only of monatomic height. A carbon film is deposited over this thin layer, and upon removal the nuclei are extracted; this film is then examined in the electron microscope. The decoration technique was introduced by Bassett ([13]) for gold on rock salt, and has also been used with very thin deposits of germanium and silver on rock salt by Sella and Trillat ([14]), gold on graphite by Henning ([15]), and gold on MgO by Robins and Rhodin ([16]).

The decoration technique has found little use in illustrating the surface texture of thin films. Its concern to thin-films specialists, however, lies primarily in its ability to display the texture of a number of cleavage surfaces that have found use as substrates for the epitaxial deposition of thin films.

2.1.3. Reflection Electron Diffraction

Information on the texture of single-crystal surfaces may also be obtained through a careful study of the reflection electron diffraction pattern from those surfaces. The reflection diffraction method is illustrated in Fig. 2 for three types of surface texture. The incident electron beam makes an angle φ of $\sim 1°$ with the surface; the resulting diffraction beams typically produce a pattern covering a semicircular area (slightly less than half the pattern produced in transmission studies).

The surface texture influences the diffraction pattern in two ways, and the result for the three different textures is also given in Fig. 2.*

In the rare case where the diffracting surface is atomically smooth and φ is the true angle of incidence to the surface (and not to a surface average), Bragg's law is modified to become $\sin^2 \varphi = \sin^2 \theta - (\mu^2 - 1)$, where μ is the refractive index across the surface [Pinsker ([17]), Chapter 6]. Although diffraction beams are lost for cases where $(\mu^2 - 1) > \sin^2 \theta$, the beams are displaced in a direction toward the surface or "shadow edge" for larger Bragg angles. Considering a typical electron-beam width of $10\,\mu$, the maximum surface length irradiated is near 1 mm. Over the macroscopic distance, changes in surface texture are likely to occur, with the result that the final diffraction spot on the screen becomes a cumulative record of different refraction corrections to the main beam. An illustration of this effect for polycrystalline MgO is found in Heidenreich ([3]), p. 185. In the case of spot patterns obtained from single crystals or from polycrystalline materials whose crystallites are all approximately oriented in the same way ("mosaic" structures, see Section 2.2.1), refraction produces an elongation

---

*In the illustration it is assumed that the incident electron beam is parallel to a direction of the type $\langle 100 \rangle$ in a cubic crystal.

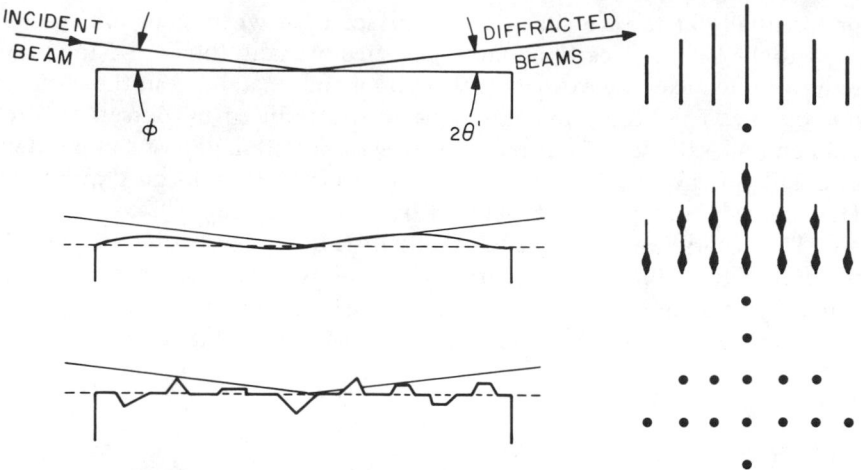

Figure 2. Illustration of the formation of reflection electron diffraction patterns from single-crystal surfaces showing the influence on the pattern of the substrate surface texture. In the upper drawings the surface is atomically flat and the pattern consists of streaks normal to the shadow edge; in the lower drawings the surface texture is rough and the diffraction process is one of transmission through protuberances; the center drawings show an intermediate case.

of the spots in a direction normal to the surface of the crystal toward the straight ("shadow") edge of the pattern.

A second influence of surface texture on the diffraction pattern results from the effect of the texture on the penetration depth of the electron beam into the sample. A diffraction spot becomes symmetrically elongated in a direction normal to the shadow edge, the elongation, E, increasing with decreasing penetration, p, as $E = 1/2p$. If the maximum penetration depth into a surface is, say 500 Å, then the total elongation of a spot is $\sim 0.05 \text{ Å}^{-1}$. The spacing between spots in a cubic pattern from gold is 0.42 Å^{-1}, and the portion of diffracted beams (for a particular (hkl) reflection) occurring during the first eighth of the total penetration depth is, therefore, sufficient to cause a merging of diffraction spots located on the same row normal to the shadow edge; this effect is illustrated in Fig. 2, upper drawing, and an example of such a pattern is shown in Fig. 3.

In summary, refraction has the effect of producing a one-sided elongation of diffraction beams toward the shadow edge, while a shallow penetration of the incident beam produces a symmetrical elongation of diffraction beams normal to the shadow edge. In practice, although refraction effects have been noted in diffraction patterns from polycrystalline specimens [Heidenreich ([3]), Sturkey and Freval ([18]), Cowley and Rees ([19]), and

Figure 3. Reflection electron diffraction pattern from an atomically smooth surface of NaCl.

Honjo ([20])] the effect of limiting penetration generally overshadows that of refraction in single-crystal patterns.

Real surfaces often provide enough protuberances at the surface so that the diffraction effect is more nearly one of transmission through the protuberances rather than reflection from a surface. The resulting reflection electron diffraction pattern then consists of spots in their "proper" positions as illustrated in the lower drawings of Fig. 2. The center drawings show an intermediate case.

Although it is extremely difficult to obtain a quantitative statement about surface texture from reflection electron diffraction patterns, the technique can be a useful, nondestructive,* qualitative test for surface smoothness on an atomic scale.

2.2. Texture: Crystalline Size and Shape

Surface protuberances that give rise to transmission-like reflection diffraction patterns (see above) or to rough texture in replicas are not necessarily crystallites, but may be aggregates of crystallites. The surface texture of polycrystalline materials is not a good indication of crystallite size, and other techniques must be used for obtaining information about the crystallite size and shape or "volume texture." Three electron-optical techniques are available: studies of the gross appearance of the diffraction pattern; line-broadening studies of diffraction rings; and direct examination of the specimen by transmission electron microscopy.

---

*Although this procedure is nominally nondestructive, a polymerized carbon film which forms on the surface during electron-beam irradiation sometimes precludes the use of this surface for subsequent experiments.

2.2.1. General Appearance of Diffraction Pattern

If the portion of metal film under irradiation by the incident electron beam has one crystallographic orientation, the diffracted beams will consist of a series of well-defined rays and produce a pattern of spots in the diffraction pattern. If the irradiated volume of film contains a very large number of randomly oriented crystallites, the diffracted beams appear in the form of concentric cones and produce circles on the flat viewing screen. Arcs result when the crystallites deviate by an amount greater than $\sim 1\%$ from a particular orientation, the arc lengths being proportional to the deviation. Finally, if the irradiated material contains no atomic ordering above the most simple nearest-neighbor ordering of atoms, there is little selective reinforcement of scattered rays and the diffraction pattern will display a continuous fall-off of intensity along a radius; this latter case is quite rare.

Although a single crystal produces a "spot" diffraction pattern, spots will also appear from a polycrystalline sample whose crystallites are within $\sim 1°$ of an absolute orientation; diffraction from this "mosaic" structure is discussed by Pinsker ([17]), p. 83, and Vainstein ([21]), p. 31.

Care must be exercised in characterizing the degree of preferred orientation in a macroscopic film from observations on one or two transmission diffraction patterns. Particularly when a selected area aperture is used and the transmission diffraction pattern is obtained from a thin-film area less than $5\,\mu$ across, a generalization based on a sample area of $2 \times 10^{-5}\%$ (for a film 1 cm in diameter) is hardly to be trusted. A more meaningful sampling of the film structure is obtained by viewing the reflection diffraction pattern while moving the sample in a direction normal to the beam, thus sweeping across the film surface.

2.2.2. Line-Broadening Studies

It was stated above that the relationship between the elongation of a diffraction spot E and the penetration depth p of the electron beam is (approximately) $E = 1/2p$. If the penetration depth is now limited by the crystallite size, the expression then gives the relationship between the broadening of a diffraction ring (for diffraction from polycrystalline material) E and the crystallite size p. A more exact expression is the Scherrer formula which gives the relationship between the angular width at half maximum intensity $D(2\theta)$ and the crystallite size [Guinier ([22])]: $D(2\theta) = \lambda/(p \cos \theta)$, where θ is the Bragg angle and λ is the wavelength of the radiation. However, due to the small value of λ in high energy electron diffraction studies compared with X-ray diffraction, the accuracy of the measurement is much poorer for electron diffraction. A simple illustration will show this. X-ray diffraction from a 2.25-Å spacing in a polycrystalline sample of 100-Å crystallite size using Cu $K\alpha$ radiation and a 60-mm camera radius will produce a line width of 1.0 mm. Over an effective camera length near 100 cm, 100 kV electrons produce a line-broadening of slightly less than 0.2 mm for the same reflection. Since the accuracy of measurement on an electron diffraction plate is seldom better than 0.1 mm, the technique is seen to be of use only for crystallites much smaller than ~ 100 Å.

2.2.3. *Examination by Electron Microscopy*

A more accurate description of crystallite size (as well as shape) results from direct examination of the specimen in thin-film form in the electron microscope. Contrast in an electron microscope image results from scattering losses of the electron beam due to changes in specimen thickness, changes in scattering power of the material (as in a two-phase sample), or from diffraction of the beam by the material.* The first two influences are always present, but diffraction contrast predominates almost to exclusion for nonamorphous films [cf. Thomas ([5]), Chapter 2]. Diffraction contrast enables crystallites to be identified in a number of ways.

Crystallites in a given field of view (say at 20,000 $\times$) are seldom aligned perfectly parallel to each other. They are therefore in different diffracting position, with the result that contrast in the final image will change abruptly across grain boundaries. If the misalignment is described in terms of the deviation of the normal of a certain crystallographic plane about a fixed direction, then the minimum tilt φ_m of two crystallites below which contrast differences tend to disappear can be approximately computed. If s is half the length of the reciprocal lattice point causing the (diffraction) contrast† [cf. Thomas ([5]), pp. 38–41], then the tilt is given as $\varphi_m = s/(1/d)$ where d is the corresponding Bragg spacing. Since $s \sim 1/\tau$ where τ is the crystallite thickness, $\varphi_m \sim d/\tau$. For the case of a polycrystalline gold film 200-Å thick where the (111) reflection provides contrast, $\varphi_m = 0.67°$. Figure 4 is an electron micrograph of a polycrystalline film of tantalum; these contrast effects are plainly evident.

Contrast effects are often enhanced by the presence of bend extinction contours. Thin metal films are invariably buckled during examination in the microscope, and different regions under one field of view (at 20,000 $\times$) of a single-crystal film will be in different diffraction positions resulting in the large-scale contrast changes known as bend extinction contours [Heidenreich ([3]), p. 256; Thomas ([5]), pp. 59–65]; an example is the series of dark bands shown in Fig. 5. Different grains (crystals) in a polycrystalline

---

*Phase contrast is used under special conditions.
†This length is related to the diffraction-spot elongation discussed above.

will show this. X-ray diffraction from a 2.25-Å spacing in a polycrystalline sample of 100-Å crystallite size using Cu $K\alpha$ radiation and a 60-mm camera radius will produce a line width of 1.0 mm. Over an effective camera length near 100 cm, 100 kV electrons produce a line-broadening of slightly less than 0.2 mm for the same reflection. Since the accuracy of measurement on an electron diffraction plate is seldom better than 0.1 mm, the technique is seen to be of use only for crystallites much smaller than ~ 100 Å.

2.2.3. Examination by Electron Microscopy

A more accurate description of crystallite size (as well as shape) results from direct examination of the specimen in thin-film form in the electron microscope. Contrast in an electron microscope image results from scattering losses of the electron beam due to changes in specimen thickness, changes in scattering power of the material (as in a two-phase sample), or from diffraction of the beam by the material.* The first two influences are always present, but diffraction contrast predominates almost to exclusion for nonamorphous films [cf. Thomas ([5]), Chapter 2]. Diffraction contrast enables crystallites to be identified in a number of ways.

Crystallites in a given field of view (say at $20,000\times$) are seldom aligned perfectly parallel to each other. They are therefore in different diffracting position, with the result that contrast in the final image will change abruptly across grain boundaries. If the misalignment is described in terms of the deviation of the normal of a certain crystallographic plane about a fixed direction, then the minimum tilt φ_m of two crystallites below which contrast differences tend to disappear can be approximately computed. If s is half the length of the reciprocal lattice point causing the (diffraction) contrast† [cf. Thomas ([5]), pp. 38–41], then the tilt is given as $\varphi_m = s/(1/d)$ where d is the corresponding Bragg spacing. Since $s \sim 1/\tau$ where τ is the crystallite thickness, $\varphi_m \sim d/\tau$. For the case of a polycrystalline gold film 200-Å thick where the (111) reflection provides contrast, $\varphi_m = 0.67°$. Figure 4 is an electron micrograph of a polycrystalline film of tantalum; these contrast effects are plainly evident.

Contrast effects are often enhanced by the presence of bend extinction contours. Thin metal films are invariably buckled during examination in the microscope, and different regions under one field of view (at $20,000\times$) of a single-crystal film will be in different diffraction positions resulting in the large-scale contrast changes known as bend extinction contours [Heidenreich ([3]), p. 256; Thomas ([5]), pp. 59–65]; an example is the series of dark bands shown in Fig. 5. Different grains (crystals) in a polycrystalline

---

*Phase contrast is used under special conditions.
†This length is related to the diffraction-spot elongation discussed above.

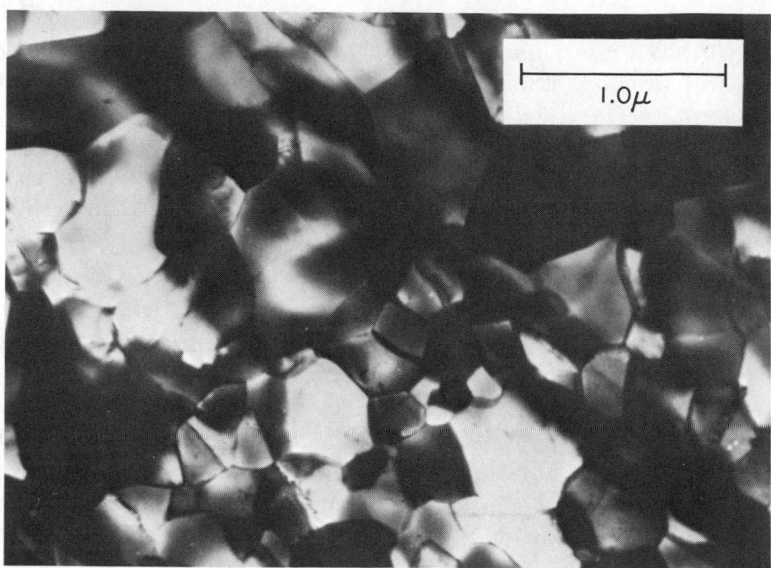

Figure 4. Electron micrograph of polycrystalline tantalum film. Grain boundaries are clearly evident; contrast between grains is enhanced by the appearance of different grains under differing diffraction conditions.

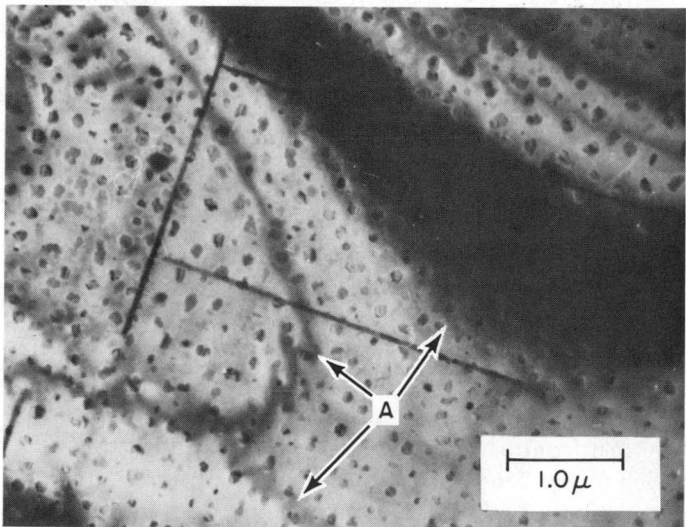

Figure 5. Electron micrograph of an oxidized single crystal film of copper showing bend extinction contours at A.

film are sometimes easily identified because of the abrupt change across a grain boundary of one or more of these contours.

Small crystallites less than 100 Å tend to be difficult to distinguish. Their appearance is made more prominent by dark-field illumination. In the simplest use of this technique a small objective aperture (~ 20–$50\,\mu$) is placed over a part of a diffraction ring, and the intermediate lens current raised to image those crystallites that contribute to that portion of the ring. Since this number is a small fraction of the total number of crystallites in one field of view, the many small dark regions on the image corresponding to these crystallites are easily identified. An example of the use of this technique is shown in Fig. 6; the left photograph is a bright-field micrograph; the tantalum crystallites are more clearly visible in the dark-field micrograph on the right.

Since diffraction contrast occurs for crystallites of different structures as well as for crystallites of the same structure but different orientation, the crystallite components of a multiphase film are easily distinguished. An example is the contrast difference between the grains of Cu_2O and the copper in Fig. 5.

3. CRYSTAL STRUCTURE

The term "crystal structure" in its strictest sense refers to the unit cell structure and the atomic ordering of atoms within the unit cell. As

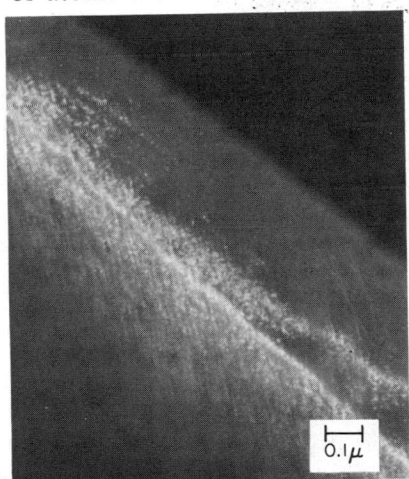

Figure 6. Electron micrographs of a composite film of carbon, single crystal MgO, and very thin (~ 50 Å) tantalum. The bright-field photograph is on the left; the tantalum crystallites are more obvious in the dark-field micrograph on the right, made from a portion of a tantalum diffraction ring.

The third limitation in the accuracy of the reflection technique in identification of structure is due to the charging-up of insulating samples, and is the most serious of the three. As an illustration of this effect, Table I shows the unit cell size, a_0, for evaporated polycrystalline tantalum films

Table I. Data from Selected Reflection Electron Diffraction Patterns of bcc Tantalum Showing the Effect of Surface Charging

(hkl)	Film A		Film B		Film C	
	a_0	Δr	a_0	Δr	a_0	Δr
(110)	3.49	0.25	3.94	0.80	3.56	0.35
(200)	3.38	0.15	3.48	0.35	3.44	0.25
(211)	3.36	0.10	3.42	0.25	3.38	0.15
(220)	3.35	0.10	—	—	—	—
(310)	3.33	0.05	3.26	-0.20	3.33	0.05
(222)	—	—	—	—	—	—
(321)	3.33	0.10	—	—	3.32	0.05

on fused silica substrates as computed from their reflection diffraction patterns. The true value of a_0 for these films is 3.31 Å; the numbers reach a maximum of 3.9 Å. In the table, $\Delta r = r_t - r_m$, where r_t would be the radius to an (hkl) reflection that would correspond to $a_0 = 3.31$ Å, and r_m is the radius measured in mm. The decrease in the error term Δr with increasing 2θ suggests a positive charging of the specimen surface; it is, in fact, possible to choose new diffraction pattern centers farther from the shadow edge resulting in a consistent calculation of the correct value for a_0. On other occasions unusual surface textures produce field gradients skew to the film surface resulting in a deflection of the diffraction pattern in a different direction from the surface normal; the displacement can be as much as 1.0 mm. The positive charge build-up on insulating substrates during reflection electron diffraction studies was first reported by Brubaker and Fuller ([26]). The most effective remedy against this disturbance is the spraying of a volume of residual gas near the surface with low-energy (~ 200 V) electrons during examination. Another, more tedious, remedy in the case of a conducting film on an insulating substrate, is the grounding of the film by applying a conducting coating such as carbon or gold.

A common problem in thin-film studies is the identification of two or more phases from one diffraction pattern. The problem is simplified for a two-phase sample in the case where the phases possess different degrees of orientation, such as small crystallites of random orientation imbedded in a mosaic or single crystal matrix. Figure 7 is a transmission diffraction pattern of this type, with polycrystalline tantalum on a single-crystal mica film. The tantalum and mica give rise to rings and spots, respectively.

In the case where two or more phases are well-ordered, the resulting spot diffraction pattern is a composite of the contribution from each phase. This is observed for both reflection and transmission electron diffraction in cases of epitaxial deposition of separate islands onto single crystal substrates, as, silver on mica by Allpress et al. ([27]), copper on rock salt by Kehoe ([28]), GaAs on germanium by Yurasova et al. ([29]), and germanium on silicon by Heidenreich ([3]), p. 298; in studies of chemical reaction products occurring on metal surfaces as in the oxidation of copper by Marcus and Brockway ([30]), Lawless and Mitchell ([31]), Takahashi and Trillat ([32]), and Jellinek ([33]), and the oxidation of stainless steels by Shimaoka ([34]), in the sulfuration of silver by Schlötterer ([35]); in studies of phase transformation in solids as in the formation of ordered structures in tantalum reported by Steeb and Renner ([36]), Villagrana and Thomas ([37]), Seraphim et al. ([38]), and Marcus ([39]); ordered structures in nickel by Alessandrini and Freedman ([40]); ordered structures in gold by Sato ([41]); and in many papers on the precipitation of ordered structures in a crystalline solid. In these cases the phases are most easily identified by a combination of dark-field electron microscopy with transmission diffraction. After a few such observations on one viewing area it should soon become readily apparent that one set of images (such as precipitate particles) are produced from one collection of diffraction spots, while the negative of this image (such as the host film) is produced from the remaining spots; in this way the two or more diffraction patterns can be defined and the phases identified. In addition, the crystallites corresponding to each phase can be identified.

Dark-field images from selected spots are made either by tilting the

Figure 7. A transmission electron diffraction pattern of polycrystalline tantalum on a single-crystal mica film. The tantalum and mica are easily identified because of the difference in ordering, giving rise to rings and spots respectively. (Photo courtesy of C. J. Calbick.)

gun so that the selected diffraction beam passes through the centered objective aperture and the optical axis of the remainder of the column, by producing the same effective tilt by electrostatic deflection, or by moving the aperture to select that reflection. Although the latter procedure introduces distortion of the image through spherical aberration, it is far easier to use and is generally suitable for routine identification in the instruments not possessing an electrostatic tilting facility. As an illustration of this procedure, Fig. 8 shows the dark-field technique applied to the study of long-range ordered precipitates in tantalum. The total diffraction pattern from an area of $20\,\mu^2$ is shown in Fig. 8a; Fig. 8b is a bright-field micrograph from this area. Placing an objective aperture of $30\,\mu$ diameter over spots 1 and 2 (Fig. 8a) produced dark-field micrographs 8c and 8d, respectively.

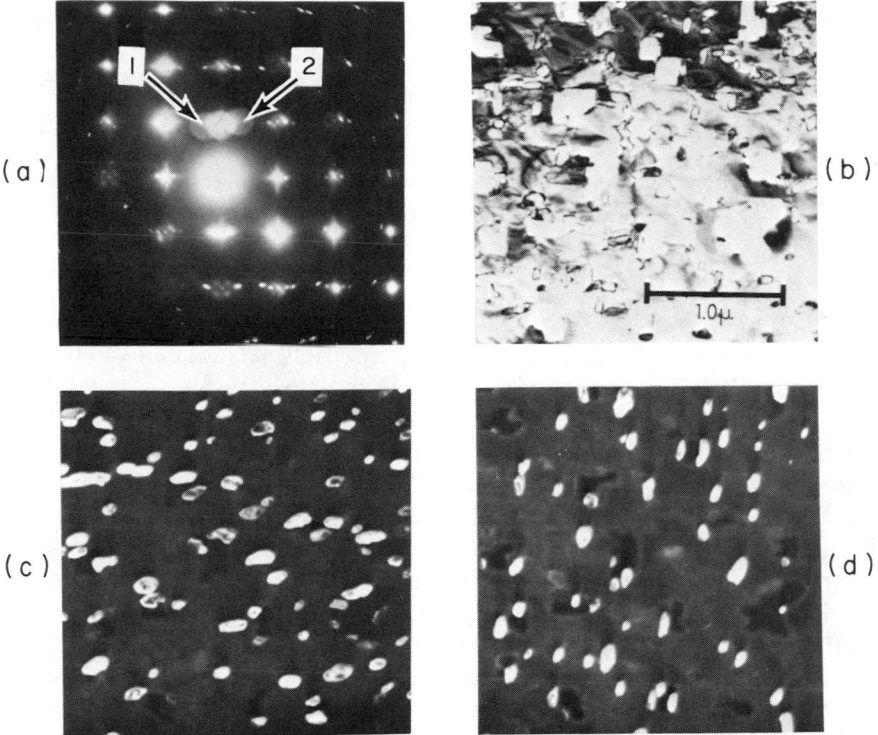

Figure 8. An application of the dark-field technique to the study of ordered precipitates in tantalum. Dark-field micrographs (c) and (d) are made from diffraction spots 1 and 2, respectively; (b) is a bright-field micrograph.

3.2. Crystal Structure: Structure Analysis

The determination of a unit cell and the arrangement of atoms within the unit cell is usually carried out by techniques of X-ray analysis. In some cases, however, it may be inconvenient to prepare materials of sufficient bulk to form good X-ray patterns, and a thin-film form may be more suitable. Also, if a polycrystalline sample has a grain size of $\sim 10\,\mu$, then a selected area transmission diffraction pattern can be made from only one crystal while an X-ray beam will produce a ring pattern from many crystallites; it is far easier to elucidate a structure from a single-crystal "spot" pattern and electron diffraction may, therefore, be preferred.

Extensive work in the determination of crystal structure by electron diffraction has been carried out by Vainstein ([21]). The procedure is to determine the unit cell type from the geometry of spots in one or more diffraction patterns (obtained by tilting the specimen with respect to the beam), find the possible space groups by an examination of symmetry and extinctions (missing reflection), and then decide among the space-group possibilities and determine the position of atoms within the unit cell by measuring intensities and using Fourier techniques. Examples of the use of this technique are given by Vainstein ([21]); some recent applications of the technique are the structure determination of low temperature phase of $\alpha - Ag_2Se$ by Pinsker et al. ([42]), $GeBi_2Te_4$ by Ageav and Semiletov ([43]), and $AgTlSe_2$ by Imanov and Pinsker ([44]).

4. CRYSTAL PERFECTION

Transmission electron microscopy is the only technique available at present for forming images of lattice defects with a resolution near 5 Å. Although defect structures can be imaged with the scanning electron microscope [Chang and Nixon ([45]), Pease and Nixon ([46])] or by X-ray topography [Lang ([47]), Young et al. ([48]) and Newkirk and Wernick ([49])], the best resolutions presently routinely obtainable with these techniques are in excess of 200 Å. The crystal defects successfully and now routinely imaged by transmission electron microscopy are vacancy clusters, dislocations, stacking faults, and microtwins; grain and domain boundaries are also easily observed. Point defects such as single vacancies have not been seen.

The use of electron microscopy as a tool in characterizing the defect structure of crystals suffers from two limitations. The technique is at times a destructive one; samples ordinarily not in thin-film samples are often on substrates from which they cannot easily be separated. Techniques for thinning a large number of inorganic and metal bulk specimens are given by Pashley ([50]) (Chapter 2) and Brammer ([51]). A second limitation depends upon the crystallography and surface density of the defects. Requiring as a conservative estimate that one defect be observed per viewing area in order to make a statistically valid statement about the state of perfection of a crystal, then the minimum surface density of defects for a viewing area ~ 35 cm^2 becomes 10^7 cm^{-2} at a magnification of 20,000 $\times$; 2.5 $\times$ 10^6 cm^{-2} at 10,000 $\times$; 6 $\times$ 10^5 cm^{-2} at 5000 $\times$; and 2.5 $\times$ 10^4 cm^{-2} at 1000 $\times$. At a magnification of 20,000 $\times$, therefore, a dislocation density of 10^3 cm^{-2} as in carefully prepared silicon [Govorkov et al. [52], Alexander and Mader [53]], may be far too low to observe by transmission electron microscopy at 20,000 $\times$; observations of dislocations with these low densities will still be possible, though, if the dislocations lie parallel to the film surface and extend long distances, as dislocations in the basal plane of graphite [Williamson [54]], and mica [Amelinckx and Delavignette [55]]. Dislocations in face-centered cubic crystals frequently lie in directions of the type $\langle 110 \rangle$. The projection of such a dislocation which extends to both surfaces in a film with a {100} orientation onto the film surface is ~ 700 Å. If we require the length of the dislocation on the viewing screen to be larger than 1 mm for ease in viewing, then the minimum magnification necessary to form such an image is 14,000 $\times$. At this magnification, the minimum surface density of dislocations for detection (at the rate of one per viewing area) is 5.5 $\times$ 10^6. It is fortunate (for viewing purposes) that dislocation densities are very often near 10^9 cm^{-2}; in the same manner it is fortunate that the surface densities of oxide grain formed on metals under conditions of low pressure oxidation are also often found to be near 10^9 cm^{-2}.

The contrast variations across an electron micrograph of a single-crystal film result from diffraction effects within the crystal, and these need to be understood if the defects are to be successfully identified. The kinematic theory of diffraction neglects all interactions between diffracted beams; its use in understanding electron microscope imaging from defects in crystals was developed by Hirsch et al. [56] and later described by others [Pashley [50], Chapter 5; Heidenreich [3], pp. 212–244; and Thomas [5], Chapter 2]. A better understanding of image contrast requires the use of the dynamical theory; this approach has been used by Hashimoto et al. [57], Whelan and Hirsch [58], Heidenreich [3], and others. Because of the successful use of the kinetic theory in understanding and predicting many features of micrographs arising from diffraction contrast, this approach will be briefly outlined before discussing the application of electron microscopy to the study of crystal perfection.

The kinematic theory is most easily applied to electron microscopy through consideration of diffraction by columns of crystals one unit cell in width [after Hirsch et al. [56]]. The incident beam k_0 is assumed normal to the foil surface, and the particular diffracted beam k_1 giving rise to contrast is parallel to the column direction as in Fig. 9; a is the unit cell spacing and $|k_1| = |k_0| = 2\pi/\lambda$. The intensity of the diffracted beam at the bottom of the column can be shown to be given by $I = (\sin^2 \pi s \tau)/(\pi s)^2$ where s is the elongation of the reciprocal lattice point corresponding to the reflection k_1 (related to the elongation E discussed above) and τ is the crystal thickness (column length). Replacing τ by the variable z which has limits 0 and τ, the expression shows that $I = 0$ with a periodicity $z = 1/s = t_0'$; t_0' is the depth periodicity of intensity oscillations. Thus, a length of column t_0' will result in zero amplitude on the viewing screen, and a wedge-shaped crystal will produce a series of fringes whose period corresponds to integral changes of t_0' in the wedge. An example is the fringe contrast appearing at the edge of the Cu_2O grain, marked A in Fig. 10. Table II lists extinction distances calculated by Hirsch *et al.* [56] using the Born approximation and neglecting relativistic corrections; relativity reduces extinction distances by about 20% at 100 kV [Calbick [59]].

The phase difference of waves scattered by two points in the column is given by $\varphi = 2\pi s z$, and for a small increment of distance δz the phase difference becomes $\delta\varphi = 2\pi\delta z$. This phase relationship can be illustrated through use of the amplitude phase diagram shown in Fig. 11. The radius of the circle is $(2\pi s)^{-1}$. The point O in the figure represents the center of the column of crystal; the phase difference between the center of the column and a point along the column a distance z from the center is given by the interior angle as indicated, and the amplitude scattered by this length of column z is given by the chord $\mathbf{OP'}$, which is the vector sum of $\mathbf{\delta A}$, where

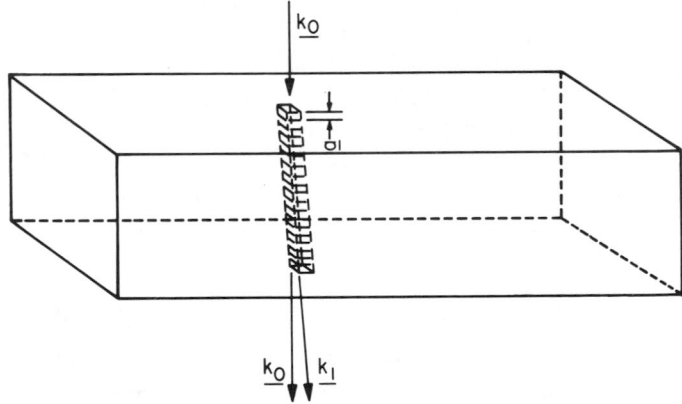

Figure 9. Representation of one column of crystal parallel to the diffracted beam k_1. The calculation of the intensity of the beam at the bottom of the column is discussed in the text. [After Hirsch, Howie, and Whelan [56].]

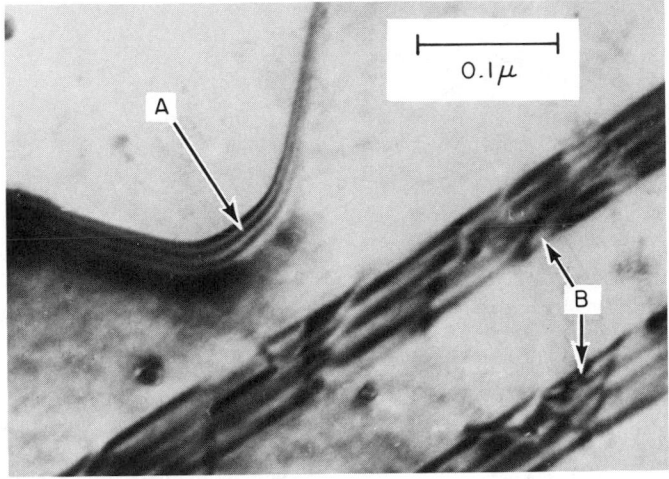

Figure 10. Cu_2O grain on copper single-crystal film. Fringe contrast appears at the edge of the grain at A; a complex stacking fault appears at B.

Table II. Extinction Distance (Å) for 100 keV Electrons (Hirsch)
***et al.* ([56])**

Metal	z^*	ρ^*	Reflection		
			(111)	(200)	(220)
Al	13	2.7	646	774	1240
Ni	28	8.90	258	302	468
Cu	29	8.94	268	308	472
Ag	47	10.5	250	285	403
Pt	78	21.45	165	188	262
Au	79	19.32	181	204	281

*The atomic numbers and densities appear under z and ρ, respectively.

each $\delta\mathbf{A}$ is the amplitude scattered by a small increment of column δz with phase difference $\delta\varphi$.

Beginning at the center of the column and going a distance $\pi/2$ to one surface, point P', starting at O, moves along the circumference of the circle and makes a complete revolution each time a distance t_0' is covered. A complete revolution corresponds to a circumference $2\pi \times$ radius of $1/s$ where, as has been shown above, $I = 0$.

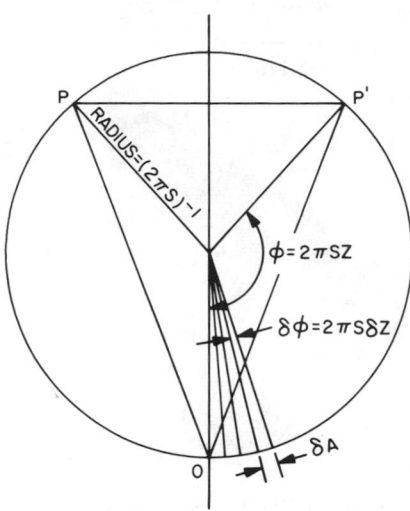

Figure 11. Amplitude–phase diagram for a perfect crystal. An incremental change in phase $\delta\varphi$ along a diffracting column produces an amplitude difference measured by the chord length δA.

Beginning at the center of the column and moving toward the other surface moves point P around the circle a number of times in the opposite direction. Thus, $\mathbf{OP} = \mathbf{OP'}$ if the origin of the amplitude–phase diagram was chosen at the center, and $\mathbf{PP'}$ is the total amplitude diffracted by the column.

It should be emphasized that the kinematic approach becomes less accurate as the reflection producing the contrast becomes stronger, the limiting case being when the reciprocal lattice point corresponding to the reflection falls exactly on the Ewald sphere.* A general discussion of the application of the two theories to electron microscopy is given by Calbick [59].

4.1. Crystal Perfection: Dislocations

Dislocations enter into a large number of solid state phenomena. They serve as diffusion channels for transport of matter [Dash [60], Frank [61]]. Their presence intimately affects the strength of materials [cf. Fisher *et al.* [62]]. Dislocations may serve as active sites for the occurrence of chemical

---

*The orientation of the diffracting crystal with respect to the incident electron (or X-ray) beam is usually represented geometrically by the construction of the Ewald sphere and the reciprocal lattice; conditions corresponding to diffraction are then easily computed. Each point in the reciprocal lattice represents a set of (hkl) planes, and a point touching the surface of the sphere represents a set of (hkl) planes in position to produce a diffraction beam.

reactions,* as, oxygen on graphite [Glenda Hughes et al. ([63])]; oxygen on copper [Young ([64]), Hondros and Oudar ([65]), and Suzuki ([66])]; and H_2S on silver [Phillips ([67])]. Dislocations influence electrical conductivity [Basinski et al. ([68])] for gold [Siegel ([69])]; tungsten and tantalum [Krautz and Schultz ([70])]; niobium and vanadium [Narlikar and Dew-Hughes ([75])]; aluminum [Joiner ([76]), Yoshida et al. ([77]), and Rider and Foxon ([78])]; and copper [Andrews ([79])]. The importance of dislocations in accommodating strain between phases is discussed by Frank and Van Der Merwe ([80]) and demonstrated by Gradmann ([81]) and Krause et al. ([82]), and their role in epitaxial growth is discussed by Pashley ([50]), pp. 217–221. In all of these cases the two features of dislocations that generally need to be understood are their number, expressed as a surface or volume density [cf. Hirsch et al. ([1]), pp. 422–424 and Foxon and Rider ([83])] and their crystallography (e.g., the direction of the dislocation and the size and sign of the Burgers vector b).

Dislocations and other lattice defects have been observed directly by imaging sets of lattice planes, indirectly through the use of moiré techniques, and by diffraction contrast along the lines presented in the previous section. If the objection aperture is positioned to pass one or more diffracted beams as well as the undeviated beam, then the periodicity of a set of lattice planes can be produced in the microscope image and dislocations can be easily seen. This approach to the study of crystal structure was first used by Menter ([84]), but has found only very limited application because of the wide lattice spacing requirement for imaging.

An indirect method of producing periodic contrast from lattice spacings is the use of moiré imaging, introduced by Pashley et al. ([85]). Under certain conditions lattice spacings in two overlapping single-crystal films behave as overlapping line gratings, and a beat (moiré) pattern appears. If the two gratings correspond to parallel lattices with spacings d_1 and d_2, the moiré spacing is $D = d_1 d_2 / |d_1 - d_2|$ and the "moiré magnification" becomes $M = d_{1 \text{ or } 2} / |d_1 - d_2|$. If the spacings are identical but rotated with respect to each other by an angle α then $D = d / [2 \sin (\tfrac{1}{2}\alpha)]$ and $M \sim 1/\alpha$. In both cases M is usually sufficiently large to produce readily observable fringes in the microscopic image.

Dislocations produce singularities in the moiré pattern as at A in Fig. 12. Both screw and edge type dislocations can be seen, and their Burgers vectors can generally be determined from the requirement that

---

*Although the literature abounds with recipes for producing selective etch pitting presumably at sites of emergence of dislocations to a surface, the evidence supporting this correlation is far from conclusive, as demonstrated for example by Ruff ([71]) and Fleischer and Walker ([72]). A correlation between etch pitting and dislocations has been found for SnO_2 crystals by Koffyberg ([73]) and for MgO by Stablein ([74]).

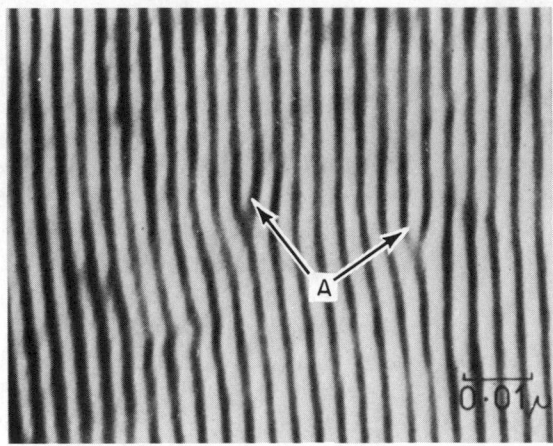

Figure 12. Moiré pattern from overlapping layers of
gold and palladium. Dislocations are seen at A. [After
Pashley *et al.* ([85]); photo courtesy of *Nature*.]

$\mathbf{g} \cdot \mathbf{b} = 0$ if the dislocation is to be invisible [cf. Hirsch *et al.* ([1]), Chapter
7, and below], where $\mathbf{g}$ is the reciprocal lattice vector of the diffracting beam.
Interfacial dislocations can also be imaged by moiré techniques and have
been observed in platinum on gold by Jesser *et al.* ([86]), oxide on iron by
Hart and Maurin ([87]), after formation of the η phase in a Ni–Cr–Ti alloy
by Merrick ([88]), and in overlapping crystals of MoS_2 by Kamiya *et al.* ([89]).

Information on the size and sign of the Burgers vector and the dislocation direction is most readily obtained by direct imaging with transmission electron microscopy. The introduction of a dislocation in a single-
crystal film produces a phase difference $\varphi = 2\pi \mathbf{g} \cdot \mathbf{R}$ between waves
scattered by displaced and nondisplaced crystal regions, where $\mathbf{R}$ is the
displacement vector. The approach has been to calculate $\mathbf{R}$ for the various
dislocation geometries in crystals and to then determine the influence
through φ on the image contrast. Once this is done certain rules can be
set up relating image contrast to dislocation geometry and applied to
practical laboratory cases.

The vector $\mathbf{R}$ has been determined for a number of special orientations
of dislocations, and the influence of the displacements on image contrast
has been calculated from the kinematic theory by Hirsch *et al.* ([56]), and
from the dynamical theory by Howie and Whelan ([90]). For the case of a
general dislocation the displacement is

$$\mathbf{R} = \frac{1}{2\pi}\left\{ \mathbf{b}\varphi + \mathbf{b}\frac{\sin 2\varphi}{4(1-\nu)} + \mathbf{b} \times \mathbf{u}\left(\frac{1-2\nu}{2(1-\nu)} \ln |r| + \frac{\cos 2\varphi}{4(1-\nu)} \right) \right\}$$

where $\mathbf{R}$ is determined at a point (r, φ) from the dislocation, ν is Poisson's ratio [Hirsch et al. [1], p. 176], and $\mathbf{u}$ is a unit vector along the positive direction of the dislocation. Dislocations are, therefore, invisible when both $\mathbf{g} \cdot \mathbf{b}$ and $\mathbf{g} \cdot \mathbf{b} \times \mathbf{u}$ are simultaneously equal to zero. The former condition occurs when $\mathbf{b}$ lies in the reflecting plane, as with an edge dislocation where $\mathbf{u} \parallel \mathbf{g}$ or with a screw dislocation where $\mathbf{u} \perp \mathbf{g}$. The latter condition arises when both $\mathbf{b}$ and $\mathbf{u}$ lie in a plane normal to k_0, as with an edge dislocation lying in a slip plane normal to k_0.

The symmetry of the dislocation image is different for the two cases where $\mathbf{g} \cdot \mathbf{b}$ and $\mathbf{g} \cdot \mathbf{b} \times \mathbf{u}$ operate to give contrast. In the former case the contrast is asymmetrical on both sides of the dislocation and in the latter case the contrast is symmetrical [Howie and Whelan [90]]. Also, the intensity of the image is usually considerably weaker in the latter case.

The procedure for determining the Burgers vector of a dislocation, then, is to observe the image of the dislocation under dark field with different selected reflections, and find those reflections for which the dislocation is invisible. From a few such observations $\mathbf{b}$ is readily determined from the criterion $\mathbf{g} \cdot \mathbf{b} = 0$ for invisibility, assuming that the contribution from $\mathbf{g} \cdot \mathbf{b} \times \mathbf{u}$ is negligible.

As an illustration of the determination of $\mathbf{b}$, consider the dislocations shown in bright field contrast in Fig. 13a. The film is epitaxially deposited tantalum, rapidly cooled after intense heating ($\sim 2000°C$) in the electron microscope. The film surface is (001), and projections of the dislocations

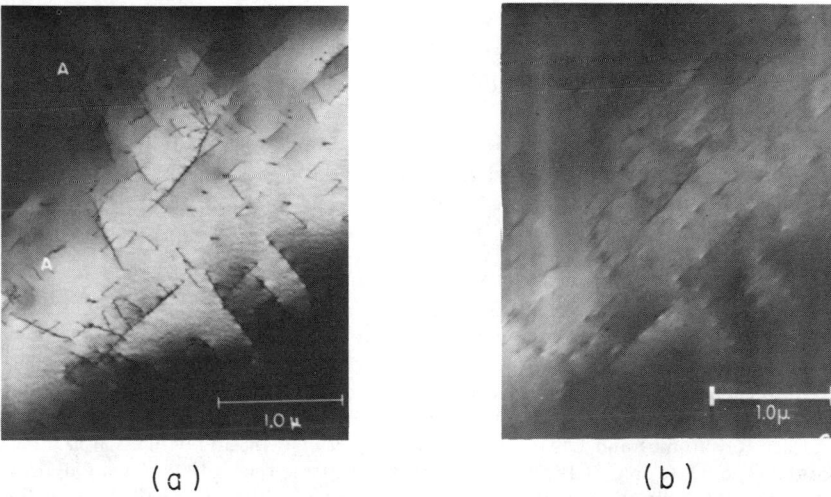

$$(a) \qquad\qquad (b)$$

Figure 13. Bright field electron micrograph of quenched epitaxial tantalum film (a). One type of dislocation has disappeared in the dark-field micrograph using a 110 reflection (b).

on the film surface are in directions [110] and [1$\bar{1}$0] as shown. From the lengths of the dislocations, their geometry upon tilting, and the known film thickness, it is concluded that they lie along $\langle 111 \rangle$ directions and intersect both film surfaces. A dark-field micrograph of this region using the 110 reflection causes one set of dislocations to disappear (Fig. 13b); this would occur if **b** for this set were $\frac{1}{2}[\bar{1}11]$. Dark field from the 1$\bar{1}$0 reflection causes the orthogonal set of dislocations to disappear (the other set being imaged) and it is concluded that the dislocations are of screw type.

Another example of the determination of the Burgers vectors of dislocations in a bcc metal is found in Ohr and Beshers ([91]); examples for fcc materials including the determination of **b** for partial dislocations is found in Hirsch *et al.* ([1]), Chapters 7 and 11, and Thomas ([5]), Chapter 5, and a comprehensive study of Burgers vector determination for partial dislocations is found in Silcock and Tunstall ([92]).

4.2. Crystal Perfection: Stacking Faults and Microtwins

In addition to the importance of planar defects in determining mechanical properties of solids and in phenomena involving mass transport, stacking faults and twins are of concern in two research areas of current interest. These are epitaxial growth studies and investigations into the electrical properties of solids. Pashley *et al.* ([93]), and more recently Jacobs *et al.* ([94]), described the formation of double-position twin boundaries,* stacking faults, and microtwins† produced during epitaxial growth of fcc metals. Discussions of the appearance of planar defects in semiconductor materials are given by Pankey and Davey ([97]) for GaAs, Mendelson ([98]) for silicon, and Catlin and Humphris ([99]) for germanium. Lattice disregistry at a fault–twin boundary causes extra scattering of conduction electrons; this is discussed in general terms by Freeman ([100]), and specifically for aluminum by Kino *et al.* ([101]) and Yoshida *et al.* ([77]), for gold by Siegel ([69]) and De Jong and Koehler ([102]), and for copper and copper alloys by Hiki *et al.* ([103]).

---

*When rotational symmetry about the substrate normal is different for the substrate and epitaxial nuclei, then adjacent nuclei often grow with a doubly positioned relationship to each other. For example, Cu_2O nuclei produced during low pressure oxidation of copper {100} surfaces often grow with a plane of the form {111} parallel to the surface [Gwathmey and Lawless ([95]), Brockway *et al.* ([96])], and with a Cu_2O direction of the type $\langle 110 \rangle$ parallel to a copper direction of the type $\langle 100 \rangle$. Two Cu_2O nuclei with the [110] direction parallel to Cu [100] and Cu [010] respectively, are doubly positioned.

†Microtwins are lamellae a few tens of Å or less in thickness that bear a twin relationship to the matrix.

4.2.1. *Identification from Diffraction Patterns*

The reciprocal lattice for material containing stacking faults differs from the reciprocal lattice for unfaulted material by the presence of streaks through certain of the main lattice points. These diffraction effects were first calculated for close-packed structures by Hendricks and Teller ([104]) and Mering ([105]). Whelan and Hirsch ([58]) showed that {111} faults with **f**-vectors [Read ([106]), p. 95] of the type $\frac{1}{6}\langle 112 \rangle$ found in fcc structures produce elongations of those reciprocal lattice points for which $(h + k + l) = 3N \pm 1$, when N is an integer. The elongations are in directions normal to the fault planes, and their lengths increase with increasing density of faulted material. These protuberances can give rise to extra "satellite" reflections in the diffraction pattern, as described by Hirsch *et al.* ([1]), p. 107, and illustrated in Fig. 14. In general, films are sufficiently buckled so that a region under illumination contains a continuum of deviations (between limits) from a Bragg condition, with the result that crosses, rather than distinct satellite spots, intersect those lattice points of the type $3N + 1$. This type of situation is illustrated in Fig. 107 [Pinsker ([17]), p. 225] and is similar to the one-sided streaking of reflection-diffraction patterns resulting from refraction, as discussed above. Often the degree of buckling is minimal and streaking is weak relative to the intensity of satellite spots. In this case the presence of streaks in the reciprocal lattice (whose intersections with the Ewald sphere produce the satellites) can be demonstrated by slightly tilting the film during examination, resulting in a motion of the satellite spots along straight lines through the matrix points.

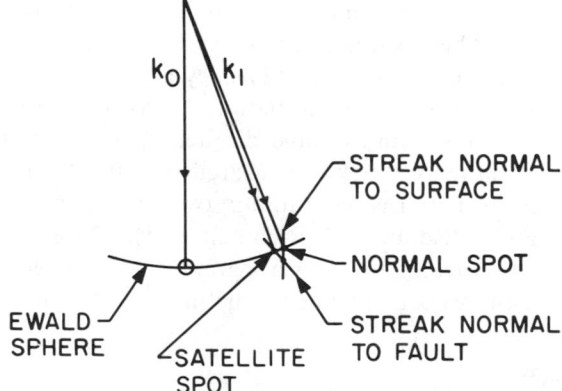

Figure 14. Faults in a thin crystal film produce streaks through reciprocal lattice points in a direction normal to the fault surface, giving rise to satellite spots in the transmission diffraction pattern.

If a transmission or reflection diffraction pattern is made from a region that contains two or more twin-related crystals, then each twin will contribute its own diffraction pattern to the composite whole. If the twinning plane for a given structure is known or, as is so often the case, suspected, then a relationship between twinned reciprocal lattice points can be defined by transformation formulae. For a cubic crystal twinned on planes of the form $\{hkl\}$, the reciprocal lattice point pqr can be shown [Göttsche (^{107})] to transform to the point $\tilde{p}\tilde{q}\tilde{r}$ where

$$\tilde{p} = \frac{h}{3}(h_p + k_q + l_r) - p$$

$$\tilde{q} = \frac{k}{3}(h_p + k_q + l_r) - q$$

$$\tilde{r} = \frac{l}{3}(h_p + k_q + l_r) - r$$

These formulae are obtained by rotating about certain reciprocal lattice axes and are used, for instance, by Pashley and Stowell (^{108}) to describe fcc material containing twins on planes of the type $\{111\}$.

A diffracted beam from one crystal passing across a twin boundary may be of sufficient intensity that it is again diffracted by the twin. Such events are common in the case of transmission diffraction patterns from single-crystal films containing microtwins. The resulting diffraction pattern then consists of three classes of spots: diffraction spots from the matrix (assuming one twin orientation describes the predominant structure in the field under view); diffraction spots from one or more twins; and "double-diffraction" spots. The resulting reciprocal lattice for the case of $\{111\}$ twinning in fcc materials is shown in Pashley and Stowell (^{108}). A similar construction derived from a transformation matrix describes the reciprocal lattice for $\{112\}$ twinning and double diffraction in bcc materials, and is shown in Fig. 15 [after Calbick and Marcus (^{109})]. Other derivations of electron diffraction patterns containing twin reflections are given by Crocker (^{110}) and Meieran and Richman (^{111}). Once the presence of twins is made known and the crystallography determined from the diffraction pattern, the various twinned structures can be identified by dark-field techniques.

4.2.2. Identification by Electron Microscopy

Stacking faults and twins are made visible in the electron microscope by diffraction contrast imaging. The kinematic contrast due to a stacking fault is best presented with the aid of the amplitude–phase diagram dis-

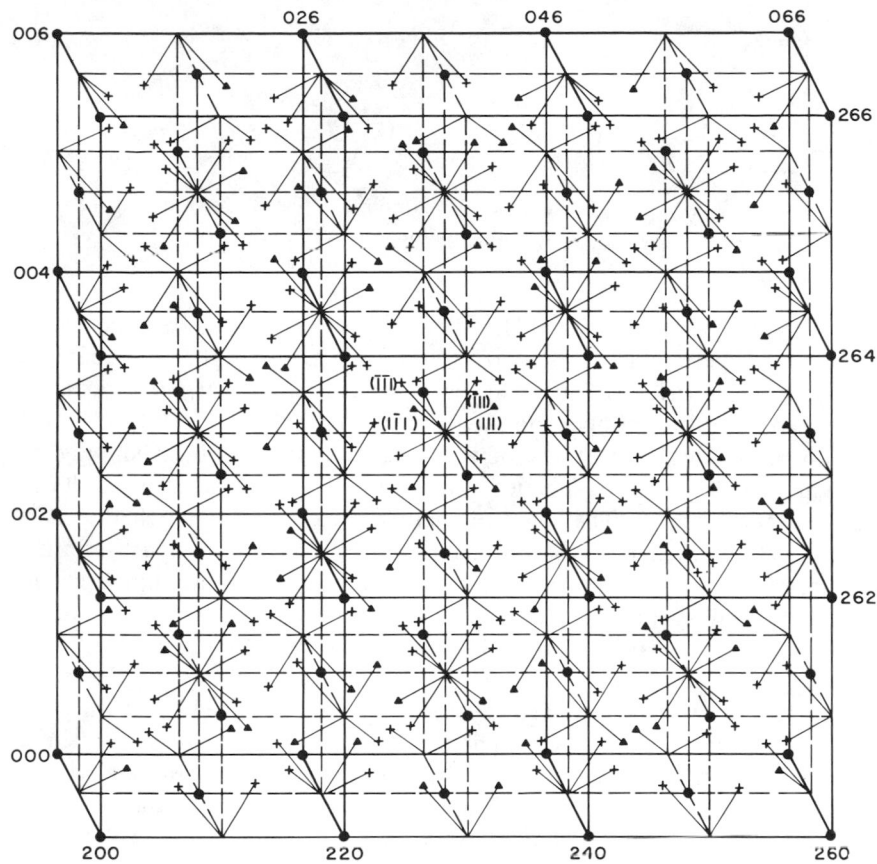

Figure 15. Portion (2 × 6 × 6) of generalized reciprocal lattice for a bcc crystal; complete unit is (6 × 6 × 6) for centered lattices. (●), fcc host reciprocal lattice points; (Δ), {111}, {211} twin points; (+) double-diffraction points.

cussed earlier, following Hirsch *et al.* ([56]). If a fault runs obliquely across a foil, then the two parts of the crystal are displaced from each other by a vector **R** lying in the fault plane. If $\mathbf{R} = \frac{1}{6}[112]$ as in fcc material, then the phase difference φ is $2\pi\mathbf{g} \cdot \mathbf{R} = \frac{1}{3}\pi[h + k + 2l]$ where **g** is the reciprocal lattice vector corresponding to the set of (hkl) planes producing the reflection. In fcc material $h + k + 2l = 2n$ where n is an integer, and $\varphi = 0°$ or $\pm 120°$. The amplitude–phase diagram for the case where $\varphi = -120°$ is shown in Fig. 16. If the intensity at the bottom of a column of crystal one unit cell in width is considered, O represents the center of the column, P the upper surface, and P' the lower surface. If the column intersects a fault at a distance Q from the center, then a second circle is drawn,

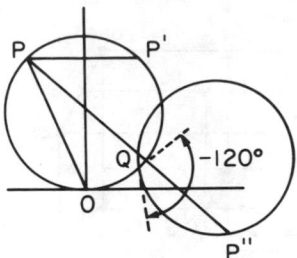

Figure 16. Amplitude–phase diagram for an fcc crystal containing a stacking fault.

with P'' as the lower surface. The total amplitude of the scattered wave, PP'', changes periodically as the position of the column in the fault changes, giving rise to a series of fringes in the micrograph. Such fringes appear in the micrograph of a copper film at B in Fig. 10.

Some important features of stacking faults are obtained only by applying results of the dynamical theory of images of stacking faults in electron micrographs. The sense of inclination of the fault [whether it is (111) or ($\bar{1}\bar{1}1$) when viewed from a [001] direction] is obtained by noting the appearance of the fringe contrast. This contrast is asymmetrical in dark field and symmetrical in bright field; the edge of the fault image where the contrast is the same in bright and dark field corresponds to the top of the foil [Hashimoto et al. ([112,113])]. The sign of the phase angle α and, therefore, the displacement vector **R** can be obtained from the contrast of the outermost fringes (light or dark) in bright field; the intrinsic or extrinsic nature of the fault can then be obtained from the knowledge of **g**, **R**, and the fringe contrast. The theory for this analysis was given by Hashimoto et al. ([112,113]), and is illustrated in Hirsch et al. ([1]), pp. 229–237. A similar application of the dynamical theory to the case of intersecting stacking faults is found in Hashimoto and Marukawa ([114]).

Twin lamellae are frequently confused with stacking faults in electron micrographs, particularly when the twins form wedge-shaped boundaries and produce fringe contrast. Although thick twin lamellae are often "easily recognized by their projected width in the image plane" [Jacobs et al. ([94])], the distinction between the two is best made by considering differences in the transmission diffraction pattern, as described above.*

4.3. Crystal Perfection: Volume Defects

In addition to line and planar defects, three-dimensional defects are amenable to identification and analysis by electron diffraction and micro-

---

*In the limit as lamellae grow thinner, the distinction between twin lamellae and stacking faults disappears.

scopy. The analysis of solid precipitates was already discussed: the analysis of voids is now considered.

Voids have been produced by two procedures. One procedure is quenching, as described by Mori and Meshii [115] for gold, and by Chen and Meshii [116] and Eddington and West [117] for aluminum. Another procedure is particle bombardment such as, nuclear irradiation followed by quenching, described by Whapham [118], xenon bombardment of platinum, described by Kelly and Ruedl [119], and electron bombardment of lead iodides, described by Forty [120]. General discussion of this field appears in Cotterill et al. [121].

A recent analysis of electron microscope diffraction contrast from small voids was given by Van Landuyt et al. [122]. They concluded that three absorption and diffraction effects contribute to the final image of voids in crystal films:

1. The total electron scattering from a region containing a void should be less than scattering from surrounding material, thus producing an image of the void brighter than the background.
2. When a Bragg condition is exactly fulfilled a light or dark image which depends on the void thickness will be produced; the contrast is reversed in bright- and dark-field images.
3. If the Bragg condition is not exactly fulfilled the contrast then additionally depends on the deviation from this condition and on the position of the void in the foil.

Vacancy clusters can form into a multilayered "planar" defect, for example, as described by Eddington and West [117]. In this case the micrograph is analyzed by examining the bounding partial dislocations, using the development of Silcock and Tunstall [92].

5. SUMMARY

The foregoing is an attempt to describe the kind of information on the physical structure of solids that can be obtained from the modern commercial electron microscope, including discussions of the way this information is obtained. Certain topics were omitted because they are less related to structure characterization but more toward techniques of electron diffraction and microscopy, or are variations of standard techniques. Examples are: the recent developments in the use of Kikuchi patterns for obtaining accurate measurements of film orientation in the microscope, described by Okamoto et al. [123] and Levine et al. [124]; quantitative analysis of the chemical composition of thin films by the use of an X-ray spectrometer attachment, by Fuchs [125]; various in situ studies; and the use of scanning techniques and ultrahigh voltage electron microscopy (cf. Proceedings of the Sixth International Congress for Electron Microscopy, 1966).

REFERENCES

1. P. B. Hirsch, A. Howie, R. B. Nicholson, D. W. Pashley, and M. J. Whelan, Electron Microscopy of Thin Crystals, Butterworths, Washington (1965).
2. D. H. Kay, Techniques for Electron Microscopy, F. A. Davis Co., Philadelphia (1965).
3. R. D. Heidenreich, Fundamentals of Transmission Electron Microscopy, Interscience, New York (1964).
4. P. Grivet, Electron Optics, Pergamon, New York (1965).
5. G. Thomas, Transmission Electron Microscopy of Metals, John Wiley & Sons, New York (1962).
6. B. M. Siegel, Modern Developments in Electron Microscopy, Academic Press, New York (1964).
7. C. E. Hall, Introduction to Electron Microscopy, McGraw-Hill, New York (1966).
8. V. G. Zworykin, G. A. Morton, F. G. Ramberg, J. Hillier, and A. Vance, Electron Optics and the Electron Microscope, John Wiley & Sons, New York (1945).
9. V. E. Cosslett, Practical Electron Microscopy, Butterworths, New York (1951).
10. D. E. Bradley, *in* Techniques for Electron Microscopy (D. H. Kay, ed.) 2nd Ed., Chapter 5, F. A. Davis Co., Philadelphia (1965).
11. C. J. Calbick, *Bell System Tech. J.* **30**, 798 (1951).
12. C. J. Calbick, private communication (1966).
13. G. A. Basset, *Phil. Mag.*, **3**, 72 (1958).
14. C. Sella, and J. J. Trillat, *in* Single Crystal Films (M. H. Francombe and H. Sato, eds.) pp. 201–218, Macmillan, New York (1964).
15. G. R. Hennig, *Appl. Phys. Lett.* **4**, 52 (1964).
16. J. L. Robins, and T. N. Rhodin, *Surf. Sci.* **2**, 346 (1946).
17. Z. G. Pinsker, Electron Diffraction, Butterworths, New York (1953).
18. L. Sturkey, and L. K. Freval, *Phys. Rev.* **68**, 56 (1945).
19. J. M. Cowley, and A. L. G. Rees, *Proc. Phys. Soc.* **59**, 287 (1947).
20. G. Honjo, *J. Phys. Soc. Japan* **2**, 133 (1947).
21. B. K. Vainstein, Structure Analysis by Electron Diffraction, Pergamon, New York (1964).
22. A. Guinier, X-ray Diffraction, p. 124, W. H. Freeman Co., San Francisco (1963).
23. R. H. Wade, and J. Silcox, *Phys. Stat. Sol.* **19**, 63 (1967).
24. Y. Drahos, and A. Delong, *Nature* **209**, 801 (1966).
25. H. Mahl, and W. Weitsch, *Z. Naturforsch.* **15**, 1051 (1961).
26. D. G. Brubaker, and M. L. Fuller, *J. Appl. Phys.* **16**, 128 (1945).
27. J. G. Allpress, H. Jaeger, P. D. Mercer, and J. V. Sanders, *in* Proceedings of the 6th International Congress for Electron Microscopy, Vol. I. pp. 289–90, Maruzen, Tokyo (1966).
28. R. B. Kehoe, *Phil. Mag.*, **2**, 1 (1957).
29. V. E. Yurasova, Y. A. Prochorov, L. B. Sheljakin, and L. N. Nevzorova, *in* Proceedings of the 6th International Congress for Electron Microscopy, Vol. I., pp. 509–510, Maruzen, Tokyo (1966).
30. R. B. Marcus, and L. O. Brockway, *Mem. Sci. Rev. Met.* **LXII**, 61 (1965).

31. K. R. Lawless, and D. F. Mitchell, *Mem. Sci. Rev. Met.* **LXII**, 41 (1965).
32. N. Takahashi, and J. J. Trillat, *Acta Met.* **4**, 201 (1956).
33. G. Jellinek, *Z. Krist.* **110** 5/6, 335 (1958).
34. G. Shimaoka, *J. Electrochem. Soc.* **110**, 1177 (1963).
35. H. Schlotterer, *Phys. Stat. Sol.* **11**, 219 (1965).
36. S. Steeb, and J. Renner, *J. Less Common Met.* **10**, 246 (1966).
37. R. E. Villagrana, and G. Thomas, *Phys. Stat. Sol.* **9**, 499 (1965).
38. D. P. Seraphim, N. R. Stemple, and D. T. Novick, *J. Appl. Phys.* **33**, 136 (1962).
39. R. B. Marcus, *J. Appl. Phys.* **37**, 3121 (1966).
40. E. I. Alessandrini, and J. F. Freedman, *Acta. Cryst.* **16**, 54 (1963).
41. H. Sato, *in* Single Crystal Films (M. H. Francombe and H. Sato, eds.) pp. 341–60, Macmillan, New York (1964).
42. Z. G. Pinsker, Ching-Liang Chou, R. M. Imanov, and E. L. Lapidus, *Sov. Phys. Cryst.* **10**, 225 (1965).
43. K. A. Agaev, and S. A. Semiletov, *Sov. Phys. Cryst.* **10**, 86 (1965).
44. R. M. Imanov, and Z. G. Pinsker, *Sov. Phys. Cryst.* **10**, 148 (1965).
45. T. H. P. Chang, and W. C. Nixon, *in* Proceedings of the 6th International Congress for Electron Microscopy, Vol. I, pp. 193–194, Maruzen, Tokyo (1966).
46. R. F. W. Pease, and W. D. Nixon, *J. Sci. Inst.* **42**, 81 (1965).
47. A. R. Lang, *J. Appl. Phys.* **29**, 597 (1958).
48. F. W. Young, Jr., F. A. Sherril, and M. C. Wittels, *J. Appl. Phys.* **36**, 2225 (1965).
49. J. B. Newkirk, and J. H. Wernick, *in* Direct Observation of Imperfections in Crystals, p. 471, Interscience, New York (1962).
50. D. W. Pashley, *in* Modern Developments in Electron Microscopy (B. M. Siegel, ed.), Academic Press, New York (1964).
51. I. S. Brammer, *in* Techniques for Electron Microscopy (D. H. Kay, ed.) 2nd Ed., Chapter 12, F. A. Davis Co., Philadelphia (1965).
52. V. G. Govorkov, Y. U. Malov, V. I. Nikidenko, and I. S. Smirnova, *Kristallografyia* **11**, 259 (1966).
53. H. Alexander and S. Mader, *Acta. Met.* **10**, 887 (1962).
54. G. K. Williamson, *Proc. Roy. Soc.* (4), **257**, 457 (1960).
55. S. Amelinckx, and P. Delavignette, *Nature* **185**, 603 (1960).
56. P. B. Hirsch, A. Howie, and M. J. Whelan, *Phil. Trans. Roy. Soc.* (*A*), **252**, 299 (1960).
57. H. Hashimoto, M. Mannami, and T. Naiki, *Phil. Trans. Roy. Soc.* (*A*), **253**, 459 (1961).
58. M. J. Whelan, and P. B. Hirsch, *Phil. Mag.* **2**, 1121; 1303 (1957).
59. C. J. Calbick, *in* Physics of Thin Films (G. Hass and R. E. Thun, eds.), Vol. 2, pp. 63–145, Academic Press, New York (1964).
60. W. C. Dash, *J. Appl. Phys.* **27**, 1193 (1956).
61. F. C. Frank, *in* Dislocations and Mechanical Properties of Crystals (J. C. Fisher, W. G. Johnston, R. Thomson, and T. Vreeland, Jr., eds.) pp. 408–411, John Wiley & Sons, New York (1957).
62. J. C. Fisher, W. G. Johnston, R. Thomson, and T. Vreeland, Jr., Dislocations and Mechanical Properties of Crystals, John Wiley & Sons, New York (1957).
63. E. E. Glenda Hughes, B. R. Williams, and J. M. Thomas, *Trans. Far. Soc.* **58**, 2011 (1962).
64. F. W. Young, Jr., *Acta Met.* **8**, 117 (1960).
65. E. Hondros, and J. Oudar, *Compt. Rend.* **256**, 2386 (1963).
66. H. Suzuki, *J. Phys. Soc. Japan* **10**, 981 (1955).

67. V. A. Phillips, *J. Appl. Phys.* **33**, 712 (1962).
68. Z. S. Basinski, J. S. Dugdale, and A. Howie, *Phil. Mag.* **8**, 1989 (1963).
69. R. W. Seigel, *Phil. Mag.* **13**, 359 (1966).
70. E. Krautz, and H. Schultz, *Z. Angew. Phys.* **15**, 1–4 (1963).
71. A. W. Ruff, Jr., *J. Appl. Phys.* **33**, 3392 (1962).
72. R. L. Fleischer, and R. M. Walker, *Phil. Mag.* (*A*) **250**, 1083 (1966).
73. F. P. Koffyberg, *J. Appl. Phys.* **36**, 844 (1965).
74. P. F. Stablein, *Appl. Phys. Lett.* **4**, 117 (1964).
75. A. V. Narlikar, and D. Dew-Hughes, *Phys. Stat. Sol.* **6**, 383 (1964).
76. W. C. H. Joiner, *Phys. Rev.* **137A**, 112 (1965).
77. S. Yoshida, T. Kino, M. Kirtiani, S. Kabemoto, H. Maeta, and Y. Shimomura, *J. Phys. Soc. Japan* **18**, (Supplement II), 98 (1963).
78. J. G. Rider, and C. T. B. Foxon, *Phil. Mag.* **13**, 289 (1966).
79. P. V. Andrews, *Phys. Lett.* **19**, 588 (1965).
80. F. C. Frank, and J. H. Van der Merwe, *Proc. Roy. Soc.* (*A*), **198**, 205 (1959).
81. U. Gradmann, *Ann. Physik* **13**, 213 (1964).
82. G. Krause, C. Menzel-Kopp, and E. Menzel, *Surf. Sci.* **3**, 421 (1965).
83. C. T. B. Foxon, and J. G. Rider, *Phil. Mag.* **14**, 185 (1966).
84. J. W. Menter, *Proc. Roy. Soc.* (*A*) **236**, 119 (1956).
85. D. W. Pashley, J. W. Menter, and G. A. Bassett, *Nature* **179**, 752 (1957).
86. W. A. Jesser, J. W. Matthews, and D. Kuklmann-Wilsdorf, *Appl. Phys. Lett.* **9**, 176 (1966).
87. R. K. Hart, and J. K. Maurin, *in* Proceedings of the 6th International Congress for Electron Microscopy, Vol. I., pp. 539–40, Maruzen, Tokyo (1966).
88. M. F. Merrick, Ph.D. Thesis, Cambridge University (1963).
89. Y. Kamiya, K. Ando, M. Nonyama, and R. Uyeda, *J. Phys. Soc. Japan* **15**, 2025 (1960).
90. A. Howie, and M. J. Whelan, *Proc. Roy. Soc.* (*A*) **267**, 206 (1962).
91. S. M. Ohr, and D. N. Beshers, *Phil. Mag.* **8**, 1343 (1963).
92. J. M. Silcock, and W. J. Tunstall, *Phil. Mag.* **10**, 361 (1964).
93. D. W. Pashley, M. J. Stowell, M. H. Jacobs, and T. J. Law, *Phil. Mag.* **10**, 127 (1965).
94. M. H. Jacobs, D. W. Pashley, and M. J. Stowell, *Phil. Mag.* **13**, 129 (1966).
95. A. T. Gwathmey, and K. R. Lawless, *in* The Surface Chemistry of Metals and Semiconductors (H. C. Gatos, ed.), pp. 283–521, John Wiley & Sons, New York (1960).
96. L. O. Brockway, R. B. Marcus, and A. P. Rowe, *in* Single Crystal Films, (M. H. Francombe and H. Sato, eds.) pp. 231–39, Macmillan, New York (1964).
97. T. Panky, and J. E. Davey, *J. Appl. Phys.* **37**, 1507 (1966).
98. S. Mendelson, *J. Appl. Phys.* **35**, 1570 (1964).
99. A. Catlin, and R. R. Humphris, *in* Basic Problems in Thin Film Physics, (Proceedings of the International Symposium at Clausthal-Göttingen, September 6–11, 1965) pp. 175–80, Vandenhoeck & Ruprecht Co., Göttingen.
100. S. Freeman, Jr., *J. Phys. Chem. Solids* **26**, 473 (1965).
101. T. Kino, S. Kabemoto, H. Maeta, and T. Yamageta, *J. Phys. Soc. Japan* **18**, 1846 (1963).
102. M. DeJong, and J. S. Koehler, *Phys. Rev.* **129**, 49 (1963).
103. Y. Hiki, T. Suzuki, and K. Yajima, *J. Phys. Soc. Japan* **18**, (Supplement II), 105 (1963).
104. S. Hendricks, and E. Teller, *J. Chem. Phys.* **10**, 147 (1942).

105. J. Mering, *Acta. Cryst.* **2**, 371 (1949).
106. W. T. Read, Dislocations in Crystals, McGraw-Hill, New York (1953).
107. H. Göttsche, *Z. Physik* **134**, 517 (1953).
108. D. W. Pashley, and M. J. Stowell, *Phil. Mag.* **8**, 1605 (1963).
109. C. J. Calbick, and R. B. Marcus, *Acta. Cryst.* **23**, 12 (1967).
110. A. G. Crocker, *Trans. AIME*, **233**, 17 (1965).
111. E. S. Meieran, and M. H. Richman, *Trans. Met. Soc. AIME*, **227**, 1044 (1963).
112. H. Hashimoto, A. Howie, and M. J. Whelan, *Phil. Mag.* **5**, 967 (1960).
113. H. Hashimoto, A. Howie, and M. J. Whelan, *Proc. Roy. Soc.* (*A*) **269**, 80 (1962).
114. H. Hashimoto, and K. Marukawa, *J. Phys. Soc. Japan* **20**, 1035 (1965).
115. T. Mori and M. Meshii, *Acta. Met.*, **12**, 104 (1964).
116. K. Y. Chen, and M. Meshii, *in* Proceedings of the 6th International Congress for Electron Microscopy, Vol. I, pp. 345–46, Maruzen, Tokyo (1966).
117. J. W. Eddington, and D. R. West, *in* Proceedings of the 6th International Congress for Electron Microscopy, Vol. I, pp. 343–44, Maruzen, Tokyo (1966).
118. A. D. Whapham, *Nucl. Appl.* **2**, 123 (1966).
119. R. Kelly and E. Ruedl, Proceedings of 3rd European Regional Conference for Electron Microscopy, p. 185, The Publishing House of the Czechoslovak Academy of Sciences, Prague (1964).
120. A. Forty, *Phil. Mag.* **6**, 895 (1961).
121. R. M. J. Cotterill, M. Doyama, J. J. Jackson, and M. Meshil, Lattice Defects in Quenched Metals, Academic Press, New York (1965).
122. J. Van Landuyt, R. Gevers, and S. Amelinckx, *Phys. Stat. Sol.* **10**, 319 (1965).
123. P. R. Okamoto, E. Levine, and G. Thomas, *J. Appl. Phys.* **28**, 289 (1967).
124. E. Levine, W. L. Bell, and G. Thomas, *J. Appl. Phys.* **37**, 2141 (1966).
125. E. Fuchs, *Rev. Sci. Inst.* **37**, 623 (1966).

VI. THE EMISSION-SPECTROGRAPHIC AND ATOMIC-ABSORPTION ANALYSES OF METALLIC THIN FILMS

J. D. Nohe

Western Electric Co., Inc., Engineering Research Center
Princeton, New Jersey

Three areas of thin-film analyses will be discussed. These include: (1) the determination of trace impurities in several types of metallic thin films by emission spectroscopy, employing the graphite-substrate technique for film removal and the dilution technique for standard preparation; (2) the determination of silicon, nitrogen, and trace impurities in silicon nitride films by plasma arc excitation; (3) composition determination of binary and ternary alloy films by atomic absorption. Where possible, collaborative data by other analytical techniques will be employed to substantiate or cross check the analytical results of the techniques described.

1. INTRODUCTION

In order to appreciate the necessity for analyzing thin films and to understand inherent differences, it is useful to consider some of the basic techniques used for film preparation ([1]). Most films are deposited by either vacuum evaporation, cathodic sputtering, or plating. In evaporation, the source material is heated to a temperature where at least some vaporization occurs. Multicomponent materials tend to deposit at a different composition than the source material. This is principally due to the differences in evaporation rates. Therefore, the composition of the film will usually not be the same or even similar to that of the source material. Cathodic sputtering poses a somewhat different problem because the bulk temperature of the source is usually well below its melting point. Sputtered materials usually deposit with the same composition as the source, except for impurities acquired from the gas phase or sputtering from objects in the apparatus. Plates may also be considered a thin film. The compositional and impurity variations are principally due to changes in plating parameters, such as current, flow rates, plating solutions, etc.

It must be remembered that both optical emission and atomic absorption are comparison techniques which require standards. Unfortunately, standards are usually not commercially available and must be prepared synthetically as powders or solutions. Unless a deposition system is highly developed and operated with little change in conditions and materials, changes will occur in both the film's impurities and composition. Therefore, with a general survey instrument such as the spectrograph, it is advisable to check routinely for as many elements as possible and include these elements in the synthetic standards. These are the principal problems encountered for any analytical technique which must rely on film recovery prior to comparison analysis.

2. EMISSION-SPECTROGRAPHIC ANALYSIS

Emission spectroscopy has a definite and important role in the development of thin-film microcircuitry. Films are produced by a number of deposition techniques, usually from ultrapure materials under a vacuum of 10^{-5} or $^{-6}$ torr. However, even under these conditions many elements can be added to the films as impurities. Therefore, the two principal advantages of the emission technique for film analyses are its sensitivity and the simultaneous detection of many elements. The principal disadvantages are: (1) the technique is destructive, and (2) the precision is fair as compared to other analytical techniques.

2.1. Film Composition and Postdeposition Contamination

Two subtle differences, which may seem obvious, should be emphasized. A sample must be removed from its substrate free of postdeposition contamination. These two sources of extraneous elements should be distinguished. Contamination of a film sample is easier than with most other samples. The films may be contaminated by substrate materials, the mechanical removal process, acid impurities, human handling, etc. On the other hand, trace impurities are usually attributed to the original source material or elements absorbed by the film during production. Analysis of the source material and the resulting film will distinguish absorbed film impurities.

2.2. Film Recovery

As pointed out in the introduction, a film must be recovered for analysis. Arcus has described several types of chemical and mechanical removal techniques ([2]). A good example to demonstrate film-removal problems is that of tantalum deposited on glass substrates ([3]). Tantalum films are one of the principal materials used in much of the microcircuitry manufactured in the Bell System. Because tantalum is reactive with only hydrofluoric acid or concentrated caustic under ordinary conditions, the choice of reagents to be used for chemical removal is limited ([4]). The supporting glass substrates are etched by both of these reagents, which consequently eliminate chemical removal as a film recovery method. It is impossible to determine if elements present in the substrate and detected in the film are substrate etchings or film impurities. Substrate materials have also been detected in films removed both mechanically and by means of an intermediate parting layer of graphite evaporated on the glass substrate to deposition. The intermediate parting layer does not permit the film to adhere well to the substrate. If the film is thermally oxidized, it will separate from the substrate as small flakes. Mechanical removal is also facilitated by the parting layer. However, the films almost invariably bond to at least a portion of the substrate, and small amounts of substrate material are removed with the film due to variable adhesion. This source of contamination can be eliminated, as shown in Table I. Because graphite electrodes are employed for most DC arc methods, it was the most obvious choice as a substrate material.

The mechanics of tantalum film recovery from graphite substrates is accomplished in three steps: (1) air oxidation in a muffle furnace at 600°C for two hours, (2) mechanical removal by scraping the surface with a platinum spatula, and (3) addition of graphite as a buffer to provide a one-to-one ratio of sample or standard to graphite.

There are several advantages of graphite substrates. Graphite is spectroscopically pure, inexpensive, relatively unreactive, has little outgassing, and has a low vapor pressure.

It should be pointed out that the graphite substrate technique has been applied to several types of films, such as metals, semiconductors, cermets, and insulators. These films have been produced by several processes, such as evaporation, sputtering, and plasma deposition.

2.3. Standards

Let us briefly mention the relationship of samples and standards for tantalum films. Because the bulk tantalum used as the cathode during sputtering is high purity, trace impurities are usually below 100 ppm each. However, many elements could occur in the resulting films which might not be anticipated. When the sources of film contamination, such as the various alloys used in deposition systems, the gases employed, the composition of the substrates, etc. are considered, possibly one-half of the elements in the periodic chart could be added to the film as impurities. It

Table I. Substrate Effects ([3])

Glass composition		Film impurities	
		Parting layer	Graphite substrate
Si	23%	0.3%	0.0015
B	4	0.02	ND <0.0005
Ba	21	0.03	ND <0.001
Al	4	0.02	0.0005

ND = Not detected.

is therefore safe to assume that, although certain elements should be present as a film impurity, practically any may occur. This point is important since spectrographic analyses must employ standards of known composition. The occurrence of an element never detected previously could leave the analyst without proper standards. In addition, the absence of certain elements and a knowledge of their detection limits can furnish valuable information.

2.4. Discussion

As stated in the introduction, it was assumed at the beginning of the investigation that many elements could be present as impurities. This assumption has not only proven valid, but extremely useful. For at least preliminary investigation, standards should be synthesized from a base containing many elements. The multielement base, covering the range of 1–1000 ppm, is useful for determining detected elements and assigning limits to undetected elements. In order to illustrate this point, two opposite examples are useful. First, a boron carbide plug was added as a deflector to the gas-introduction point of a sputtering system. Although in this case a boron analysis was requested, boron was present in the standards and had been regularly checked in previous films. It could be stated that, although boron had never been detected previously, it was now being contributed at about the 5 ppm level by the boron carbide plug. An opposite example would be unsuspected impurities. During a modification to some sputtering equipment, a bismuth solder was mistakenly employed, and large amounts of bismuth and other solder components were detected in a group of films during routine analysis. Because the standards contained bismuth and the other components, their concentration could easily be determined. The above also points to the necessity of monitoring film-impurity levels on a routine basis.

3. SILICON NITRIDE FILMS

Silicon nitride films provide an interesting analytical problem. It is interesting to note that they are employed as a barrier or encapsulation medium for silicon semiconductor devices due to their inactivity. Because several techniques are employed for film deposition, a rapid method to determine silicon, nitrogen, and trace impurities in many samples is desirable. An emission technique was suitable for the nitride analyses due to its small sample capability, sensitivity, speed, and the simultaneous determination of trace elements.

Our laboratory employed the device which is shown in cross section in Fig. 1 to gas stabilize a direct current arc. The emission spectra produced by the apparatus revealed a complete absence of the spectral interference due to excited cyanogen molecules. It should be realized that the arc is stabilized at atmospheric pressure with no special vacuum equipment for eliminating the CN spectral interference. A method for determining nitrogen (in addition to other metallics) by producing cyanogen excitation from carbon in graphite and nitrogen in a sample was investigated ([5,6]).

Film-recovery techniques are also important in silicon nitride analyses. Other workers have employed classical chemical techniques for film analyses and usually recover the nitrided films by chemical removal of the silicon substrate material ([7]).

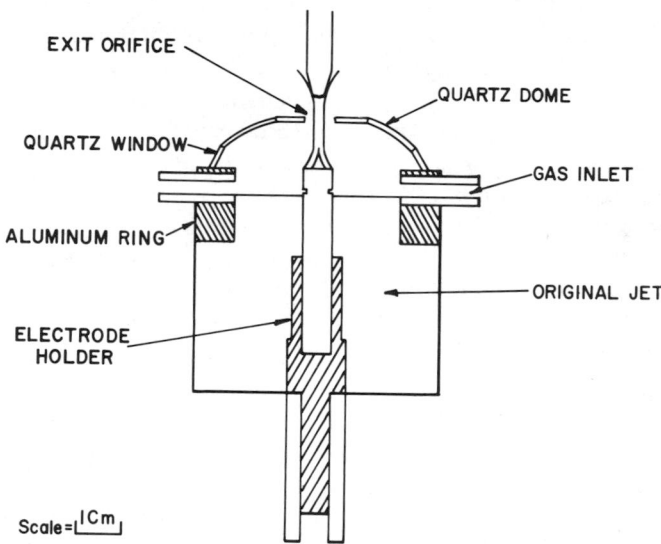

Figure 1. Solids device.

3.1. Samples

Once again for this application, substrates other than silicon offer attractive sampling procedure. Flat 2×2 cm graphite substrates were employed for film deposition. The films were consequently removed by abrading the surface with platinum. At this point, one of two techniques may be employed. The graphite may be removed by air oxidation in a muffle furnace, or it may be retained and included with the film sample. For this work the unwanted graphite was removed by oxidation in order to obtain a total film weight which was dependent only on the balance accuracy. The reason for this action was that the samples were manufactured at a higher temperature in an ammonia atmosphere. It should be emphasized that the only purpose of the firing step was to recover the film itself for microbalance weighing. In practice, this step is not necessary, as the determined total weights of silicon and nitrogen may be employed to calculate silicon and nitrogen percentages. However, these percentages are then subject to the errors for the determinations rather than the smaller error of the microbalance.

Standards were prepared by blending 325 mesh Si_3N_4, graphite and the internal standard, germanium dioxide in $3 \times 1\frac{1}{4}$ in. polystyrene vials. The tangential gases employed for arc stabilization were argon and oxygen. If oxygen is not added, the graphite electrodes and samples are not consumed and the cyanogen molecules are not formed. Two additional points are important. First, the arc will not start if oxygen is being added to the argon. Secondly, the rate of gas introduction is important. If the full flow is introduced immediately, powdered samples are often expelled from the electrodes. However, if a needle valve is added to the gas line and both gas flows are increased slowly, the samples are not expelled.

3.2. Nitrogen Blanks

Blanks on both solid materials and gases must also be considered. Both argon and oxygen must be checked for the presence of nitrogen with blank graphite electrodes. Although nitrogen has not been detected to date in the cylinder of commercial-grade argon employed for this work, commercial-grade oxygen has not proved satisfactory. However, when research-grade oxygen was employed, satisfactory blanks were obtained. It is interesting to note that the total weight of nitrogen (about 28 μg), which is contributed by the oxygen during the arcing cycle, is several times higher than the detection limit per electrode for nitrogen in the solid sample (1–5 μg). This apparent contradiction is most probably explained by observing the device and considering the excitation mechanism. Most of the oxygen is transported with the argon through the device's orifice with little sample contact. In addition, cyanogen excitation takes place in the arc's interconal region and probably decreases rapidly away from this region.

The electrodes, graphite, and GeO_2 have consistently yielded no nitrogen or blank analyses. Apparently, little or no nitrogen from air is occluded in these materials. It is interesting to note that most of the available nitrogen is detected as excited cyanogen molecules, and little or no excited atomic nitrogen is detected as indicated by the atom line at 8216 Å.

3.3. Precision

The coefficient of variation at 1θ for eighteen nitrogen and silicon demonstrations performed by one operator on three different days was determined at 6.6% for nitrogen and 7.0% for silicon. The parameters employed for the analyses are listed in Table II.

Table II. Silicon Nitride Emission Parameters

1	DC arc	16 A
2	Slit	35 μ
3	Exposure	60 sec
4	Emulsion	SA #1
5	Gas flows	Ar; 7 (l/min)
		O_2; 3 (l/min)
6	Sample weight per electrode	0.025 g
7	GeO_2	0.1%
8	Analytical lines	Ge; 3269 Å
		Si; 2987 Å
		CN; 3883 Å

3.4. Discussion

By way of review, the gas-stabilized arc permits the extension of the emission technique to include sample nitrogen. These determinations may be made easily at atmospheric pressure with little modification of most emission spectrographic equipment. If sufficient graphite is present for quantitative cyanogen formation, the basic technique should be applicable to nitrogen determinations in many types of samples.

4. ATOMIC ABSORPTION

The final subject to be considered is atomic absorption (A.A.) and its role in thin-film analyses.

Most of the sampling techniques employed for optical emission analyses may be applied to A.A. as the samples must be recovered in both cases. There are a few general, pertinent remarks which should be pointed out for A.A. analyses. The principal advantages of the A.A. technique are (1) detection limits which are about $1 \, \mu g/ml$ for most elements, and (2) reproducibility with a coefficient of variation of less than one to a few percent of the amount present.

It is important to remember that thin-film samples are always solids and usually small. It is therefore necessary to transfer the solid to a solution phase which immediately points out that the technique is destructive. In addition, sensitivity is decreased on dissolution and dilution of the sample. The decrease in sensitivity is a controversial point because one may question methods of comparing detection limits for various analytical techniques. It should be noted that for atomic absorption, if the atoms in question were freed to the neutral atomic phase directly from the solid more rapidly than from the solution, detection limits should be greater for solids.

On conversion from the solid to liquid sample phase several additional points are apparent. In order to obtain maximum sensitivity, it is often necessary to keep sample volumes small. Use of small volumes can lead to human errors in the dissolution step because of the difficulties in removing a sample from or completely dissolving a substrate. However, these problems are essentially microchemical mechanics.

Because most A.A. techniques utilize single channel units, problems can also result when performing multielement determinations. Each element determined consumes its own volume of the sample total. If the available sample is small, the time for solution nebulization must be short. This can result in insufficient burner flushing and small measurement times of the absorption signal. Both of these factors can affect the precision of the measurement.

It is also useful to mention something that should be obvious but can be a source of problems. Solutions present homogeneous samples. However, the solutions are only indicative of the solid starting material. Since the amounts of solid film is usually quite small, it is not wise to assume that it was originally homogeneous. The best solution to the problem is the use of multiple samples, which should obviate shortcomings in the sampling procedure.

So much for some of the general remarks on film analysis: let us now conclude with a few examples. The A.A. technique is an extremely convenient method of determining small amounts of material. This has really been one of the principal uses of the technique in the Bell System, as well as other industries. Weights of gold, silver, tin, lead, and a myriad of other metals are now routinely determined on piece parts that vary from extremely fine wire to printed circuit boards, and from biological samples to plating solutions.

An interesting example of thin film analysis by A.A. was based on an experiment by Shukovsky and Morton at the Engineering Research Center ([8]). Other authors ([9,10]) have reported a composition gradient in iron–nickel permalloy plated films, which affects their magnetoelastic sensitivity. The sign of the magnetostriction change is dependent on the iron content of the film, which decreases with increasing thickness until a limiting value is reached.

In this work, the dimensions of the plating cell were the limiting factor, so that only 1.2 cm of a pure copper wire with a diameter of $500\,\mu$ or 20 mils could be plated. The thickness of the plate was varied from 250 to 12,500 Å by varying the plating time. This represented a total weight of 3.6 μg of plate, or 1.5 and 2.1 μg of iron and nickel for the 1.2-cm length of the smallest sample. The copper wire itself weighed 0.018 g/cm.

The important point to emphasize here is convenience of the A.A. technique for determining small weights. A series of standards were prepared by simply adding iron and nickel solutions to measured lengths of pure copper wire. The final volume selected was 10 ml for the measured length of 1.2 cm of plated wire.

The results of these determinations for both nickel and iron are given in Fig. 2, which illustrates the composition gradient as a departure from the straight line curve.

5. SUMMARY OF THIN-FILM ANALYSES

The following is a brief summary of the three types of thin-film analyses described in this chapter.

1. Optical emission spectroscopy is employed for film-impurity determinations. The problem of postdeposition contamination may be reduced by samples prepared on graphite substrates. Film samples are compared to standards prepared from a multielement base which permits the determination of detected elements and assigning detection limits to undetected elements.

2. The solids plasma device will eliminate air and permit the determination of nitrogen and silicon nitride films. Deposition of the nitrided films on graphite substrates, in place of the usual silicon, permits rapid film recovery.

3. Atomic-absorption spectroscopy is a convenient method for determining alloying components in thin films.

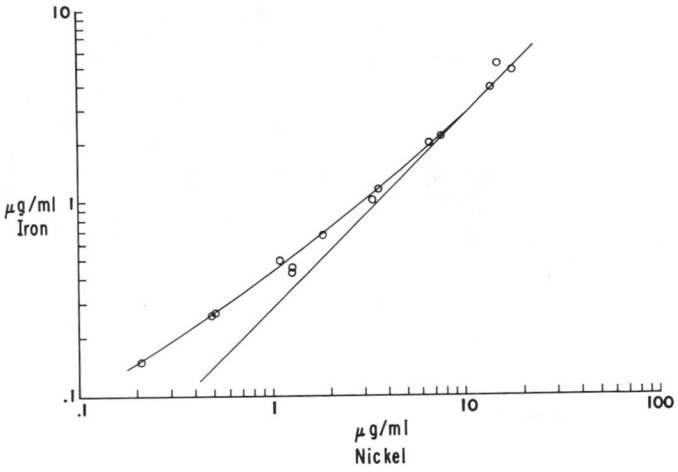

Figure 2. Composition gradient.

ACKNOWLEDGMENT

The author wishes to thank Mr. K. L. Morton for his assistance and suggestions in much of the work described, and Dr. C. Altman for his help in preparing the paper.

REFERENCES

1. K. H. Behrndt, Preparation of Thin Films, Trans. ASM Thin Film Seminar, 1963, ASM, Metals Park, Ohio, pl. 1964.
2. A. A. Arcus, Emission Spectrographic Analyses of Thin Films and Residues, paper presented at the International Conference on Spectroscopy, University of Maryland, June 1962.
3. J. D. Nohe, Emission Spectrographic Analyses of Tantalum Thin Films, *Appl. Spectr.* **21**, 364 (1967).
4. *Handbook of Chemistry and Physics*, Hodgman, C. D., ed., Chemical Rubber Publishing Co., Cleveland, Ohio, 1960–61, 42nd Ed., pp. 666–667.
5. L. D. Frederickson, Jr. and L. Smith, *Anal. Chem.* **23**, 742–744 (1951).
6. E. F. Runge and F. R. Bryan, The Determination of Nitrogen in Austenitic Steels Using a Cyanogen Bond Head, *Appl. Spectr.* **10**, 68 (1956).
7. C. H. Lee, T. L. Chu, and G. A. Gruber, Properties of Silicon Nitride Films, paper presented at Symposium on Silicon Nitride, Electrochemical Society, Philadelphia, Pennsylvania, October 1966.
8. H. B. Shukovsky and K. L. Morton, unpublished work, Western Electric Co., Inc., Engineering Research Center, Princeton, New Jersey, 1967.
9. I. W. Wolf, Composition and Thickness Effects on Magnetic Properties of Electro-deposited Thin Ni–Fe Films, *J. Electrochem. Soc.* **108**, 959 (1961).
10. M. E. Henstock and E. S. Spencer-Timms. The Composition of Thin Electro-deposited Alloy Films with Special Reference to Nickel–Iron, *Trans. Inst. Metal Finishing* **40**, 179–185 (1963).

VII. RF SPARK SOURCE MASS SPECTROMETRY FOR THE ANALYSIS OF SURFACE FILMS

D. L. Malm

Bell Telephone Laboratories, Incorporated
Murray Hill, New Jersey

The RF spark source mass spectrograph is applicable to a wide variety of surface film studies by virtue of its high sensitivity and surface-sensing ability. This paper describes some of the more unique applications of these features. These applications include the determination of dopant levels in the ten to ten thousand ppm atom fraction range in sputtered tantalum capacitor films 4000 Å thick, the detection and identification of films equivalent to 0.04 of a monolayer in thickness, the detection of impurities in the 1×10^{-9} atom fraction range in a drop of liquid by sampling the residue left after evaporation, and the detection of micro and nanogram quantities of elements in the form of precipitates collected on silver membrane filters. Included with the discussions are descriptions of the sampling techniques appropriate to each application along with some recent innovations which are increasing the present scope of the method.

A brief history of the development of the technique and a description of the instrument is included.

1. INTRODUCTION

The inherent high sensitivity and surface-sensing ability of the RF spark source mass spectrograph make it a logical approach for analysis in a wide variety of surface film problems.

For example, recent analytical demands in thin-film technology require a means for quantitative measurements of intentionally added impurities in sputtered tantalum capacitor films. To a large degree the RF spark source has fulfilled this need.

In addition, the detection and identification of films equivalent to 0.04 of a monolayer in thickness have been demonstrated under controlled conditions, thus indicating the method's usefulness for the detection and identification of very small amounts of foreign material present on a surface.

The technique has been further exploited for the analysis of impurities in liquids by first evaporating the liquid on a specially prepared surface and then sampling the residues.

Improved sampling techniques such as the spinning electrode approach, which minimizes the interference from the substrate, are constantly increasing the scope of useful applications for the analysis of thin films.

2. HISTORY

Professor A. J. Dempster and his associates first demonstrated the possibilities of the spark source for mass spectrometric work in 1934 ([1]). During World War II the further development and application of this method indicated that it was not only a very sensitive technique but also one of broad applicability.

In 1951 Gorman, Jones, and Hipple, utilizing standard samples and electrical detection, demonstrated that the results could be made quantitative ([2]).

Hannay, at Bell Telephone Laboratories, selected the spark source for general analytical work on the grounds that it should be relatively nonselective in that all elements should have about the same detection sensitivity, and a substantial gain in sensitivity could be obtained utilizing the best photographic plates available. This unit consisted of a double focusing mass spectrograph utilizing the Mattauch Herzog geometry with a pulsed, radio-frequency spark source ([3]). With this arrangement, all masses of an unknown sample could be simultaneously recorded. Subsequently, Hannay and Ahearn demonstrated that impurities of at least 0.1 ppm atom fraction could be detected and that the mass spectrographic response was directly proportional to the concentration over a large range.

Finally, in 1958, the first commercial instruments became available. These greatly improved versions can, under favorable conditions, achieve sensitivity levels in the ppb range.

3. INSTRUMENTATION

A diagram of a typical spark source mass spectrograph of the Mattauch–Herzog design is illustrated in Fig. 1. In order to discuss the method of ion formation and mass analysis utilizing this geometry, the

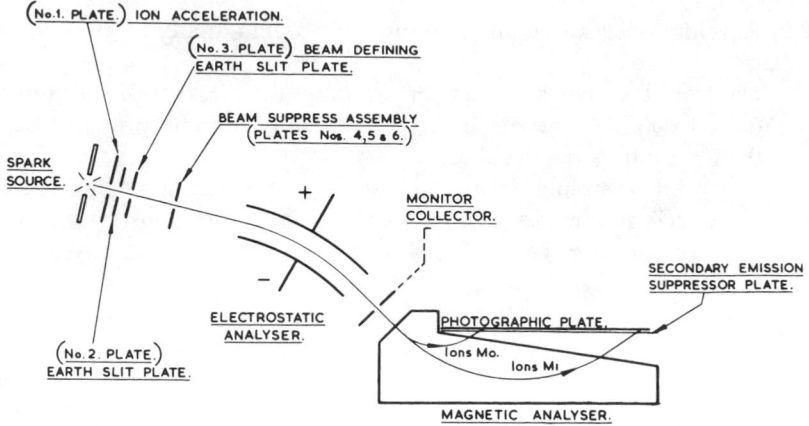

Figure 1. Mattauch–Herzog mass spectrograph.

components, all enclosed in a high vacuum, may be conveniently divided into three groups.

First, the RF spark source: Here, positive ions are produced for analysis. The spark is formed utilizing a trigger circuit which provides pulses to control the operation of an RF oscillator power amplifier arrangement coupled to the electrodes via a high-voltage, high-frequency transformer. The electrodes forming the spark normally consist of the sample material being analyzed.

Second, the electrostatic and magnetic analyzers: The spark source, being a high voltage device, does not produce monoenergetic ions. In fact, the ions exhibit an energy spread of 2–3 kV. This characteristic imposes the necessity for velocity focusing in addition to the conventional requirement of directional focusing. The Mattauch–Herzog geometry copes with this problem by providing a combination of electric and magnetic fields connected in tandem. As the ion beam passes through the electrostatic analyzer, velocity dispersion occurs. The exit slit allows only a narrow energy band of ions to pass through to the magnetic sector where mass analysis occurs.

Third, the detector: As the ions with divergent paths emerge from the magnetic analyzer they are brought into focus in a plane beyond the analyzer exit. The photoplate, which is positioned in this plane, intercepts and records the density and mass positions of the ions produced in the spark. In spite of some disadvantages, the photoplate is used almost to the exclusion of other devices for general analytical work because of its integrating qualities and its ability to record simultaneously nearly the entire mass range found in the periodic table of the elements.

4. APPLICATIONS

The spark source is being used in a wide variety of analytical applications for the study of solids. There are several reasons for its popularity and growth.

First is its very high detection sensitivity, whether defined in terms of low concentrations of impurities in a matrix (ppb atom fraction range) or by the total amount of sample needed for detection (10^{11} atoms).

Second, the method is relatively nonselective for the elements in that the detection sensitivity for most elements is within a factor of 5.

In addition, the RF spark source is inherently well suited for sampling surfaces in that the very nature of the method provides for the vaporization, ionization, and removal of successive layers of surface material as sparking progresses with time.

5. SURFACE STUDIES

Surface-film analyses have been applied to a number of problems. In order to characterize these more clearly, several distinctions will be made. The first involves alien surface contamination; second, intentional surface contamination; and third, sputtered films.

The general technique used is to scan the sample surface with a probe electrode. Variations in this approach are necessary for specific applications and their description will be included with the discussion of the individual categories.

5.1. Alien Surface Contamination

Alien surface contamination may be described as an unwanted surface film on a substrate. It may range in thickness from fractional portions of a monolayer to several microns and may have varying degrees of uniformity. This category includes material which may have been chemically or mechanically deposited on a surface. These could be residues left as a result of poor cleaning techniques, machining, polishing, or etching processes, or from the condensation of vapors on a surface, just to name a few.

The importance of the detection and identification of this type of contamination both in the solid state material sciences and in critical electronic applications is immediately apparent. Normally, the qualitative identification of surface films in this instance is relatively straightforward.

5.1.1. *Detection*

The primary problem in studying films less than $5\,\mu$ thick is distinguishing the surface contamination from bulk impurities in the substrate.

This is due to the fact that the spark normally will penetrate completely through the surface film being analyzed. This complicates the spectra by including the substrate material as well as the thin impurity surface layer.

Early applications of intentional contamination to problems of this nature demonstrated how this distinction can be made ([4]). As was previously noted, the spark initially contacts the sample surface and continues to erode material away as sparking time increases. If an impurity is present in the substrate the characteristic line of that impurity will persist in successive recordings of that spectra. However, if an element were present only on the surface the characteristic line would show a marked decrease in intensity after the first recording.

This differentiation is illustrated in Fig. 2. In exposures A, B, and C, the Al^{+2} line is monitored in a matrix of nickel. In each case the same total number of ions was recorded on the photoplate. It is apparent that

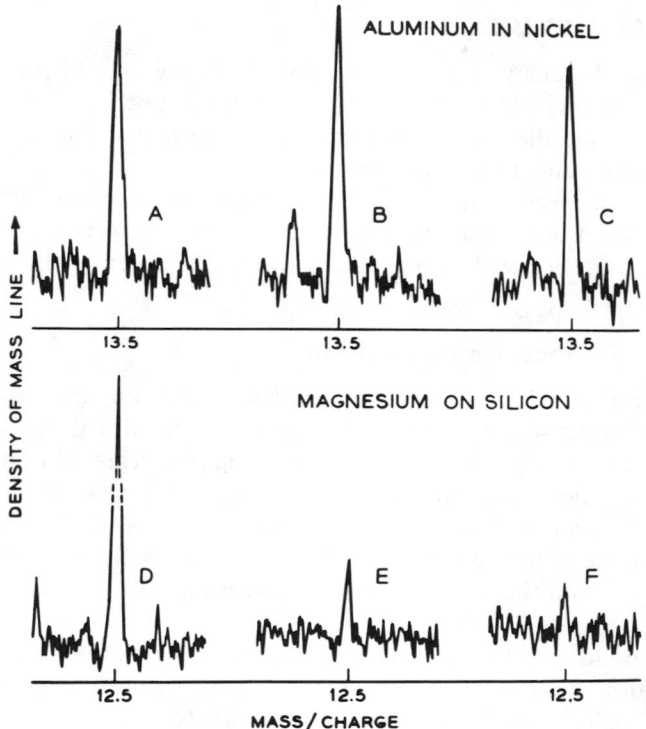

Figure 2. Density records for mass line of bulk impurity *vs.* surface contaminant. (A, B, C) aluminum as a bulk impurity in nickel. Mass line 13.5 (Al^{+2}) in successive spectra; (D, E, F) magnesium as surface contaminant on silicon. Mass line 12.5 (Mg^{+2}) in successive spectra ([4]).

there is no significant deterioration of the line intensity, therefore indicating that aluminum exists as a bulk impurity.

Conversely, exposures D, E, and F, illustrate the Mg^{+2} line from a silicon spectrum. Here, as successive spectra are recorded, a reduction in line intensity of about ten is apparent, thus indicating the magnesium is a surface contamination.

These, of course, are prime illustrations. Many times in work of this sort the distinction is not as apparent, as in the case of surface residues left by exacting semiconductor cleaning operations, in which only very minute quantities of foreign material may be present on the surface and cannot be distinguished from bulk impurities.

5.2. Intentional Surface Contamination

5.2.1. *Residues*

The use of controlled-deposition techniques of residues and films on surfaces has been helpful in the determination of sensitivity and detection limits in many surface study problems.

For example, the ultimate film thickness that can be detected is determined by the area that is available to the spark for sampling. In early work, surface contaminants that were equivalent to 0.04 monolayer were detected and identified. In this experiment, one monolayer of indium was deposited on a pair of germanium electrodes with the geometry illustrated in Fig. 3. The point-probe electrode scanned the 0.080 in. area indicated. The density record obtained is shown in Fig. 4. The detection of the two isotopes of indium, 115 (96% abundance) and 113 (4% abundance), was easily done. The response from the indium 113 line is then equivalent to

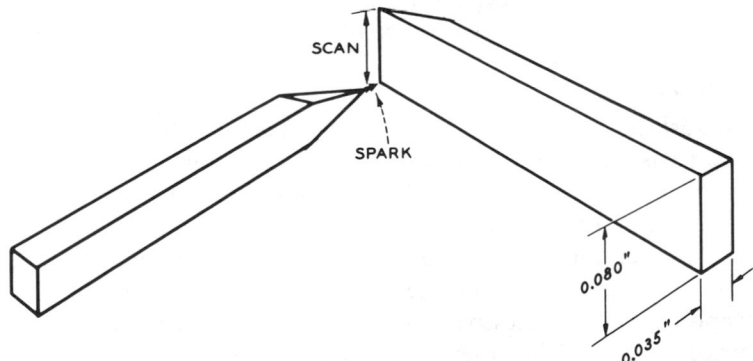

Figure 3. Electrodes for surface contamination studies in which area explored by spark is increased by manual scanning ([4]).

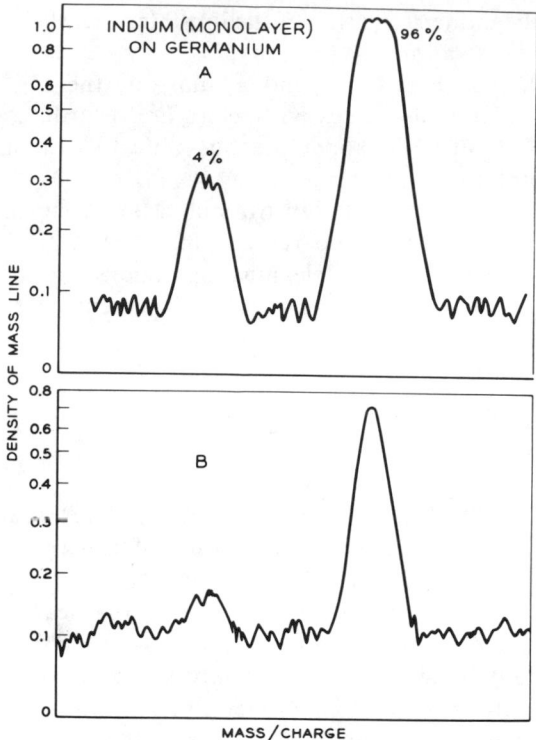

Figure 4. Density record for indium mass lines from one monatomic layer deposited on germanium surface ([4]).

0.04 of a monolayer. It is evident from this experiment that the equivalent to 0.01 of a monolayer can be detected.

5.2.2. *Liquids*

The surface-sensing ability for the study of intentional surface contamination has been further exploited to study impurities in liquids. This is accomplished by first evaporating the liquid under study on a clean surface consisting of a material which will produce a minimum of spectral interference. The liquid evaporates and leaves an irregular film of residue on the prepared surface which is then spark-scanned with a probe electrode. The evaporation of successive droplets of liquid also serves as a preconcentration method in order to improve sensitivity.

Ahearn ([4]), in an early fluid drop experiment, utilized a deionized water sample doped with beryllium, sulfur, chromium, copper, arsenic, silver, and lead. One drop of this doped water was dried on the tip of a high-purity silicon electrode and allowed to evaporate. All of the dopants were detected in the subsequent mass spectrum.

Table I lists the concentration of the particular isotope of the dopant used for detection along with the density of the corresponding mass line. These data indicate that impurities equal to or less than a concentration of 1×10^{-9} atom fraction can be detected with this method.

Table I. Mass Spectrographic Detection of Impurities Introduced into Deionized Water ([4])

Impurity	Isotope	Mass line m/c	Density	Concentration, atom fraction
Beryllium	9	9	0.44	1.1×10^{-9}
Chromium	53	53	0.12	1.0×10^{-9}
Copper	65	65	0.06	0.9×10^{-9}
Arsenic	75	75	0.33	1.0×10^{-9}
Silver	107	107	<0.02*	1.2×10^{-9}
Lead	207	103.5	0.04	5.8×10^{-9}
Sulfur	32	10.67	0.11	22.0×10^{-9}

*Visually detected.

This technique has been successfully used by Chastagner ([5]) for the detection of impurities in the 1 ppb range in 30-mg drops of heavy water moderator from water-moderated nuclear reactors. The small amount of sample required was an added incentive in this case, due to the problems involved in handling a radioactive moderator.

When low concentrations of impurities are being sought in a comparatively large matrix of solute, such as encountered in electroplating solutions, microcrystals of the solute may form on the substrate surface as the amount of evaporated residue increases. These microcrystals often will not adhere to the surface when subjected to the conditions existing in the spark. In this special case preconcentration by evaporation of more drops becomes self-defeating.

5.2.3. Precipitates

A recent investigation by Luke at BTL ([6]) may significantly overcome this problem of matrix interference resulting from preconcentration by evaporation mentioned above. In this case a coprecipitating element and a suitable precipitating reagent are used to precipitate microgram amounts of most elements quantitatively, leaving the larger mass of solute in solution. Microgram quantities are well within the limits of sensitivity of the spark source. However, Luke has exploited the X-ray spectrograph for rapid semiquantitative analysis of 64 elements down to the 1–0.1 μg range. For spark source application, samples of the precipitates have been collected on silver membranes and the residue spark scanned with a gold probe electrode. Preliminary tests of the feasibility of this approach for spark source work yielded 0.1 ng sensitivity for Sn, 1.0 ng for B, Fe, and Cu and at least 10 ng for Be. These sensitivities were obtained under very unrefined conditions which are now in the process of being improved. The ultimate sensitivity will, of course, be limited by the interference from all sources, such as the blank, and the ability to obtain quantitative precipitation at low levels. The spark source will not compete with the speed, accuracy, and precision in the useful range of the X-ray spectrograph. However, it may, in many instances, supplement the X-ray work by virtue of increasing the sensitivity for many elements into the nano- and picogram ranges and by including Na, F, B, Be, and Li, which are either difficult or impossible to work with in X-ray spectrographic analysis. The application of this preconcentration method for spark source study has just recently been introduced in our laboratory and therefore many questions are yet to be answered.

In any of the above applications it is imperative that suitable blanks be run to determine the presence of unwanted interference from the substrate. In the case of the fluid drop evaporation technique a high-purity semiconductor material such as silicon or germanium is suitable. In examining precipitates one is presently limited to the porous silver membrane which, in theory, is quite desirable.

The water drop experiment by Ahearn and the utilization of the precipitation method by Luke for preconcentration are more impressive when applied to water pollution studies and water samples of geochemical interest. Biological applications may include the study of body fluids.

5.2.4. Techniques

In spite of the fact that the method can detect very thin films it lacks precise control of the depth of spark penetration into the sampled layers of atoms. This deficiency is evident in the study of diffusion boundaries and interface problems. In these instances it is very difficult to distinguish any change in the concentration of the diffused element with depth. The problem is that the depth to which the diffusion boundary extends is usually less than the total depth of penetration of the spark. As the entire volume of the diffusion layer is consumed in one scan, no change in the concentration of the diffusion material can be detected. The sampling depth of $3-5\,\mu$ experienced with slow scanning techniques is much too gross for the more critical needs just mentioned.

In an effort to circumvent the problems of controlling the sampling depth, controlled-etching techniques have been used to remove comparatively small amounts of the diffusion layer systematically. After each etching operation a spark scan of the remaining total surface volume was made. Crude estimates of the diffusion rate may be made by monitoring the decrease in the concentration of the diffused element as successive portions of the diffusion layers are removed. This is a laborious operation at best, but has been used as a stopgap solution when other factors limited the use of alternative methods. Some control over the sampling depth may be regulated instrumentally by adjusting the spark intensity and by controlling the time the spark is permitted to continue at a given point on the surface.

The spark intensity may be adjusted by changing the spark parameters: i.e., repetition rate, pulse length, and spark voltage. However, the minimum intensity needed for only superficial penetration of the surface is limited in that the spark must still be intense enough to produce an ion current which is adequate to satisfy the transmission requirements of the instrument in order to obtain a spectrum in a reasonable time period; it is therefore of only minor importance. The time that the spark remains at any one point can be controlled by moving the surface being tested under a stationary probe electrode. This is accomplished mechanically with varying degrees of complexity ranging from single spark, manual scanning of the surface with a suitable electrode, to a high-speed rotating disc, depending on the particular depth resolution requirement of the surface under study.

Sweeney *et al.* ([7]) recently described a method whereby the depth resolution is significantly improved by effectively limiting the penetration of the spark sampling by utilizing the source arrangement shown in Fig. 5.

The sample to be analyzed is in the form of a disc mounted on the shaft of a battery-powered electric motor and rotated at 1750 rpm. A stationary electrode of a noninterfering high-purity metal is located near the edge of the disc and less than $25\,\mu$ from the surface in order to form a spark. This system presents fresh material to the spark on each half-cycle of the spark. The volume of material excited at these half-cycle intervals was estimated to be about $10^{-12}-10^{-14}$ cc. The time involved for the ionization of each increment is estimated to be only a fraction of a microsecond.

Spectra were obtained using a silicon disc and a gold probe which revealed lines corresponding to gold, silicon, carbon, and oxygen. It was later established that concentrations in the order of 0.1% were

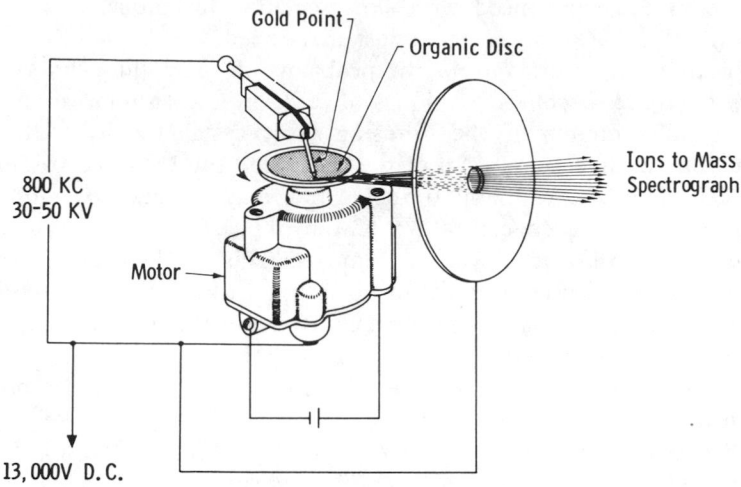

Figure 5. Mass spectrographic rotating electrode source ([7]).

obtainable with this small sample volume. The depth of sampling was established by making electron micrographs of the silicon surface as shown in Fig. 6 ([8]). The craters are in the order of 4000 Å in diameter and have a depth of about 2000 Å. This graphically illustrates the large reduction in sampling depth made possible by the spinning electrode technique.

Scala *et al.* ([9]) suggested that because the spinning electrode distributes the spark energy over a large area, there is a significant reduction of time during which the sampled volume is at the temperatures attained in the spark. This characteristic offers great possibilities in the study of organic films; the catalytic degradation of the sample on prolonged exposures to the elevated temperatures encountered with slower scanning techniques is minimized with the spinning sample, because new undegraded material is continually being made available for sparking.

Another innovation in surface sampling devices which is being developed at BTL is shown in Fig. 7. It utilizes an external motor coupled magnetically through a viewing port to the sampling device mounted in the source vacuum chamber. The external variable speed motor is a simplification of similar devices used in the source chamber.

In addition to the variable speed rotation of the sample beneath the stationary electrode, which allows the sampling of a track along the diameter of the circular disc, the center of the disc may move along the axis of the instrument, to provide a larger annular area of sampling and thus increase the amount of available sample significantly.

Figure 6. Replica electron micrograph on silicon illustrating half-cycle sampling and one-cycle sampling ([7]).

Initial experiments with palladium films 5000 Å thick sputtered on prepared copper discs showed that the contribution to the spectrum from the copper substrate and gold probe electrode was only from 1–5 % of the total ions recorded. This is a reduction by about two orders of magnitude compared to results from the slower scanning techniques. This significant reduction of interference from the probe and substrate yields a corresponding increase in sensitivity for elements in the film which would often be masked by their presence in the substrates and should help to increase the scope of application to thin film problems.

5.3. Sputtered Films

Recent analytical demands in thin-film technology require a means for quantitative measurements of intentionally added impurities in sputtered

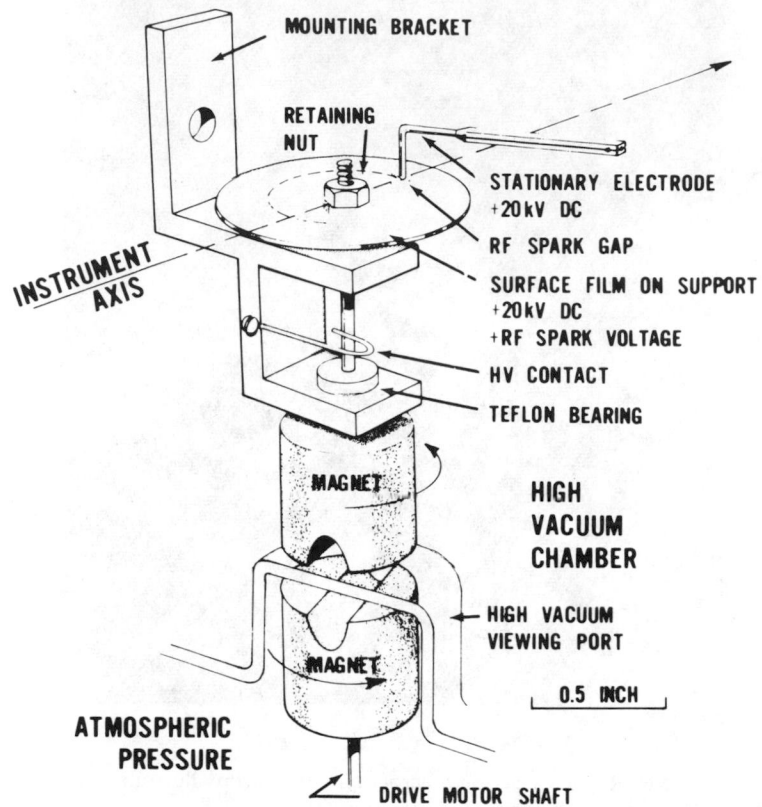

Figure 7. Thin film sampling device.

tantalum capacitor films. It has been demonstrated that with the aid of an internal standard and a sample-scanning technique which samples the film on the substrate, thus eliminating any chemical separations, quantitative estimates of molybdenum additive in films 4000 Å thick can be made with an average relative error of ±23% ([10]).

A concentration range of 0.02–3.1% atomic fraction of molybdenum in tantalum films was studied. Because adequate sensitivity is attained without consuming the entire available sample, it is reasonable to predict that sensitivities of 10 ppm atomic or less may be reached.

Results show a linear increase in the molybdenum concentration as the molybdenum–tantalum sputtering surface ratio increases. Once this relationship has been established, films with the desired molybdenum concentration can be produced without the need for further chemical analysis. Mass spectrographic results also indicate that the molybdenum additive is homogeneously distributed in the tantalum film.

For the purpose of this study, eight groups of tantalum films 4000 Å thick were sputtered on spectrographically pure carbon blocks with a surface area of about 40 mm^2. Increasing amounts of molybdenum were simultaneously sputtered with the tantalum in each group. The method used to add the molybdenum to the film consists of simply affixing wires of the additive to the tantalum cathode. The control is achieved by varying the ratio of the area of the additive wire to that of the tantalum cathode by changing the number and diameter of the molybdenum wires as described by Axelrod *et al.* ([10]). In this study, increasing numbers of 0.010-in. molybdenum wires were added, with the exception of two groups, one of which utilized a 0.005-in. wire, and one of which utilized a 0.001-in. wire. However, with this method only a limited estimate can be made of the additive concentration in the film. Therefore, further mass spectrographic study was necessary.

5.3.1. *Method*

The analyses were made with an Associated Electrical Industries, Ltd., MS-7 mass spectrograph. The positive ion source is a pulsed vacuum spark between a probe electrode and the sample surface. The spark voltage was ~20 kV, the pulse length 25 μsec, and the repetition rate 10 pulses/sec. These conditions were maintained throughout the analyses. The vacuum conditions with the spark off were ~3–5 × 10^{-9} torr in the source and analyzer of the instrument.

This method produces a constant ion contribution from the film to the spectrum during sparking, and allows a graded series of photographic exposures to be made in which the ion intensity measured from the photoplate is directly proportional to the ion exposure measured at the monitor. The exposures used ranged from 0.003 × 10^{-9}–10 × 10^{-9} C depending on the amount of molybdenum in the film. The optical transmission of the lines in question was measured with a microphotometer and converted to ion intensity by means of a photographic plate calibration. From the plots in Fig. 8 of the molybdenum ion intensity and that of the niobium internal standard as a function of the exposure, the concentration of the molybdenum can be derived from the ratio of the niobium exposures for a given ion intensity.

The sample configuration when mounted in the source is shown in Fig. 9. The probe is a 0.020-in. gold wire, and the substrate on which the film is deposited is a spectrographically pure carbon block, 0.1 × 0.5 × 0.05 in. thick. The probe and substrate were previously analyzed and were found

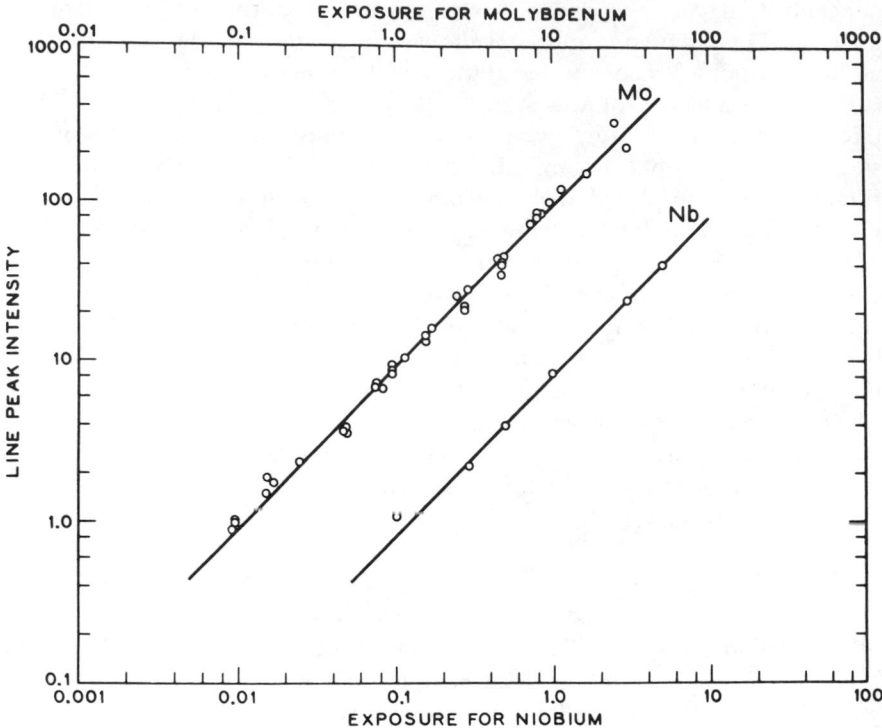

Figure 8. Log/log plot of peak intensity *vs.* ion exposure.

free from the additive, internal standard, and interfering lines. The spark is formed between the stationary gold probe and the surface on which the film has been deposited. It penetrates the sample surface to a depth of about three microns, which is enough to consume the film and part of the substrate. In order to obtain a constant ion contribution from the film, the necessary sensitivity, and a graded series of exposures, a fresh sample surface must be continuously presented for sparking.

This is attained by providing a continuous motion of the sample beneath the gold probe while constantly maintaining the spark. The uniform motion of the sample across the short axis is provided by a slow speed motor, which is connected to the sample manipulator from outside the source. After each traverse, the spark is stopped and a fresh surface made available by manually shifting the sample in the long-axis direction. This routine is repeated until the desired exposures have been completed.

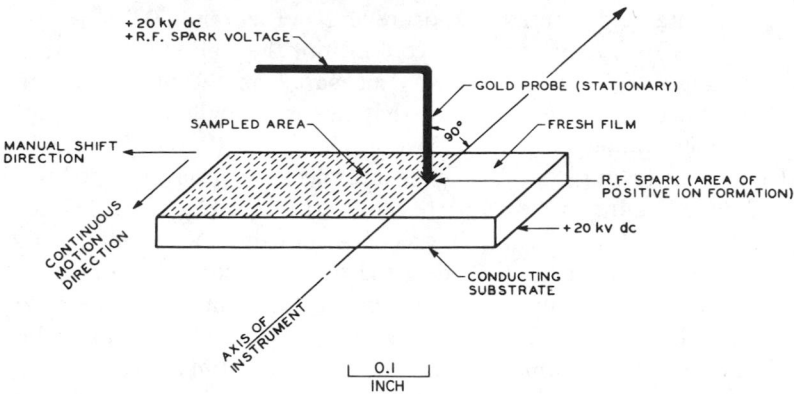

Figure 9. Electrode configuration for sample scanning technique surface film study.

5.3.2. Results and Discussion

The mass spectrographic results for the molybdenum concentration in the tantalum film are shown in Table II. Cross checks were obtained in two cases with a photometric method and are included for comparison.

Normally, an isotope line from the matrix material is selected as the internal standard. However, in this case the ^{181}Ta (99.988% abundant)

Table II. Molybdenum Additive Tantalum Film

Number of 0.010-in. Mo wires added	MS-7 wt.% Mo	Photometric value (wt.% Mo)
8	1.62	1.79
6	1.3	—
4	0.72	0.8
3	0.63	—
2	0.35	—
1	0.18	—
0.5	0.098	—
0.1	0.015	—

Note: The designation "number of Mo wires added" refers to the number of 0.010-in. Mo wires that were affixed to the tantalum sputtering cathode. The 0.5 and 0.1 designate a 0.005-in. and 0.001-in. wire.

line is not suitable, because at exposure levels of less than 0.001×10^{-9} C, which are necessary for the plate calibration, the ion exposure measured at the monitor and the ion intensity measured on the photoplate are no longer proportional. It is suspected that this is partially due to inaccurate exposure measurements at these levels. The ^{180}Ta (0.012% abundant) is inadequate in the longer uniform exposures because of serious line broadening and plate fogging in the area adjacent to the line. Therefore the niobium impurity in the tantalum cathode was chosen as the internal standard. The niobium value was predetermined in the tantalum cathode to be 144 ppm atomic. This value was obtained with a photometric method and is accepted in this experiment as a standard value. The mass spectrographic value for niobium in the same sample was determined as 305 ppm atomic without the aid of prepared standards. A relative sensitivity coefficient (RSC = mass spectrographic value/standard value) of ~ 2.1 is therefore assumed, and all mass spectrographic values for niobium are adjusted to conform with the standard value.

The data plotted in Fig. 8 shows the mass spectrographic value of the niobium intensity to be directly proportional to the exposure. This indicates that the internal standard niobium and therefore the tantalum contribute a constant fraction of ions being analyzed, and that the molybdenum is homogeneously distributed when compared to the niobium and therefore to the tantalum film.

The straight line curve of Fig. 10 made from the data in Table II indicates that, under the sputtering conditions used, the rate of deposition of the molybdenum is proportional to the molybdenum area of the sputtering surface. Also, with this information, if the number, diameter, and position of the molybdenum wires on the tantalum cathode are duplicated in subsequent film sputtering, satisfactory concentration values can be obtained directly from the curve, thus eliminating the need for further chemical analysis.

The possibility that there may be interference caused by a ^{92}Mo^{1}H (m/e 93) with ^{93}Nb is minimized, as there is no evidence for the ^{98}Mo^{1}H (m/e 99) in the clear mass position on the photographic plate.

The photometric results for molybdenum in the tantalum film when compared with the mass spectrographic result indicate an RSC value slightly greater than one. Considering the analytical error, no correction was made.

From this study it is evident that the analysis of molybdenum additive in tantalum films can be accomplished with a mass spectrograph and the sample scanning technique. There are good indications that other additives in tantalum films can be studied, if the sampling probe and substrate material are carefully selected so that their contribution to the spectrum

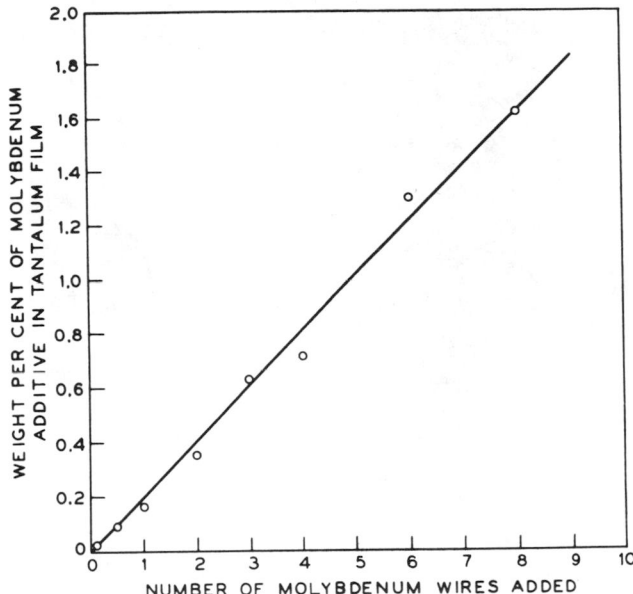

Figure 10. Linear plot of molybdenum concentration *vs.* number of molybdenum wires added to tantalum sputtering cathode for film deposition.

does not interfere with the additive or standard isotope lines. Other tantalum film studies are in progress where useful information is being gathered concerning contamination of the films during sputtering. It is interesting to note here that recent films studied with the slow scanning technique were deposited on glass, ceramic and sapphire. The 5000 Å thick Ta films, when properly prepared for spark source analysis, conduct very well in spite of the insulating substrate. An enlarged view of a spark-scanned Ta film deposited on a sapphire substrate is illustrated in Fig. 11. The spark "track" is 0.020-in. wide and close examination reveals closely spaced and overlapping spark craters produced during the slow scanning technique. This is in marked contrast with high speed disc depicted in Fig. 6. However, the slower scanning was adequate for this study.

6. SUMMARY

Certain factors concerning the spark source for use as an analytical approach to surface film studies should be emphasized.

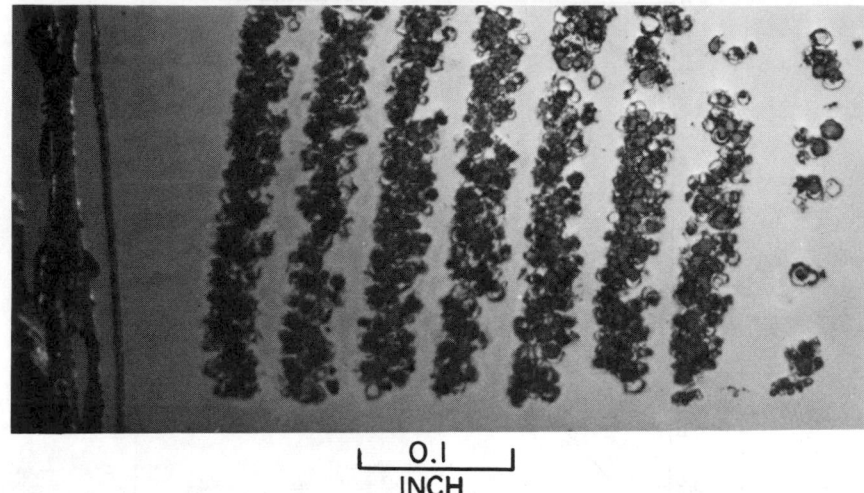

Figure 11. Enlarged view of spark scanned tantalum film 5000 Å thick on sapphire.

First, in the absence of reliable prepared standards the results in most cases are semiquantitative. The exceptions are the recent application of the precipitation technique, where standards may be more readily produced and certain sputtered film problems, where internal standards are present in the form of inherent homogeneous impurities.

Second, the nature of the problem precludes preliminary surface treatment for the purpose of eliminating secondary contamination introduced during handling. Therefore, it is necessary that procedures include the use of positive pressure, filtered air hoods during all phases of preparation, and judicious use of airtight containers for transporting, in order to insure that the surface condition of interest remains unaltered.

However, in spite of these difficulties, the method has been successfully used in numerous surface study problems and provided analytical data that could not be obtained by any alternate method. The unique combination of high sensitivity and surface-sensing ability, relatively equal sensitivity for all the elements, the simultaneous recording of almost the entire range of elements found in the periodic table, and the elimination of chemical separation of the film from the substrate make it a powerful tool for thin-film investigations.

REFERENCES

1. A. J. Dempster, *Proc. Phil. Soc.* **75**, 755 (1935); *Rev. Sci. Instr.* **7**, 46 (1936).
2. J. G. Gorman, E. J. Jones, and J. A. Hipple, *Anal. Chem.* **23**, 438 (1951).

3. N. B. Hannay, *Rev. Sci. Instr.* **25**, 644 (1954).
4. A. J. Ahearn, *J. Appl. Phys.* **32**, 1197–1201 (1961).
5. P. Chastagner, Presented at Twelfth Annual Conference on Mass Spectrometry and Allied Topics, June 7–12, 1964, Montreal, Canada, Paper No. 55.
6. C. L. Luke, *Anal. Chim. Acta*, April (1968) in press.
7. G. G. Sweeney, W. M. Hickham, and L. B. Crider, Fourteenth Annual Conference on Mass Spectroscopy and Allied Topics, May 22–27, 1966, Dallas, Texas, Paper No. 44.
8. W. M. Hickham and Y. L. Sandler, *Surface Effects in Detection* (J. I. Bregman and A. Dravnieks, eds.) pp. 192–196, Spartan Books (1965).
9. L. C. Scala, G. G. Sweeney, and W. M. Hickham, *Analysis of Organic Thin Layers Using the Spinning Electrode Spark Source Mass Spectrograph*, Fourteenth Annual Conference on Mass Spectroscopy and Allied Topics, May 22–27, 1966, Dallas, Texas, 1966, Paper No. 43.
10. N. N. Axelrod, B. H. Vromen, H. G. Guberman, D. J. Harrington, and N. Schwartz, *Asymmetric Conduction in Anodic Oxides Formed from Sputtered Tantalum Alloy Films*, Electro-Chemical Society Meeting, Cleveland, Ohio, May 1–5, 1966.

VIII. CHEMICAL AND STRUCTURAL EVALUATION OF THIN GLASS FILMS

W. A. Pliskin

IBM Components Division, East Fishkill Facility
Hopewell Junction, New York

Due to the importance of thin-film insulators for diffusion masking, crossovers insulation, and for surface passivation of semiconductor devices, a great deal of interest in glass and oxide films has been generated. To evaluate and compare various glass films with regard to composition, structure, and water and chemical stability, a combination of optical and spectroscopic techniques have been used.

The evaluations include the effect of various treatments such as thermal annealing and densification, exposure to high humidity and temperature, etching, etc. on the film properties. The use of these techniques will be discussed in detail. Comparisons will be made among insulating films formed by RF sputtering, fusing sedimented glass, pyrolysis, and electron-gun evaporation, and also with thermally grown silicon dioxide.

1. INTRODUCTION

With the increased use of microminiaturization it has become important to evaluate various thin glass films for prospective use in the manufacture of devices ([1-4]). These glass films must satisfy a variety of requirements. They may serve as diffusion masks, crossover insulators, or as passivating films for complicated monolithic devices. In addition they must be water and chemically stable and above all compatible with the structure of the device. It would be difficult to evaluate on actual devices all the various glass films which could be made. Methods were therefore sought to make it relatively easy to perform a chemical and structural evaluation of the glass films prior to application on actual device structures. If the preliminary evaluations showed specific glass films to be satisfactory, they then could be tested on device structures. A combination of optical and spectroscopic techniques were found to be very useful in evaluating and comparing various glass films with regard to composition, structure, and water and chemical stability. No one technique in itself was sufficient for the evaluation of the films, but from a combination of these techniques useful evaluations could be made.

The evaluations include the effect on the film properties of various treatments such as thermal annealing and densification, high humidity and temperature, etching, etc. The use of these techniques will be discussed in detail. Comparisons will be made among insulating films formed by RF sputtering, fusing sedimented glass, pyrolysis, and electron-gun evaporation, and also with thermally grown silicon dioxide. By showing the use of these simple techniques for various specific examples, the method can best be elucidated. Although the main emphasis is on infrared spectroscopy, its application is to some extent limited and it must be used with caution, as is shown with specific examples.

2. EXPERIMENTAL TECHNIQUES

2.1. Infrared Spectroscopy

In some cases, compositional and structural evaluation of glass films can be made easily by use of infrared spectroscopy. By comparing the intensities of various infrared absorption bands, one can determine the relative amounts of various components in the glasses. In the case of transmitted spectra, the absorption band intensities are roughly proportional to the film thicknesses, i.e., they obey Beer's law fairly well and are much better for quantitative determinations than are reflective spectra [5]. Although the intensity of the absorption is given best by the integrated intensity, in many cases, sufficiently accurate composition comparisons can be made utilizing the optical density (O.D.) of absorption bands [5].

In addition, infrared spectroscopy is especially useful for detecting the presence of impurities such as water and silanol groups in the glass by their characteristic absorption bands, about 3400 cm^{-1} for water, and about 3650 cm^{-1} for hydrogen bonded silanol groups [6,7]. The intensity of these bands is an indication of the number of water or silanol groups present and indirectly is an indication of the porosity of the glass film.

Information can also be obtained from the exact position and half-width of some absorption bands. For example, the exact half-width and position of the Si–O stretching band at ~ 1050–1100 cm^{-1} in SiO_2 is strongly influenced by the bond strain, stoichiometry, and porosity of the film [7] and it is also influenced by the presence of other components in the glass [5,8].

Films in question are generally examined on silicon substrates since most of our interest is with silicon devices. Other substrates can also be used but silicon is very useful for a variety of reasons. It is stable at very high temperatures and films formed at high temperatures can be deposited on the substrate. It is chemically stable and generally not very reactive. It is excellent for optical studies of the deposited films in the visible region. It has no very strong lattice absorption bands in the useful region of the infrared and thus can be used for transmission studies. To correct for the lattice absorption bands in silicon, a reference silicon wafer slightly thinner ($\sim 10\%$ for SiO_2 and many silicate glass films on silicon) than the sample silicon wafer containing the deposited glass film is used in the reference beam of the double-beam spectrophotometer. The reason for using a slightly thinner wafer in the reference beam is that the effective path length through the sample wafer is less than the path length through the bare silicon wafer ([9]). The requirement that the silicon wafers be transparent in the infrared necessitates the use of fairly-high-resistivity material (≥ 5 Ω-cm). For best results, the use of float-zone or Lopex material rather than pulled crystals is recommended, because the latter have varying amounts of dissolved oxygen, which can result in a fairly strong absorption band near 1100 cm^{-1} close to the absorption band for silica and various silicates. The wafers should be either chemically polished or mechanically polished (both surfaces) to eliminate radiation losses due to light scattering. Finally, the wafers should be about 30 mils thick (depending on the resolution of the spectrophotometer), so that interference fringes are not formed due to the thickness of the silicon wafer itself.

In checking for the presence of small quantities of water, silanol groups, or other impurities, the absorption bands may be too weak to detect, especially if the film itself causes interference fringes in the spectrum. In this case, the weak absorption band may be at a position corresponding to the position of a steep slope in the interference spectrum, and it would cause an imperceptible perturbation on the slope. This problem is avoided by replacing the bare silicon wafer in the reference beam with a wafer containing a pure and dry film of approximately the same refractive index and thickness as the sample wafer. The interference fringes are thus in effect cancelled and the infrared spectrum can be amplified for the detection of weak bands. For most glass films having refractive indexes in the range of 1.4 to 1.6, the reference wafers and films can be thermally oxidized silicon wafers. If the wafers were oxidized in steam then they should be dried in oxygen or nitrogen at or above 1000°C for at least one-half hour depending on the film thickness. After oxidation, the film on one side of the wafer is removed by etching. If the refractive index of the reference film does not coincide with that of the sample film, then the proper reference film thickness is given by $n_s d_s/n_r$ where d_s is the thickness of the sample film and n_s and n_r are, respectively, the refractive indexes of the sample and reference film at the infrared wavelengths being used for examination. If the dispersions of the sample and reference films are not significantly different, then one can use the refractive indexes of the films in the visible region. A thickness match within about 200 Å of the desired thickness is generally sufficient to allow satisfactory amplification of the spectra. In our laboratories we have reference wafers with SiO_2 films ranging from 0.4 to $2.4\,\mu$ in thickness intervals of 400 Å.

2.2. Optical Techniques

Refractive indexes and film thicknesses can be measured accurately and simply by the use of VAMFO ([10-12]), which is a specially constructed interference microscope. The refractive index is an important physical property which is useful for determining the composition and density of glass films ([7,13]). For example, the percent composition of lead oxide in the film has a strong influence on the refractive index. Other compounds such as aluminum oxide also influence the refractive index but to a more limited extent. The refractive index is also influenced by the oxygen stoichiometry in the glass film ([7]). For example, glass films which are oxygen deficient will show higher refractive indexes than corresponding films which are completely oxidized. A decrease in density due to porosity will also result in a decreased refractive index. Thus, the refractive index can give information as to composition, oxygen deficiency, and density.

Accurate measurements of thicknesses are important for determining subsequent densification on heating of the glass films, for determining the stability of the glass film when subjected to various ambients, and for determining its etch stability and etching characteristics. It is important for determining the water and chemical stability of glass films, although thickness in itself often is not a good measure for this evaluation, as will be shown later.

2.3. Etching Techniques

It has been previously shown that selective etching is useful for determining the strain and density in silicon dioxide deposited films ([7]). The same can be said for various types of glass films. In addition to the effect of strain and porosity, the composition of the glass film also influences its etch rate. For example, glasses which are rich in either lead or boron have faster P-etch rates than glasses with no lead or boron oxide in them ([5,14]). Also, as far as other common compositional components of glasses are concerned, the P-etch rate of a glass can be decreased by increasing the alumina and the silica content, and in the case of some active deposition techniques, by increasing the oxygen deficiency.

For quick reference we have tabulated the influence of various film properties and composition on the refractive index, etch rate, and infrared spectra for some silicate glasses. Table I shows the value of using a combination of techniques for the examination of glass films. One of the very big advantages of nondestructive techniques such as infrared spectroscopy is that the films deposited on silicon wafers can be examined both before and after subjecting them to various chemicals or ambients at elevated temperatures.

Table I. Influence of Some Film Properties and Composition on Refractive Index Etch Rate, and Infrared Spectra for Silicate Glasses

	Density	Oxygen deficiency	Bond strain	PbO content	Al_2O_3 content
Refractive index	+	+	0	+ +	+
P-etch rate	−	−	+	+	−
1100 cm^{-1} Si–O band:					
Position ($\sim$ 1050–1100 cm^{-1})	+	−	−	−	−
Si–O band half-width	−	+	+	+	+
3650 cm^{-1} SiOH and 3400 cm^{-1}					
H_2O band intensities	−	0	0	0	0

3. APPLICATION OF TECHNIQUES

3.1. Boron Content in Borosilicate Glasses

Common glass components which give rise to strong absorption bands in the infrared are B_2O_3 and SiO_2. Since many of the glasses of interest are borosilicate glasses, it is desirable to know the relative amount of B_2O_3 and SiO_2 in the glass. In general, chemical analysis is not useful for such films. An example of the usefulness of infrared spectroscopy is shown in Fig. 1, where spectrum A is that of a borosilicate film RF sputtered from a fire-polished GSC-1 plate, and spectrum B is of a film sputtered from a target of GSC-1 whose outer layer had been ground away ([18]). It is quite obvious from a comparison of the intensity of the B–O band at 1390 cm^{-1} that the film corresponding to spectrum A is boron deficient so presumably the outer layer of the GSC-1 target was boron deficient. The target as a whole was not boron deficient as shown by the fact that the spectrum of a sedimented and fused film formed from a ground portion of the target was similar to the spectra of other fused GSC-1 glass films. The boron deficiency in the fire-polished plate arises from the fact that near the surface of fired glass objects the boron composition is low.

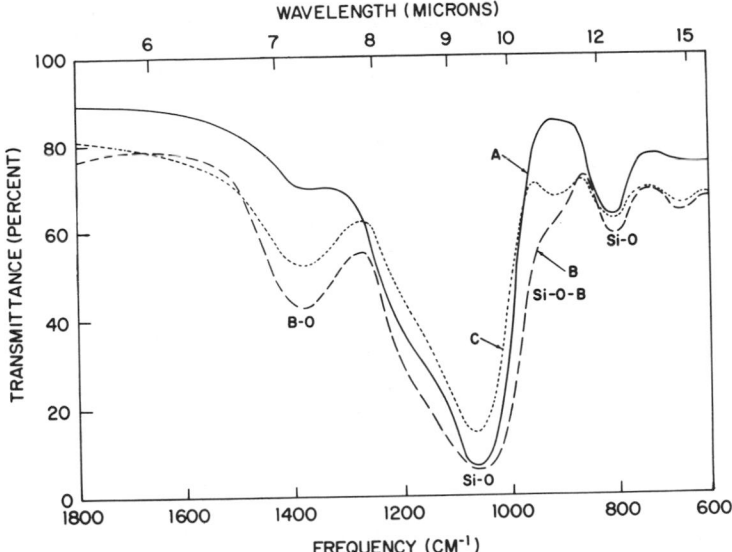

Figure 1. Infrared spectra showing effects of target surface removal and run-in time on mixed-composition glass films. (A) GSC-1 film RF sputtered from a fire polished GSC-1 plate; (B) film sputtered from same plate after removal of the outer layer of the plate by grinding; and (C) film sputtered from the same plate after grinding and run-in period ([18]).

When the borosilicate glass is fired at a high temperature, the boron near the surface of the borosilicate diffuses out causing a slower etch rate near the surface as shown in Fig. 2, where we have plotted the P-etch rate of General Electric GSC-1 borosilicate glass after having fused the sedimented powder or frit by firing for five minutes in oxygen at 1195°C ([5,15]). The slower etch rate near the surface (less than 5 Å/sec for the first 500 Å) is due to the out diffusion of some of the boron. It was necessary to remove about 4000 Å of glass before reaching a steady etch rate of 9.5 Å/sec. This glass was fired in dry oxygen, but if this same glass had been fired in a moist ambient, there would have been much more out diffusion and leaching of the boron and the etch rate would have been even slower at the surface. In the case of Pyrex, where a good glazed film can be formed by firing the sedimented powder at about 820–840°C, no significant boron out diffusion was detected when fired in a dry ambient. However, if the powder is fired in a moist ambient there is some loss in boron content depending on the firing temperature.

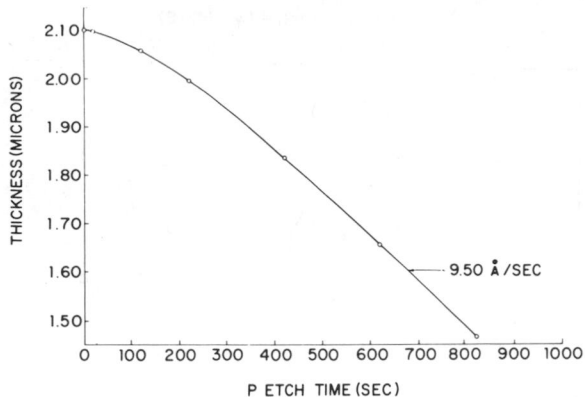

Figure 2. P-etch rate study on fused GSC-1 glass fired
5 min in dry O_2 ($\sim 1195°C$) [5].

3.2. Effect of Lead Oxide Content on the Infrared Spectra of Lead Borosilicates

Other common components such as lead oxide and alkali cannot be determined easily by infrared spectroscopy, although they do have an influence on the relative shapes and intensities of various absorption bands. The effect of lead oxide on the infrared spectrum is shown in Fig. 3. Spectrum A is for a $0.72\,\mu$ film of Drakenfeld E1527 glass which contains approximately 29 wt. % SiO_2 and 51 wt. % PbO. Spectrum B is for a 0.61-μ film of Corning X760LZ glass which contains approximately 51 wt. % SiO_2 and 29 wt. % PbO. The total quantity of SiO_2 in these two films is almost equal. Considering the density of the two glasses (4.1 g/cc for E1527 and 2.93 g/cc for X760LZ), the SiO_2 contents are equivalent to SiO_2 film thicknesses of $0.39\,\mu$ for the E1527 (spectrum A) and $0.41\,\mu$ for the X760LZ (spectrum B). Equivalent thicknesses of B_2O_3 would be $0.14_4\,\mu$ for E1527 and $0.11_4\,\mu$ for X760LZ. From a comparison of the two spectra it can be seen that an increase in lead oxide content shifts the Si–O absorption band to longer wavelengths and makes the band broader, resulting in an increased absolute (or integrated) band intensity. This shift has been observed with other glasses where the lead to silicon ratio was varied. This technique is not very sensitive for determining the lead content, but it can be used for screening the glasses as to the relative amount of lead oxide in the glass.

Introduction of other metal oxides produces a similar shift, broadening, and increased intensity of the Si–O absorption band depending on the amount added. In some borosilicates a small addition of cations will shift the Si–O band to higher frequency indicative of increased polymerization of

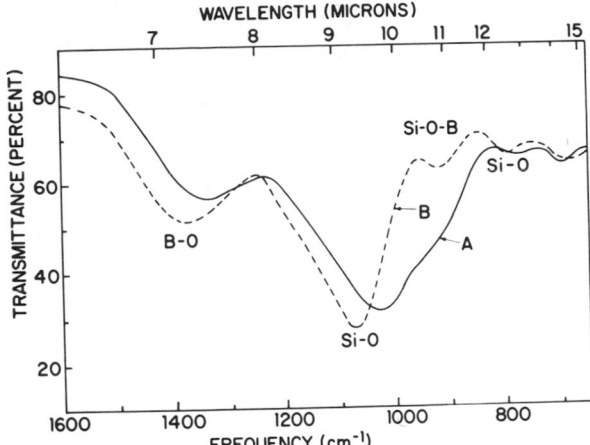

Figure 3. Effect of PbO content on lead borosilicate glasses. (A) Spectrum of $0.72\,\mu$ film of Drakenfeld E1527; and (B) spectrum of $0.61\,\mu$ film of Corning X760LZ ([5]).

SiO_4 tetrahedra ([16,17]). As shown in Fig. 3, the specific intensity of the B–O band near 1380 cm^{-1} decreases with the addition of monovalent and divalent metal oxides. In addition to the shift and broadening of the 9-μ Si–O absorption band, the absorption near 11 μ appears to be weakened very markedly by the addition of cations.

3.3. Structural Differences Between Fused and RF-Sputtered Glasses

3.3.1. GSC-1 Glass and Effect of Annealing

The study has been made of RF-sputtered-glass films and compared with those of fused-glass films to learn more about the composition and the structure of the sputtered-glass films ([18]). In this section, we will compare the spectra of different RF-sputtered glasses with the spectra of the corresponding fused glasses. In making these comparisons we shall show the effect of substrate temperature and annealing on the structure of the sputtered films. Figure 4 shows the spectrum of a GSC-1 film RF sputtered on a 100°C silicon substrate. Spectrum B is that of a fused sedimented powder of nearly the same thickness, $0.778\,\mu$ compared to $0.809\,\mu$ for the RF-sputtered film. Note that in the RF-sputtered film the Si–O–B band at 920 cm^{-1} is significantly weaker than that of the fused-glass film similar to the case of powdered-glass films compared with fused-glass films ([5]). The absorption band due to Si–O stretching in the sputtered film is at lower

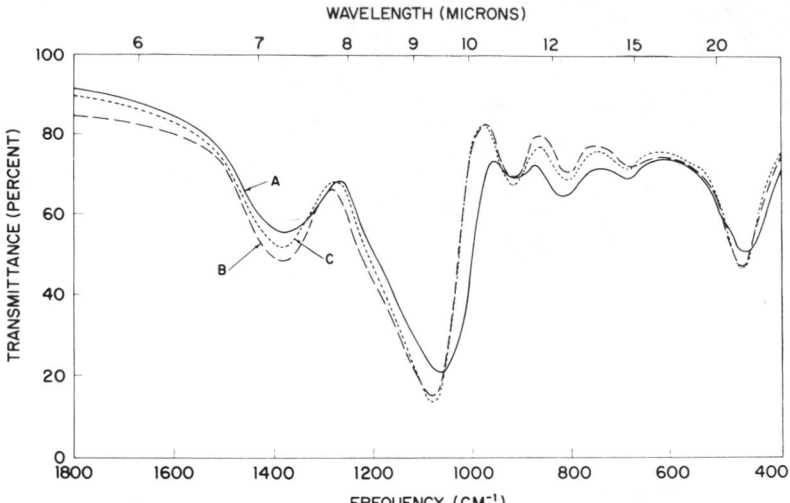

Figure 4. Infrared spectra for: (A) RF sputtered GSC-1 on ∼100°C silicon substrate $(0.809\,\mu)$; (B) GSC-1 film formed by fusing sedimented powder $(0.778\,\mu)$; and (C) GSC-1 film from (A) after heating in dry N_2 for 5 min at 965°C $(0.786\,\mu)$ [18].

frequency than that for the fused-glass film. This is attributed to the fact that the sputtered film is not quite as dense as the fused film. The shift to lower frequency and broadening of the 1100 cm^{-1} band is attributed to a slight oxygen deficiency in addition to some bond strain and some slight decrease in film density. It has been observed with silicon dioxide that strain in the film and decreased density, which is reflected in decreased polymerization of the SiO_4 tetrahedra, will cause the 1100 cm^{-1} Si–O absorption band to shift to lower frequencies and broaden the band [7]. After heating the sputtered film at 965°C for five minutes, spectrum C was obtained. This spectrum is practically the same as that of the fused-glass film. It was, therefore, concluded that the sputtered film had the same composition, for all practical purposes, as that of the fused-glass film. This is also shown by the fact that the sputtered film, after annealing, had the same P-etch rate and the same refractive index as the fused-glass film. Note also that the film densified as shown by the decrease of the film thickness from $0.809\,\mu$ to $0.786\,\mu$.

3.3.2. *Effect of Substrate Temperature on RF-Sputtered Corning 1715 Films*

The effect of substrate temperatures on RF-sputtered-glass films is shown in Fig. 5 where we show spectra A and B of RF-sputtered Corning

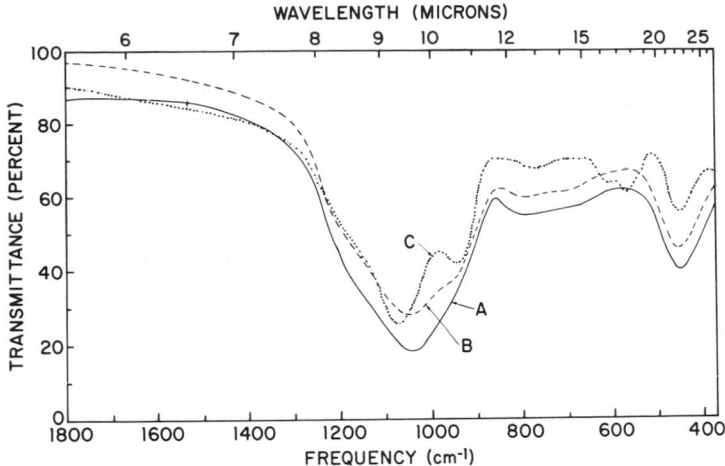

Figure 5. Infrared spectra for: (A) Corning 1715 glass RF sputtered on $\sim 100°C$ silicon substrate ($1.142\,\mu$ thick); (B) Corning 1715 glass RF sputtered on $\sim 500°C$ silicon substrate ($0.930\,\mu$ thick); and (C) film of 1715 glass formed by fusing sedimented powder at 1130°C ($0.754\,\mu$ thick) ([8]).

1715 glass deposited at substrate temperatures of $\sim 100°C$ and 500°C. This is a calcium alumina silicate glass. These are compared with spectrum C which is the spectrum of a fused-glass film of Corning 1715. It can be seen that the band near 950 cm^{-1} is more intense in the film deposited at 500°C than in the low temperature film. In the case of the low temperature film, that band only appeared as a very weak shoulder, whereas the shoulder is more pronounced on the 500°C film. When the film is heated the band at 940 cm^{-1} increases greatly in intensity. This absorption is attributed to the stretching vibration of $Si–O^{-}$, the presence of which is due to calcium cations in the glass structure.

In general, if a sputtered-glass film is structurally different from the fused-glass film, although having similar composition, then heating near or above the annealing temperature will result in a glass film more similar to the fused glass. In some cases, pronounced structural modifications will occur at temperatures well below the annealing temperature.

Note also in the initial spectra (A and B) that, as with the other sputtered films containing SiO_2, the main $Si–O$ absorption peak is at longer wavelengths and the absorption band is broader than in the fused or heated films. The sample having the higher substrate temperature is not shifted as much from the fused-glass spectrum as that having the lower substrate temperature.

3.3.3. *RF-Sputtered SiO₂ Films*

RF-sputtered SiO_2 films deposited at a substrate temperature of 450°C resemble thermally grown SiO_2 films more closely than do films deposited at 100°C. This is shown in Table II where two RF-sputtered SiO_2 films are compared to thermally grown SiO_2 films of the same thickness ([18]). Note that the Si–O band position and half-width for the higher temperature film

Table II. Comparison of RF-Sputtered SiO₂ Films with a Thermally Grown SiO₂ Film (∼5700 Å) ([18])

		Optical density OH at 3600 cm⁻¹	Si–O stretching absorption bands		
Sample	Substrate temp.		Position ν_a	Half-width ν_a	Position ν_b
RF SiO₂	100°C	0.0026	1057	107	816
RF SiO₂	450°C	0.0004	1072	98	813
Thermal (DWD)	980°C	—	1087	81	805

is more similar to that of the thermally grown SiO_2. It was also found that the P-etch rate of the higher temperature film was closer to that of thermally grown SiO_2, its etch rate being approximately 4.6 Å/sec, whereas the 100°C temperature film had a P-etch rate of 10.2 Å/sec. The P-etch rate of thermally grown SiO_2 is about 2 Å/sec.

Many cold and hot substrate samples of RF-sputtered SiO_2 films have been investigated ([18]). Part of this investigation has included an examination of the effect of a relatively mild post-heat treatment. The initial heat treatment varied from a 10- to 20-minute exposure to dry nitrogen at 500 to 540°C. We were especially interested in the possibility of structural modifications at these temperatures. This treatment was not sufficient for significant densification or permanent drying (removal of hydroxyl groups), but the treatment was sufficient to show differences between the hot- and cold-sputtered SiO_2 films. These results are summarized in Table III.

As deposited, cold-sputtered films had higher refractive indexes than hot-sputtered films. Heat treatment reduced the refractive indexes of the cold-sputtered films, especially the thinner ones. The refractive indexes of the hot-sputtered films were reduced only slightly. These differences could be attributed to the entrapment (or absorption) of gases or volatile impurities in the less dense cold-sputtered films. Because of diffusion effects, these substances are removed more readily from the thinner films on heating. During the heat treatment in nitrogen some of the film is probably oxidized

Table III. Effect of Mild Heating (15 min Dry Nitrogen at 520°C on RF-Sputtered SiO_2 Films ([18])

	Refractive index (5460 Å)		Infrared examination (film thickness 5600–8500 Å)			
			1100 cm^{-1} band position		Half-width	
Type sample	Initial	Average change due to heating	Initial cm^{-1}	Shift due to heat	Initial cm^{-1}	Decrease due to heat
RF-sputtered: Cold (50–100°C)	1.473–1.479	-0.011 $(d > 2\,\mu)$ -0.022 $(d < 1\,\mu)$	1057–1064	$+5$–7	105–107	2–6
Hot (400–530°C)	1.467–1.475	-0.002	1070–1074	$+1$–3	98–103	1
Thermal SiO_2	1.461_8	—	1087–1091	—	81–86	—

by the slight amount of moisture present in the film. This oxidation would decrease the refractive index. Since the cold-sputtered films have more moisture, as indicated by the intensity of the 3600 cm^{-1} band, one might conclude that the greater decrease of the refractive index of the cold-sputtered film on heating in nitrogen is due to this effect. But this would not explain the greater decrease of the refractive index of the thin films of the cold-sputtered SiO_2 as compared to the thick films; however, this can be explained by a volatile impurity hypothesis. Sufficient heat treatment would also tend to densify the films; this would be reflected by an increase in the refractive index. It is concluded that all these effects occur to some extent.

The infrared spectra show that the low-temperature films are more amenable to structural modification by this relatively low-temperature treatment. The heat treatment is sufficient to shift the 1100 cm^{-1} band 5 to 7 cm^{-1} toward higher frequency with a corresponding half-width decrease of 2 to 6 cm^{-1} whereas, with the samples having a high substrate temperature, the spectra are closer to that of thermally grown SiO_2 and the subsequent changes on additional heating are not as pronounced. Although the postdeposition heat treatments of the "cold" samples were in some cases for longer times and at higher temperatures than the deposition times and temperatures of the films sputtered on hot substrates, the infrared spectra show that the latter, even without any postdeposition heat treatment, are closer to thermal oxide than the cold-substrate films with post-heat treatment. This implies that the equilibrium conditions can be reached more readily if the film is heated as it grows.

Thickness changes on heating show that the cold-sputtered films are slightly less dense than the hot-sputtered films. This is also substantiated by the greater intensity of the 3600 cm^{-1} band due to hydrogen bonded silanol groups in the untreated cold-sputtered films.

RF-sputtered SiO_2 films could be made virtually indistinguishable from thermally grown SiO_2 by high-temperature baking in an oxidizing atmosphere. The 5700-Å sputtered films described in Table II were exposed to oxygen for eight minutes at 990°C. The infrared spectra of both the cold- and hot-substrate films were practically indistinguishable from that of thermally grown SiO_2. The half-widths of the main absorption band were 81 cm^{-1}, the same as for thermally grown films; the absorption bands were at 1086 cm^{-1}, only 1 cm^{-1} removed from that of thermally grown oxide; the measured refractive indexes were 1.459 and 1.462 as compared to 1.461_8 for thermally grown oxide ([11]); and the P-etch rates were practically the same as for thermally grown SiO_2.

3.4. Densification of Pyrolytic Oxides

Pyrolytic films of silicon dioxide can be obtained from the thermal decomposition of alkoxysilanes at deposition temperatures of about 600 to 900°C ([19-21]). Depending on the deposition temperature and conditions, films formed by this technique are less dense than those of thermally grown silicon dioxide. Pliskin and Lehman ([7]) have shown the importance of the combined use of refractive index, exact infrared Si–O absorption band position and half-width, close scrutiny of hydroxyl content, and densification effects in the evaluation of these and other low temperature deposited silicon dioxide films. As an example, in Fig. 6 spectrum A is that of a pyrolytic oxide formed at 675°C and spectrum B is the spectrum of the same film after densification by exposure to steam for 15 min at 975°C. For all practical purposes, spectrum B is the same as that for thermal oxides of comparable thicknesses. In the spectrum of the undensified film, the 1100 cm^{-1} band is broader and shifted to lower frequency than in the spectrum of the densified or thermal oxide, whereas the 800 cm^{-1} band is at higher frequency than in the case of the thermal oxide.

A further indication of the porosity of these films is given by their lower refractive indexes and faster etch rates ([7]). The porosity of the films is shown most clearly by the fact that they can be densified by thermal treatment. The effects of various thermal densification treatments on refractive index and film shrinkage are shown in Table IV. The influence of

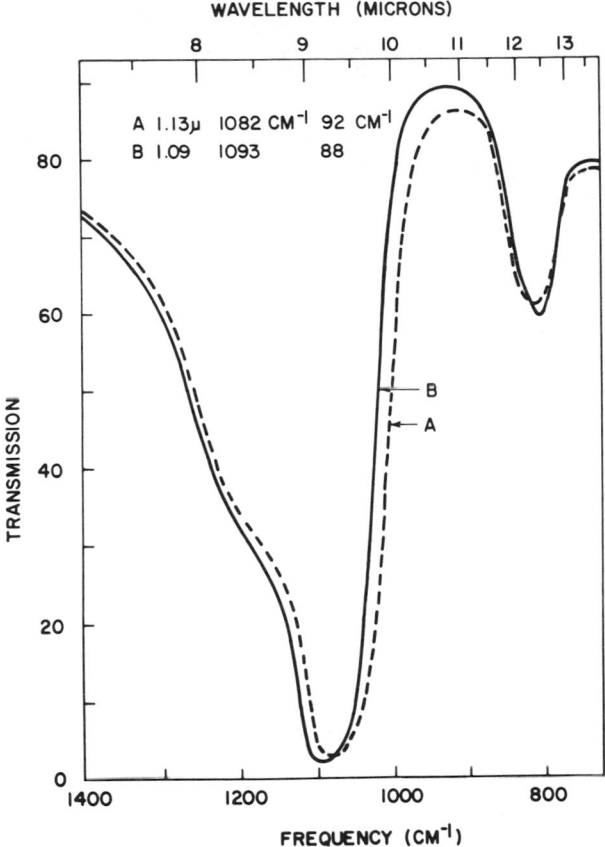

Figure 6. Steam densification of pyrolytic SiO_2: (A) T.F. pyrolytic SiO_2 formed at 675°C; and (B) densified by exposure to steam for 15 min at 975°C ([7]).

similar treatments on the refractive index and P-etch rate of pyrolytic SiO_2 films is given in Table V. These results show that heating in a moist ambient at temperatures greater than 800°C was more effective for densification than heating in a dry ambient.

3.5. Electron-Gun-Evaporated SiO_2 Films

In the evaluation of various low-temperature-deposited SiO_2 films, very interesting results with regard to electron-gun-evaporated films were obtained ([22]). It has been found that these films are more reactive with water

Table IV. Densification Produced by Various Treatments [7]

Relative quan. ads. water	Densification treatment			Refractive index		Density (g/cc)		% Densification	
	Ambient	Temp., °C	Time, min	Before dens.	After dens.	Before dens.	After dens.	By R.I.	By film shrinkage
High	Argon	800	15	1.45_0	1.45_5	2.15^b $(1.99)^a$	2.18	1.1^b $(9.2)^a$	9.0
Low	Steam	850	15	1.43_7	1.46_3	2.09	2.22	6.0	6.4
Med.	Nitrogen	975	5	1.44_4	1.45_6	2.12^b $(2.07)^a$	2.18	2.7^b $(5.2)^a$	6.3
Low	Steam	975	15	1.44_4	1.46_5	2.12	2.23	4.7	5.4

[a] Before densification, these samples contained a significant amount of water as shown by their infrared absorption spectra. The relative quantity of absorbed water was considered in calculating their densities.
[b] The water content was not considered in determining these values.

Table V. Refractive Indexes and Etch Rates of Various T.F. Pyrolytic Oxides (7)

Deposition temp., °C	Deposition time, min	Densification ambient	Densification temp., °C	Densification time, min	Thickness μ	Refractive index (5460 Å)	P-etch rate Å/sec	P-etch rate Temp., °C
675	75	—	—	—	0.78	1.44_7	13.2	25.1
675	120	Argon	800	15	1.42	1.45_2	2.9_1	25.1
675	120	Steam	800	15	1.27	1.46_0	2.1_7	25.1
675	120	Steam	975	15	1.09	1.46_3	2.0_3	25.1
835	10	—	—	—	1.56	1.45_3	6.7_5	26.0
~835	10	—	—	—	1.21	1.45_0	10.6_5	26.0
Thermal oxide					0.59	1.46_2	2.07	25.4

than most other low-temperature SiO_2 films. This reactivity was easily seen by infrared spectroscopy and by etching techniques.

The reactivity of electron-gun-evaporated films is shown quite clearly in the spectral regions given by Fig. 7. Spectrum A is the spectrum of the electron-gun-evaporated film within one day after deposition. The film was deposited on a silicon substrate held at 400°C. Spectrum B is that of the same film which had been exposed for 24 days at a temperature of 85°C in 85% relative humidity, and spectrum C is that of this film after densification at 983°C. The latter spectrum is virtually indistinguishable from the spectrum of a thermal oxide of the same thickness. As can be seen in the OH-stretching region of the spectrum, there has been a significant pickup of water shown in the $3\,\mu$ region by the increase of spectrum B over that of spectrum A. In addition the absorption band due to Si–O stretching near $9\frac{1}{2}\,\mu$ has shifted significantly to shorter wavelengths or higher frequency and has undergone a pronounced decrease in bandwidth. In previous studies of pyrolytic oxide films deposited at temperatures greater than 650°C, it had been found that this absorption band would decrease in bandwidth and shift to higher frequencies on decrease of porosity in the film (7). In this case, the porosity of the film has increased on exposure to high humidity as shown by the increase in the quantity of absorbed water and by measured increases in film thickness. In addition, spectrum B shows the presence of a new band at 935 cm^{-1}. This band is attributed to the vibration of silanol (SiOH) groups, thus showing that water has reacted with the SiO_2 to form SiOH. In addition, etch-rate data show that the etch rate of an initially deposited film is much faster than a film which has been exposed to high humidity and temperature. Pyrolytic oxides deposited at temperatures of 650°C and higher did not form silanol groups as readily

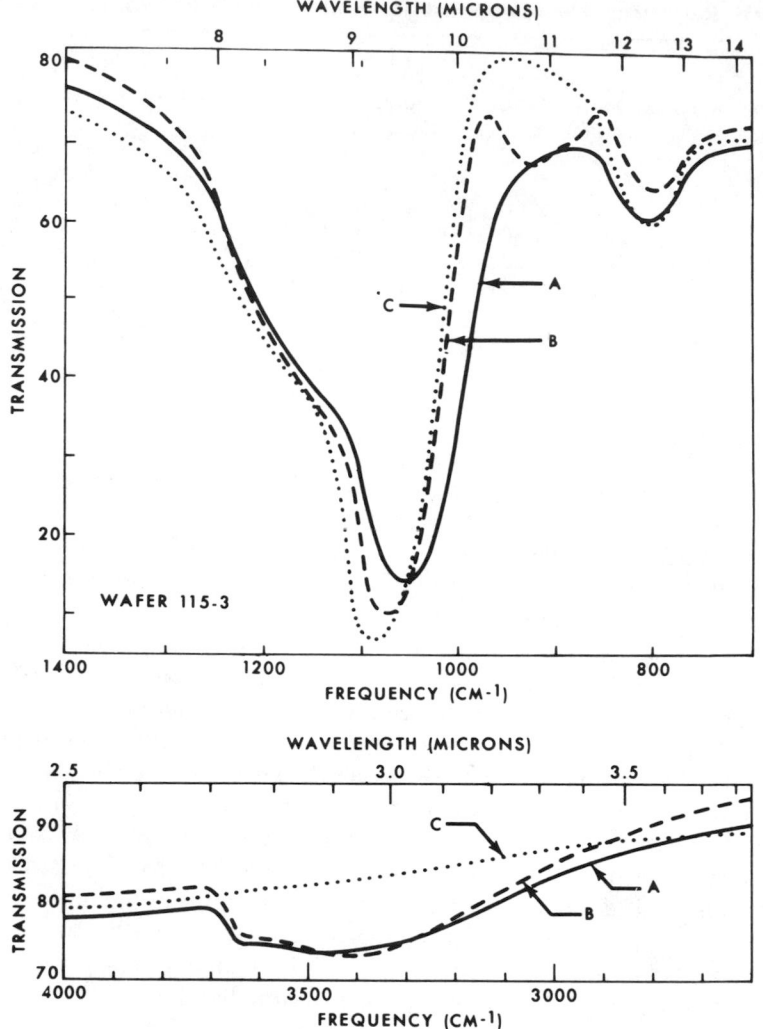

Figure 7. Effect of humidity and temperature on an electron-gun-evaporated SiO_2 film (8070 Å initially) on a 400°C substrate: (A) Initial spectrum (1 day old); (B) 24 days exposure, 85°C, 85% RH; and (C) densified 10 min in N_2 at 983°C ([22]).

on exposure to high humidity. Furthermore, the etch rate of the pyrolytic oxides decreased with a decrease in porosity ([7]), yet here it is seen that the etch rate decreased with an increase in porosity. These results can be explained on the basis of a high degree of bond strain in addition to porosity in the electron-gun-evaporated films. The broadness of the Si–O band initially is due to a great deal of strain and variation in bond energies in addition to the porosity of the film. This strain makes the oxides more reactive in addition to the fact that the porosity allows for a greater surface to hold and react with the absorbed water. On reaction of the water with the oxide to form silanol groups, strain in the bonds are relieved and the absorption band due to the Si–O stretching becomes sharper and shifts to higher frequencies. With the relief of the strain, the etch rate of the oxide decreases.

Although spectrum B was taken after 24 days exposure to high temperature and humidity, most of the observed changes occur during the first day of exposure. In other words, most of the reactivity in the high humidity temperature chamber has occurred within the first day. In fact, the reactivity of the electron-gun-evaporated SiO_2 is so great that similar changes, although to a lesser extent, can be seen by mere exposure to room ambient [22]. The degree of change is relative humidity dependent.

As part of this study, the refractive indexes, film thicknesses, and etch rates of the various films were measured before and after different ambient treatments [22]. These results, summarized in Table VI show that the various humidity or moisture treatments both increase the film thickness and refractive index and decrease the P-etch rate as previously mentioned.

Table VI. Humidity, Room Ambient, and Heating Effects on Electron-Gun-Evaporated SiO_2 Films Deposited at 400°C [22]

Wafer No.	Treatment	Average thickness Å	Refractive index	P-etch rate, Å/sec	Thickness change, %
1030-1	Initial	8127	1.476	28.3	—
	1 hr boiling water	8238	1.482	21.5	+1.4
	30 min steam, 181°C	8185	1.484	20.5	−0.7
115-3	4 days, 25°C, 25% RH	8078	1.480		
	24 days, 85°C, 85% RH	8291	1.483	14.2	+2.6
	10 min N_2, 983°C	7640	1.462		−7.9
128-2	Initial	6475	1.466	32.9	
128-3	2 days, 25°C, 25% RH	6621	1.465	30.2	
	69 days, 25°C, 25% RH	6687	1.475	22.6	+1.0
128-4	5 min N_2, 985°C	5989	1.460	3.5 (Variable)	
128-1	4 days, 85°C, 85% RH	7081	1.475	16.9	
	66 days, 25°C, 25% RH	7129	1.469	—	+0.7
	30 min steam, 450°C	6854	1.441	8.0	−3.8
	36 hr, 85°C, 85% RH	6868	1.457	8.0	+0.2
	10 min N_2, 980°C	6450	1.465	2.0	−6.1

The high porosity of the electron-gun-evaporated films is shown by wafer No. 115-3 where heating for 10 minutes in nitrogen at 983°C was sufficient to densify the film nearly 8%. After this heat treatment, the infrared spectrum of the sample and the refractive index indicated that the film was now nearly the same as thermally grown SiO_2 films.

3.6. Summary of Refractive Indexes and P-Etch Rates of Silicon Dioxides

A summary of the refractive indexes and P-etch rates of various silicon dioxides is given in Table VII. The variability in refractive index and P-etch rate can be attributed to changes in substrate temperature and deposition rate. Generally, a lower substrate temperature will result in less dense and more strained films which are characterized by lower refractive indexes and faster etch rates. Similarly, faster deposition rates will result in less density, larger strains, lower refractive indexes, and faster etch rates. Although SiO_2 films were studied in most detail, the same results were found with various silicate glasses.

3.7. Moisture Stability of Surfaces

3.7.1. *Corning 7050 Glass*

One of the requirements of an effective semiconductor insulator system is that it be impervious to attack and penetration by ambients, particularly moisture. Films of various fused sedimented glasses ([15]) have been studied for resistance to moisture attack ([6,9]). The most rapid and

Table VII. Summary: Refractive Indexes and P-Etch Rates of Silicon Dioxides[a]

Oxide type and description	Refractive index at 5461 Å	P-etch rates at 25°C, Å/sec
T.F. pyrolytic	1.44–1.45	6–20
T.F. pyrolytic, densified	1.463	2.0
CO_2 process	1.465	2.4–4.2
Reactive sputtering, deposition rate <300 Å/min	1.46	3.5–21
Reactive sputtering, deposition rate ≥700 Å/min	—	≥100
Anodized	1.30–1.49	18–228
PbO catalyzed oxidation (lead silicate)	1.72	600
Electron-gun-evaporated SiO_2	1.464–1.487	20–70
RF sputtered	1.467–1.479	4–12
Thermal	1.462	2.0

[a]From references 7, 11, 14, 18, 22, and 23.

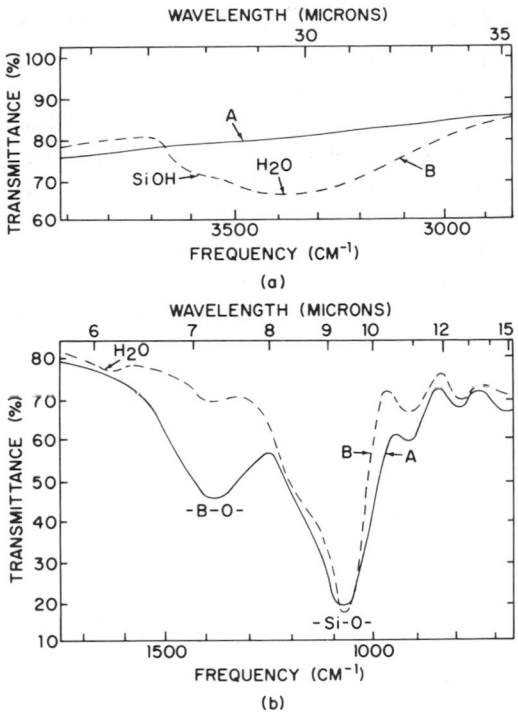

Figure 8. Effect of boiling water on 0.76-μ film of Corning 7050 glass: (A) before boiling; and (B) after boiling for one hour ([6]).

simple accelerated test of this property was found to be exposure of the glassed wafers to boiling water. Some glass films are virtually unaffected by exposure to boiling water (i.e., Pyrex and fused quartz). Those glasses which are affected by boiling in water will show a dissolution of the glass which can be detected by weight loss and a decrease in film thickness or they will show significant amounts of moisture in the film as seen by the presence of hydroxyl absorption in the $3\,\mu$ region, and they may show leaching of a soluble component oxide such as B_2O_3. Corning 7050 glass is an example of a glass which is seriously attacked by boiling water without showing any film thickness decrease. From Fig. 8 it can be seen that most of the boron oxide was leached out of the film and water was absorbed by the film. Glasses such as Pyrex (Corning Glass 7740) show no change in the infrared spectrum as a result of a similar moisture exposure. Obviously when looking for a semiconductor encapsulant film, glasses with high moisture stability like 7740 are desirable.

3.7.2. *Effect of Moisture on RF-Sputtered Glass Films*

Generally, the glasses which resist water dissolution and component leaching in fused films will show similar stability in RF-sputtered films of the same glass. Some difference in the glass film properties occur depending on the thermal history of the deposited films ([18]). Similarly, there are some differences in the water stability of RF-sputtered films depending on the deposition temperature of the film. As a representative example of a film RF sputtered from a stable glass, we have chosen silicon dioxide.

The water stability of RF-sputtered SiO_2 films was examined by use of infrared spectroscopy ([9]). The results show that films which have been

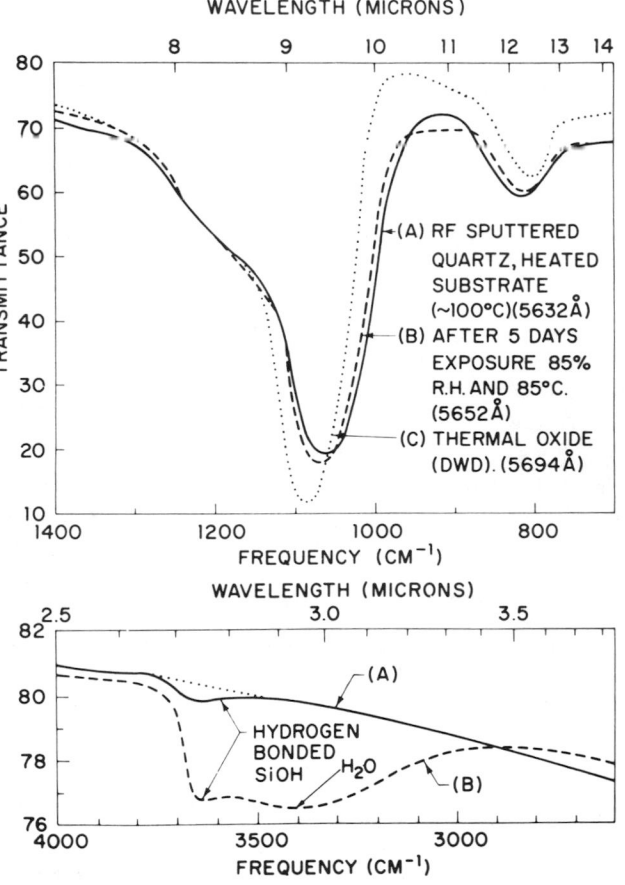

Figure 9. The effect of moisture on a RF-sputtered SiO_2 film deposited at 100°C ([9]).

deposited at low substrate temperatures ($\leq 100°C$) picked up several times as much water as films which have been deposited at higher temperatures ($\geq 300°C$). These results are consistent with other data which show that the low temperature films are somewhat less dense, have more bond straining, have initially more hydrogen bonded silanol groups, and are more dissimilar from thermal oxide than the high temperature films. These results are shown in Figs. 9 and 10. In Fig. 9 spectrum A is that of a RF-sputtered SiO_2 film which was deposited at 100°C. The spectrum shows a

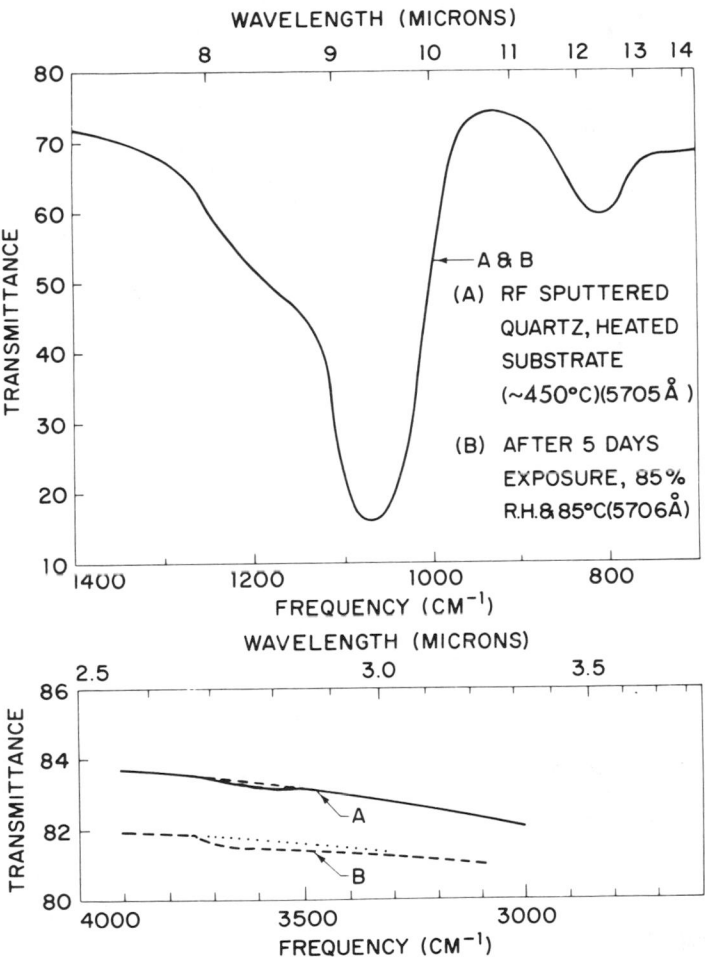

Figure 10. The effect of moisture on a RF-sputtered SiO_2 film deposited at 450°C ([9]).

very weak absorption band at 3650 cm^{-1} which is attributed to strongly hydrogen bonded SiOH groups in the sputtered film. Spectrum B was obtained after exposure to the sample to 85°C and 85% relative humidity for five days. The spectrum shows a large increase in the amount of absorbed water and hydrogen bonded silanol groups. The fact that there is actual water in the sample is shown by the presence in the spectrum of a weak absorption band at 1620 cm^{-1} which is due to the scissors (deformation) vibration of H$_2$O. (This region is not covered by Fig. 9.) It should be noted that the region of the OH stretching bands near 3 μ is amplified 5-fold from the remaining spectrum, and therefore, the amount of absorbed water is not as great as one would at first conclude. On the other hand, in Fig. 10, it is seen that the amount of water absorbed on the 450°C substrate sample after exposure for 5 days in the high humidity chamber is much less than that on the low temperature sputtered film.

It was also found that exposure to 85% relative humidity and 85°C for five days had a greater effect on the amount of moisture pickup than did boiling water for one hour. The amount of moisture pickup after boiling in water for one hour was only about $\frac{1}{3}$ that of the five day high humidity treatment. In fused glasses, the short boiling water test had been found to be more severe.

The slight increase in thickness of the low-temperature-deposited sample on exposure to moisture is real. This is similar, although to a much lesser extent, to the case previously described for the electron-gun-evaporated films (Section 3.5.). We have generally observed with porous, low temperature glass films deposited by various techniques this general phenomenon of increase in film thickness on exposure to moisture accompanied by a slight increase in the refractive index. On the other hand, heating a sample deposited at low temperature by sputtering (Section 3.3.3.) reduced the refractive index and decreased the film thickness. This effect is not very noticeable on the better-quality films deposited at high temperatures by sputtering. It is much more noticeable on the more porous electron-gun-evaporated films deposited at 400°C than on sputtered films deposited at substrate temperatures of 100°C. If the heating were insufficient for permanent densification, then subsequent re-exposure of the more porous films to moisture results in an increase in the thickness and refractive index. The phenomenon is attributed to the absorption of water and filling of the pores in the glass film.

REFERENCES

1. J. A. Perri, H. S. Lehman, W. A. Pliskin, and J. Riseman, *Surface Protection of Silicon Devices with Glass Films*, Electrochem. Soc. Meeting, Detroit, Oct. 2, 1961.

2. J. L. Langdon, W. E. Mutter, R. P. Pecoraro, and K. K. Schuegraf, *Hermetically Sealed Silicon Chip Diodes and Transistors*, Electron Devices Meeting, Washington, D.C., Oct. 27, 1961.

3. J. A. Perri and J. Riseman, New Dimensions in IC's through Films of Glass, *Electronics* **39**, 108–116 (1966).

4. W. A. Pliskin, D. R. Kerr, and J. A. Perri, in *Physics of Thin Films Vol. 4* (G. Hass and R. E. Thun, eds.), pp. 257–324, Academic Press, New York (1967).

5. W. A. Pliskin, Comparative Evaluation of Thin Glass Films, presented at Electrochem. Soc. Meeting Symposium at Philadelphia, October 1966. Also published in *Measurement Techniques for Thin Films* (B. Schwartz and N. Schwartz, eds.), The Electrochemical Society, New York (1967).

6. W. A. Pliskin, The Stability of Glazed Silicon Surfaces to Water Attack, *Proc. IEEE* **52**, 1468–1471 (1964).

7. W. A. Pliskin and H. S. Lehman, Structural Evaluation of Silicon Oxide Films, *J. Electrochem. Soc.* **112**, 1013–1019 (1965).

8. W. A. Pliskin, *The Evaluation of Thin Film Insulators*, presented at American Vacuum Society 13th National Vacuum Symposium at San Francisco, October 1966. *Thin Solid Films*, **2**, 1–26 (1968).

9. W. A. Pliskin, Am. Ceram. Soc. Meeting, Washington, D.C., May 1966 (also available as IBM preprint MP 22.0078, *The Effect of Moisture on R.F. Sputtered and Fused Glass Films*).

10. W. A. Pliskin and E. E. Conrad, Nondestructive Determination of Thickness and Refractive Index of Transparent Films, *IBM J. Res. Develop.* **8**, 43–51 (1964).

11. W. A. Pliskin and R. P. Esch, Refractive Index of SiO_2 Films Grown on Silicon, *J. Appl. Phys.* **36**, 2011–2013 (1965).

12. W. A. Pliskin and H. S. Lehman, in *Proceedings of the Symposium on Manufacturing In-Process Control and Measuring Techniques for Semiconductors*, at Phoenix, Arizona, March 1966, Vol. 1, pp. 11-1 to 11-28. (Also available as IBM Technical Report TR22.279, *Non-destructive Optical and Spectroscopic Measurements of Oxide and Glass Films*.)

13. M. L. Huggins and K-H Sun, Calculation of Density and Optical Constants of a Glass from Its Composition in Weight Percentage, *J. Am. Ceram. Soc.* **26**, 4–11 (1943).

14. W. A. Pliskin and R. P. Gnall, Evidence for Oxidation Growth at the Oxide–Silicon Interface from Controlled Etch Studies, *J. Electrochem. Soc.* **111**, 872–873 (1964).

15. W. A. Pliskin and E. E. Conrad, Techniques for Obtaining Uniform Thin Glass Films on Substrates, *Electrochem. Tech.* **2**, 196–200 (1964).

16. P. E. Jellyman and J. P. Procter, Infra-red Reflection Spectra of Glasses, *Trans. Soc. Glass Tech.*, **39**, T173–T192 (1955).

17. V. A. Florinskaya and R. S. Pechenkina, Reflection and Transmission Spectra of Potassium-Silicate Glasses in the Infrared, *Dokl. Akad. Nauk SSSR* **91**, 59–62 (1953).

18. W. A. Pliskin, P. D. Davidse, H. S. Lehman, and L. I. Maissel, Properties of Insulating Thin Films Deposited by RF Sputtering, *IBM J. Res. Develop.* **11**, 461–467 (1967).

19. E. L. Jordan, A Diffusion Mask for Germanium, *J. Electrochem. Soc.* **108**, 478–481 (1961).

20. J. Klerer, A Method for the Deposition of SiO_2 at Low Temperatures, *J. Electrochem. Soc.* **108**, 1070–1071 (1961).

21. J. Klerer, On the Mechanism of the Deposition of Silica by Pyrolytic Decomposition of Silanes, *J. Electrochem. Soc.* **112**, 503–506 (1965).
22. W. A. Pliskin, Electrochem. Soc. Meeting, San Francisco, May 1965; Also W. A. Pliskin and P. P. Castrucci, Reactivity and Bond Strain of Films Formed by Electron-Gun-Evaporation of Silicon Dioxide, *Electrochem. Tech.* **6**, 85–88 (1968).
23. R. M. Valletta, J. A. Perri, and J. Riseman, Reactively Sputtered Silicon Dioxide Films, *Electrochem. Tech.* **4**, 402–406 (1966).

INDEX